A Goodly Heritage

D1262428

A Goodly Heritage

The Life and Times of a Presbyterian Minister, Missionary, Activist

Arch B. Taylor Jr.

Copyright © 2014 by Arch B. Taylor Jr.

Library of Congress Control Number:		2014906197
ISBN:	Hardcover	978-1-4931-9696-8
	Softcover	978-1-4931-9694-4
	eBook	978-1-4931-9695-1

All rights reserved. No part of this book may be reproduced or transmitted in any form or by any means, electronic or mechanical, including photocopying, recording, or by any information storage and retrieval system, without permission in writing from the copyright owner.

This book was printed in the United States of America.

Scripture taken from the King James Version of the Bible.

Rev. date: 04/25/2014

To order additional copies of this book, contact:
Xlibris LLC
1-888-795-4274
www.Xlibris.com
Orders@Xlibris.com
546242

CONTENTS

PART FOUR
Margaret Hopper Taylor

INTRODUCTION

The lines are fallen unto me in pleasant places; yea,
I have a goodly heritage.

(Psalm 16:6, King James Version)

As I grow older year by year (I am now well past ninety), this verse from the Bible often occurs to me. I probably heard it first as a child some time when my family had daily Bible reading and prayer or in Sunday school or at church where we regularly attended. When people ask me, "How are you?" I frequently reply, "I live in a constant state of thankfulness," using a remark that my wife Margaret Hopper passed on to me from her grandfather Terry. I cannot escape the deep feeling that God has singularly blessed me, and I want to bear witness to that blessing and share it, especially with my family and friends, but also with any others who might be interested. I believe my story is worth telling. These words from the Bible seem altogether appropriate to characterize my life. The goodly heritage that I celebrate is vaster than I can adequately express in an account like this. It will be only generally chronological in order, but with some details added as I go along that actually occurred only at a later date.

Part 1 describes my family background. Chapter 1 describes my ancestors on my father's side, highlighting their connection with the Presbyterian Church and the culture of the South. Chapter 2 tells how Presbyterianism and Southern culture were strengthened by my mother's family background. I go on to describe our family life after she and my father married. I was a wanted child. I believe my parents prayed for me before I was born, and I was almost a "Christmas gift" to them, being born December 23, 1920. They always loved, appreciated, and encouraged me, as they also did my three sisters. My parents presented me as "a child of the covenant" for infant baptism in the First Presbyterian Church in Charlotte, North Carolina. I always knew that God loved me and that Jesus was my Savior. At about the age of twelve, I made a public profession of my faith in Christ and became a member of the First Presbyterian Church of Winston-Salem, North Carolina, where we had moved from Charlotte. Growing up and through my adult life, I never went through a period when I thought I was not "saved," and I was never bothered with the question "Who am I?" During my high school years, I was active in the church youth group, and I felt a call to the ministry while still a student in high school. I followed preparation for the ministry at Davidson College and Louisville Presbyterian Theological Seminary, where I received a generous scholarship. I received love, spiritual encouragement, and financial assistance from my family and the church. Details of my family life as well as my ancestral background are included here more fully

It will become abundantly clear that the culture of the South was a powerful force in the life of my family from colonial days till after the Civil War, Reconstruction, and Jim Crow. My great grandfather Henry Porterfield Taylor owned slaves, but evidently he treated them humanely. He and his family lived near Richmond, Virginia, capital of the Confederacy, where they could witness some of the military encounters and suffer the deprivations of war.

My great grandfather W. R. Boggs was a graduate of West Point and a lieutenant in the U. S. Army, but he resigned his commission and joined the forces of Georgia, his native state. One of his descendants now proudly possesses his desk, which she had suitably refinished. W. R.'s father-in-law, Colonel John Symington, did not resign from the U. S. Army. One of the family stories that I heard at home told how some of our kinfolks were driven out of their home during General Sherman's scorched earth march from Atlanta to the sea. The wife was ill and was removed from the house while lying abed. One of my sons owns portraits of her and her husband and a sofa that had belonged to them. In this way, for several generations the reality of the Civil War and its aftermath has lingered in the thoughts and emotions of some of the Taylors.

When I was a teenager and worked summers at Taylor Bros tobacco factory where most of the employees were black, both blacks and whites used the "N word" usually without malice. There was a general acceptance of the status quo and peaceful coexistence. The Southern Presbyterian Church was segregated at the time, and I grew up in that cultural environment. Privately I sensed some dissatisfaction and negative feelings, but it was only after I left home that education and other life situations contributed to some degree of maturation. This account describes partially the process by which my mind has changed. My truthful description of some of the negative aspects of my parents' attitudes in no way contradicts my appreciation for their basic humanity and Christian faith, and my gratitude for the genuine love they lavished on me and the many positive influences their example and upbringing provided.

Part 2 deals in some detail with my education in high school, college, and seminary, and my marriage to Margaret Ruth Hopper. Margaret was daughter of a Presbyterian minister in Louisville, Kentucky, and we married at the beginning of my third year in seminary. There is a brief account of our ministry in Charlestown, Indiana, while I was still a seminary student and in Buffalo Valley and Silver Point Presbyterian churches in Tennessee that followed my graduation from seminary.

Even before I finished seminary, Margaret and I had agreed to volunteer as missionaries to China. From Tennessee, we proceeded to Yale University to study Chinese language. Our status was made questionable because civil war still raged on Mainland China. After a year of language study, we finally set out for China, but circumstances prevented our going to Beijing for a second year of language study. Instead, we "refugeed" in Taiwan for a year as guests of the Canadian Presbyterian mission. Contrary to our hopes and expectations, the threat of China to invade Taiwan (which was actually forestalled by the outbreak of the Korean War) resulted in our going to Japan, where we spent the rest of our missionary career.

Part 3 is devoted to our years in Japan. We had had no specific preparation for Japan, and many details of the land, language, culture, and Christian witness in the land were unknown to us till later. I devote chapter 6 to presenting the historical background of Japan and the coming of Christianity there. Chapter 7 is devoted to our years at Shikoku Christian College, from its meager beginnings to its gradual development and growth. Margaret and I had the privilege of serving together there. She taught in the Social Welfare Department, and I taught

Bible. After we had been there for nearly twenty years, I was elected president of the college, which caused a delay in our much-needed home assignment. Those years were particularly difficult for Margaret. When we at last returned to the U.S. for home assignment, she was found to have lung cancer, which ended her life about two years after diagnosis. We were married for forty years and were parents of three sons, William, John, and Samuel.

Part 4 is chapter 8, by far the longest in this book. My wife Margaret had a powerful influence on my faith and life, and I wrote a biographical sketch of her that is an important essay in this present collection. Included in the biographical sketch is "A Lament" written by Margaret as she contemplated her impending death. She died of lung cancer at the relatively young age of sixty-three in 1984. Appended to that biography is a tribute to Margaret written by Professor Okamoto Mitsuo[1], a Japanese faculty colleague of Shikoku Christian College.

Part 5: I returned alone to Japan for a few years until I retired. In combination with the example and influence from Margaret, my study and teaching of the Bible has had a major influence on my worldview. I devoted several chapters of this book to show how my mind changed and how I was led into a life of activism for peace and justice. As a natural outcome of my teaching and activism, I have spent time writing essays and books to promote my views. By now, I have been retired for nearly thirty years, drawing Social Security and a pension from the Presbyterian Church (USA). It seems as though retirement made possible a new and different career for me. I call it retread. This time of my life was greatly enriched by my marriage to Wanda Rowe Myers.

Grace Wanda Rowe Myers was a widow who was a few years older than me and who was the mother of two daughters. The younger daughter had been killed by a drunk driver. Wanda introduced me to many cultural organizations, such as Compassionate Friends, Mothers Against Drunk Driving (MADD), and the historical societies of Louisville and Kentucky. She was a sweet, gentle companion. We lived in Louisville until we sensed the need to enter a retirement facility in

---

[1] I follow the Japanese practice of listing family name first, followed by given name.

Clarksville, Indiana, where I still live. Wanda and I were married for sixteen years before she died in 2006. These two partners, Margaret and Wanda, were truly gifts to me from God.

Part 6: During my retirement, I have not been idle. I did some occasional supply preaching in Louisville Presbytery early on, and I still preach occasionally today. Through years of living in Japan, I came to know Japanese as fellow human beings and children of God. I visited both Hiroshima and Nagasaki, which had been destroyed by atomic bombs. I studied the history of Japan and learned of the pressures exerted upon Japan by the U.S. and other Western powers. As a result of my research, I came to a radical revisionist view of the attack on Pearl Harbor on December 7, 1941, and the nuclear bombing of Hiroshima and Nagasaki on August 6 and 9, 1945. I wrote a small book dealing with these two events and their aftermath entitled *Pearl Harbor, Hiroshima, and Beyond: Subversion of Values* (2005 Trafford Publishing). In Louisville, I participated actively in the annual Hiroshima and Nagasaki observance, which the local chapter of the Fellowship of Reconciliation had begun years previously. My involvement in advocating the abolition of nuclear weapons continues unflaggingly.

On my return to Louisville, I joined the opposition to President Reagan's war against Nicaragua, arming the counterrevolutionary remnants of the Somoza dictatorship. My peace activism led to participating in two delegations to Nicaragua and active opposition to the School of the Americas, a US. training facility for right-wing armed violence in many Latin American countries. Here at home, I have been active to promote full civil rights for people of homosexual orientation and opposition to the death penalty.

Another issue to which I have devoted a great deal of attention, time, and energy is that of the state of Israel. As a modern nation state, Israel is obligated, I believe, to abide by all the requirements and conventions concerning international law and human rights. As a political state, Israel discriminates heavily against Arabs within its boundaries and commits extreme violations of the human rights of Arab Muslims and Christian Palestinians in the West Bank and Gaza. In my view, the U.S. is complicit in Israel's criminality by reason of the vast amount of economic and military aid we give Israel annually and the obvious bias we demonstrate toward Israel in its relations with the Palestinians. Chapter 14 reprints the report I wrote after participating in the Presbyterian Peace Fellowship delegation to Israel/Palestine in 2011 hosted by Christian Peacemaker Teams. In chapter 15 I summarized substantive criticisms of Israel by thoughtful Jews, and I commented on what I see as a seriously misguided national policy of the state of Israel that contradicts the ethical principles of Judaism as a religion and the Hebrew Bible, with which I am familiar by reason of its being a substantial part of the scriptures of my own Christian faith.

While remaining a loyal citizen of the United States and grateful for the quality of life that that citizenship has provided me, I cannot deny that my native land has long pursued policies of imperialism and that many of my advantages have been gained at the expense of others.

Although in a very real sense this is my story, I know that I am not alone. I am a part of a larger family and a broader culture and a part of humanity embraced in the grace of God, the Creator and Redeemer of all people. The goodly heritage that I celebrate is vaster than I can adequately express in an account like this. It will be only generally chronological, but sometimes as I pursue a particular theme, I may carry it forward beyond its proper chronological order.

As I review my personal family history, I note two features: (1) a number of my ancestors were active members of the armed forces of both the United States and the Confederacy, and (2) others were active in the ministry of the Presbyterian Church, both at home and abroad. I have devoted my career to the church, and over time, I have moved farther and farther away from the military. I consider myself a strong advocate of nonviolence and a critic of the militaristic culture that now characterizes my homeland, the United States of America. This is *my* story. I won't pretend to be objective, and I will express my own attitudes and opinions (some might call them prejudices) and indicate how my mind has changed over time. The basic principle that has had most influence on my change of mind is the conviction that there is only one God and that this one God loves and saves us all. That is the theme of my book, *God for All: the Biblical Foundation of Universal Grace* (2013, Wipf and Stock, Eugene Oregon).

PART ONE

Ancestors and Family Life

1

My Ancestors

Like the ancestors of everybody else in the world today, my earliest forebears came out of Africa, as I learned from participating in the Genographic Project of the National Geographic Society. From Africa, my people went up into Central Asia; and from there, they turned west, where they eventually separated. One branch ended in what is today the British Isles and another in Southern France close to the Iberian Peninsula.

1. The Taylors

From documentary records, I know some of my ancestors came from England, Scotland, and Ireland to North America in the colonial days. The first was a James Taylor, who emigrated from Carlisle in England to Virginia in 1658.

Of more immediate interest to me are Edmund Lewis Taylor (April 1785-September 1823) and his wife, Frances Ann Richardson (1796-1860), parents of my great-grandfather Henry Porterfield Taylor. Colonel Edmund Taylor served in the War of 1812 in the Nineteenth Virginia Volunteers and was a prominent merchant in Richmond, Virginia. Edmund Taylor owned ships and engaged in trade in New Orleans and Florida. He himself made a trip to Florida and continued overland from there to New Orleans. He planned to return home via the Mississippi and Ohio rivers, but unfortunately, he never made it. At

Roncevert, now part of West Virginia, he died of yellow fever. His body and all of his papers were burned.[2]

Henry Porterfield Taylor (October 10, 1817-November 19, 1887), referred to hereafter as HPT, was his only child. After his father's death, his mother, Frances, married the Reverend James W. Douglas, who evidently took his wife and stepson to Fayetteville, North Carolina, where he was pastor of the Presbyterian Church. HPT was instructed by his stepfather at Donaldson Academy in Fayetteville, where he prepared for college. After attending Hampden-Sydney College and Washington (later Washington and Lee) College, he went to Princeton University in New Jersey in 1835. According to the Princeton University biographical sketch of the class of 1838, HPT left college due to ill health and the death of his stepfather. He later studied at Richmond Medical College but again dropped out due to ill health. All in all, it seems to me that HPT's education was rather eclectic and unfocused, though he was praised as bright, attractive, and diligent in study, and he devoted himself to teaching.

Some of my family archives refer to him as a Presbyterian minister, which is probably incorrect, for we have no evidence of the place or nature of his ministry. According to Presbyterian polity, one can be ordained only if one has both proper training and a formal call to an authenticated ministry, which do not appear to have applied in the case of HPT. For some years, he conducted a higher English and classical school in Richmond, Virginia, and census records refer to him as a teacher. He also acted as an auctioneer during his time in Richmond, as indicated by a copy of a newspaper advertisement of his establishment announcing a coming auction of horses. He seems to have purchased a property outside Richmond, and later, census records call him a farmer. It is known that he owned slaves, fewer than a dozen, including children and elderly persons. So contrary to our family traditions, his was not an extensive plantation.

Henry Porterfield Taylor married Cornelia Storrs on April 25, 1842. My father said HPT believed bringing Africans to the U.S. was part of a

---

[2] Evelyn Rich, who has done extensive family research, supplied this information concerning Col. Edmond Taylor and the details of the life and career of Henry Porterfield Taylor. I am gratefully indebted to her and will use her initials (ER) to identify other information included in my account.

divine providence; God had given to the white people, the responsibility to Christianize and educate these people, and that the Civil War was a punishment for the failure of the whites to do so. According to ER's research, HPT wrote a book that did not condemn slavery as such but severely criticized, on one hand, those who broke up slave families and treated them cruelly and, on the other, the tactics and policies of some northern abolitionists. After the surrender of the South, HPT's wife destroyed the manuscript, lest it be used against him during reconstruction.

During the Civil War, the environs of Richmond, Virginia, were very insecure. Being the capital of the Confederacy, Richmond was the object of attack from Union troops, and some skirmishes took place at no great distance from the Taylor property. Deserters and criminal elements might be on the prowl, so the authorities determined to conscript a local militia for protection, with HPT in command. He declined, saying that he was a pacifist and opposed the use of violence to try to settle disputes among individuals or nations. When pressed, he agreed to take the post, but he would not wear a uniform or bear an arm. Dad said another accomplishment of HPT was devising the method of preparing the surface of country roads by a judicious mixture of sand and clay, what came to be known as the sand-clay road, which stood up well to traffic and weather.

HPT and his wife had five daughters before the birth of their first son, my grandfather William Barrett Taylor. In my family tradition, two of the daughters were given boys' names: Douglas married a missionary, Jonathan Graybeal, and died at a young age on the mission field (in Mexico, I believe). Another called Sidney married an Adair. Their son Lewis had five daughters. As a boy, I visited the Adairs in Richmond, and Nancy visited us in Winston-Salem. In recent years, Cornelia Adair Green and I have had some correspondence. A younger son of HPT was Jacqueline Plummer Taylor, who later was partnered with William in Taylor Bros. tobacco business (see below).

The Civil War raged nearby when William was a boy. One story my dad reported had it that a Union officer was in charge of moving a herd of horses along the road that ran near the Taylor property. One of Taylor's horses got excited by the passage and ran off to join the herd. Young William was able to accost the officer and complain about the loss. The officer said he was responsible only for the total number of animals, so he permitted the youngster to pick whichever horse was his. That done, he remarked, "You damned little rebel! You picked the best horse in the whole bunch!" William was fourteen years old when the Civil War ended, and his formal education ended at that point. I have no information concerning what happened after that—the death of the parents, the scattering of the family, and how they disposed of the property.

2. Related Families

Two families related to the Taylors by marriage deserve mention.

2a. The Boggs Family

Grandfather William Barrett Taylor married Elizabeth McCaw Boggs, daughter of General William Robertson Boggs, a native of Georgia. He graduated from West Point, and as a lieutenant in the U. S. Army, he was assigned to the Watervliet Arsenal in Troy, New York. There, W. R. Boggs married Mary Sophia Symington, daughter of the commander, Major John Symington.[3] In 1857, Boggs was transferred to the Louisiana Arsenal at Baton Rouge. In 1859, he became inspector of ordinance at Point Isobel, Texas. On December 14, 1859, he took part in an engagement with Cortino's Mexican marauders near Fort Brown, for which General Winfield Scott gave him honorable mention. Soon after, he was transferred to the Allegheny Arsenal at Pittsburgh, to which his father-in-law Major Symington had also been assigned. Before the outbreak of the Civil War, W. R. Boggs resigned his commission and joined the armed forces of Georgia, his native state.

Boggs was appointed by Georgia Governor Joseph E. Brown as the purchasing agent to procure arms, ammunition, and supplies for Georgia state's troops. Later, in the Provisional Confederate Army, Boggs's duties were again as an engineer and ordinance officer. He was never given the command of troops in combat. His major accomplishments were (1) to complete fortifications and supply depots in 1861, including the defenses of Charleston, South Carolina, and Pensacola, Florida,

---

[3] Some detail of what follows through the next two paragraphs is gleaned from Wikipedia.

and (2) to engineer Kirby Smith's invasion of Kentucky in 1862 and to assist Smith's military administration west of the Mississippi River from 1863 to 1865. In General Boggs's personal memoirs, he expressed sharp criticism for what he saw as poor planning and performance by Confederate commanders. He seems to have alternated between service to the Confederacy and to the state of Georgia.

After the war, Boggs engaged in the profession of engineering, participating in railroad construction in the West. In 1875, he was appointed professor of mechanics in the Virginia Polytechnic Institute, a position he held until a reorganization of the faculty in 1881. One of his colleagues wrote, "He was highly valued by his associates as a man of force and culture; was esteemed by the student body as an attractive and honest teacher; by the people of the community as an upright, genial, agreeable gentleman. Politics was alone responsible for his removal."

From Virginia Tech, W. R. Boggs retired to Winston, North Carolina, to live near his daughter, Elizabeth McCaw Boggs Taylor ("Mother Bess" to me). When Dad and the other grandchildren visited him, they played with the model canon that had been a wedding present from the arsenal workers when he married Commander Symington's daughter Mary Sophia. The old man kept the canon under the bed. He was getting blind, and he would stumble over the canon when the children left it out. He said Archie was the only one who ever put the thing back where it belonged, so he gave it to Dad.

When I was a child, Dad brought out the cannon on holiday occasions, charged it with black powder, and would allow one of us children to ignite the touchhole and fire the cannon. The force always drove the weapon backward, and I remember one New Year's, it set fire to the dried-out lawn in front. When Dad died, Mother passed the canon on to Karl Zipf Jr., son of my sister Bess (Elizabeth McCaw Taylor Zipf). Her husband, Karl Sr., was our contemporary military kinsman, who retired as a full colonel in the army and who is buried at Arlington Cemetery.

The Boggs ancestors came from Ireland, a fact that W. R. Boggs confirmed by correspondence with a kinsman, William Boggs of Loughbrickland, Ireland, in 1896.[4] Dad referred to these ancestors as bog-trotting Irishmen. Grandpa Boggs used to infuriate Dad by

---

4 ER's research provided the text of this correspondence.

suggesting that some of the Scots forebears in Ireland had intermarried with sailors washed ashore after the wreck of the Spanish armada, and Dad's dark hair was evidence of that.

2b. The Symington family

As noted above, W. R. Boggs had married Mary Sophia Symington, daughter of Major John Symington, commander of the Watervliet Arsenal. My second wife, Wanda, and I, on one of our annual trips to New England to visit family, stopped in at the arsenal in Troy, New York. There we saw the model of a cannon similar to the one in our family. When I informed them about the acquisition of our family's cannon, they insisted that we should return it to the arsenal, but I told them I didn't have that authority. I bought a book there that told the history of the arsenal.

John Symington was born in Delaware on December 23, 1797, and married Elizabeth McCaw Johnston at Richmond, Virginia, in 1830. They had twelve children, the eldest of whom was Mary Sophia.[5] Major Symington was the fifth commanding officer of Watervliet, which is the oldest U.S. arsenal in continuous operation. He served from October 10, 1851, to June 23, 1857. Apparently, there was a lull in the arms industry at the time; and for the first year, Major Symington was occupied in supplying materials and workers for a new arsenal the government was building in California. His chief contribution was a thorough reorganization of the shops and the workflow process. According to the book, "this general scheme, with variations caused by the extended scope of operations, is still employed, with excellent results."[6] There was a fire in the commander's residence in 1854. Major Symington was seriously affected by smoke inhalation, which made him a semi-invalid. Even so, he was left in command there until he departed in 1856; and even then, his successor was not formally installed till 1857.

---

[5] Per ER.

[6] Swantek, John, *1837-1997 The Watervliet Arsenal: A Chronology of the Nation's Oldest Arsenal.* Watervliet Arsenal, Public Affairs Office, Watervliet, NY. 1997, p. 68.

Symington did not resign from the Union, and with the rank of colonel, he was made commander of the Allegheny Arsenal near Pittsburgh. Soon after his arrival, he replaced with women two hundred teenage boys who had been working there. The boys flouted discipline and commonsense safety precautions, including playing with matches in the powder rooms. Once women were employed in the powder rooms, Colonel Symington reported no further discipline problems. Nonetheless, the Allegheny Arsenal was the scene of the most massive explosion and fire behind the Northern lines during the Civil War. Many victims were burned beyond recognition, and the exact number of victims is not known. It occurred on September 17, 1861, the same day as the battle of Antietam in Maryland, where twenty-four thousand fell. Greatest suspicion fell on the chief of the laboratory, but the actual cause of the fire was never determined. Symington, as commander, came in for some criticism. According to a statement written by Colonel Alfred Mordecai (who had succeeded Symington as commander at Watervliet), Symington, a man "unwilling to rest under reproach, however unjust, demanded an inquiry, which was accorded, and his vindication was complete." [7]

Prior to the Watervliet assignment, Symington was commanding officer at Harpers Ferry, where his organizing talents were not appreciated and he got embroiled in some serious political problems. An arsenal at Harpers Ferry had been a dream of George Washington since his early days as a surveyor. He thought the confluence of two rivers, the Potomac and the Susquehanna, at that point would provide abundant power, and it was relatively near his own home farther downstream on the Potomac. The proposal failed when knowledgeable people objected that the rivers were subject to sudden and violent floods, the climate was conducive to diseases such as malaria, and the general population was uneducated and unsuitable for labor. Washington was called from retirement to advise the government during the War of 1812, and then he finally succeeded in getting the operation going at Harpers Ferry.

All the objections proved to be valid, and on top of everything, the whole enterprise was under the control of a man named Stubblefield, head of one of five wealthy families with interrelated interests who

---

[7] <http://www.historynet.com/explosion-at-the-allegheny-arsenal.htm> supplemented by ER.

controlled all the affairs in the area. The man that got the contract to construct the waterworks did a poor job, and several times, floods washed them away. Another man owned a distillery and sold liquor to the people who worked there. Contrary to the example of Springfield Arsenal in Massachusetts that standardized production of interchangeable parts for the weapons, Harpers Ferry used the old European master craftsman system. Each master did his own thing, and the parts weren't interchangeable. Besides, they didn't want anybody to put them on a strict time schedule, so they came to work when they pleased, and they drank on the job. There were numerous complaints, especially from the War Department in Washington, which wasn't getting the desired results for their money.

Several attempts at reform failed, and at last, the army took charge of the whole operation and put Symington in command. He encountered stiff opposition at every turn, but he managed to bring about a much better organization of the workshops (similar to what he did later at Watervliet), including improving illumination by installing windows in the workrooms. He imposed regular hours on all workers including the masters and forbade any drinking on the job, but they sullenly resisted. Symington and his wife were active in the community, promoting the temperance movement, which apparently didn't go over very well.

Stubblefield and his allies complained to the War Department in Washington, but for a while, the army supported Symington. A big issue arose when Symington dismissed a fairly important subordinate from his post, unjustly, his opponents alleged. At last, Stubblefield mobilized all the political powers in the region. They took the issue to Washington where it was debated in the War Department and even at the cabinet level. In the end, politics won, and Symington was transferred. Control of Harpers Ferry reverted to Stubblefield and the other powerful families, and within a short time, the old, corrupt, inefficient order reasserted itself. I went on the Internet and discovered records of the evidence brought against Symington. I found no testimony in Symington's favor, but one charge against him was having installed the windows in the workrooms. Not too many years afterward, Harpers Ferry was the scene of John Brown's raid, which Robert E. Lee suppressed. At the outbreak of the Civil War, both southern and northern forces fought to control it.

3. The Presbyterian Church and the Taylors

As will become clearer as this account proceeds, the Presbyterian Church exerted a great influence on the Taylors and other families related through marriage, and they in turn made not inconsiderable contributions to the Presbyterian Church.

3a. Characteristics of the Presbyterian Church

Presbyterians are heirs of doctrine and form of government that originated from John Calvin (1509-1564) of Geneva, Switzerland. Calvin was a leader of a branch of Protestantism originating a little later than that of Luther in Germany. The doctrine is referred to as *reformed*, indicating its aim to reform the perceived errors of Catholic teaching and policy of the time. One should be careful to note that *reformed* is not meant to imply that final or perfect doctrine or policy has been achieved. A familiar Latin motto defines us as *ecclesia reformata, semper reformanda*—"church reformed, always to be reformed." Presbyterians should always maintain open minds and hearts to discern where further reformation may be needed in the light of scripture and a reasonable response to ever-changing conditions.

Presbyterian Church government is a form of representative government and assumes "the priesthood of all believers." *Presbyterian* derives from a Greek word meaning "elder." During both Old Testament and New Testament times, elders were men of advanced age, experience, and wisdom, who were respected by their neighbors and entrusted with important local decisions. Members of each particular Presbyterian congregation elect representatives from among their number as ruling elders who make up the Bench of Elders or Session to govern the congregation. Ordained Presbyterian ministers, who have had special training and ordination, are called teaching elders.

A number of particular churches in geographical proximity comprise a presbytery, which has considerable authority over all those particular churches, including legal trusteeship of each particular church's real property and the authority to approve or disapprove the person (teaching elder) that a particular church calls as its minister. The teaching elders are members of the presbytery but are also pastors of the congregations that call them and moderators of the sessions of such congregations.

Each presbytery determines its own organization of committees from among its churches and hires a staff to assist its affairs. Each presbytery has a fair degree of freedom in determining its schedule of meetings and its internal organization. A presbytery elects one of its members as moderator to preside over its meeting. When I was ordained by Nashville Presbytery, they elected a moderator for each meeting. Mid-Kentucky Presbytery of which I am now a member elects a moderator to serve for an entire year. By no means does the moderator have great executive authority, but only as the presbytery bylaws allow for the moderator's ex officio membership in some committee or commission, or calls for the moderator to make appointments for stated purposes. A presbytery may provide spiritual and educational opportunities for elders and may need to act in cases of alleged misconduct. It also acts on business sent up from its particular churches or sent down from the General Assembly, that is, the highest authority of the entire denomination. Each presbytery elects commissioners (i.e. representatives) in equal numbers of ruling and teaching elders to attend the meeting of the General Assembly, which now meets biennially as the entity with the highest authority.

Today, the geographical area of the U. S. and the total membership of the Presbyterian Church (USA) is such that the 144 presbyteries are grouped into sixteen synods that perform other services but do not exercise the degree of authority given to the particular churches and presbyteries. The rule is that every meeting at any upper level of governing authority in the Presbyterian Church should be attended by equal numbers of ruling elders and teaching elders. Some Presbyterians like to claim that the U. S. government was modeled on the Presbyterian, but that is probably an exaggeration, though there are recognizable similarities.

Most of my forebears grew up in the Presbyterian Church in the southern states and inevitably imbibed cultural characteristics peculiar to the South, of which slavery was a part. The southern states' insistence on greater autonomy (states' rights) has an undeniable link to the whole question of slavery and subsequent policies toward Negroes.

One should understand that the Presbyterian Church derives its name from its system of government, which is a characteristic of churches of the Calvinistic tradition in the British Isles and Ireland and in North America. Equally important is the fact that its doctrine is reformed. On the mainland of Western Europe, Calvinistic churches usually name themselves reformed to reflect their doctrine, but their form of government is Presbyterian, though they may have different terms to identify ruling elders, teaching elders, and presbyteries.[8] A common characteristic of Calvinistic churches is what we call connectionalism. While each particular church has a good deal of autonomous self-government, it is connected to other particular churches in the presbytery which has a degree of oversight of them all; and the General Assembly has final authority in all matters of doctrine and government, though the most important decisions require approval by a majority of presbyteries. The most significant articles of doctrine and government require a supermajority of presbyteries' votes.

3b.   The Civil War and the Spirituality of the Church

At the outbreak of the war, the General Assembly meeting of the Presbyterian Church of the United States of America entertained a motion (thereafter referred to as the Gardner Springs Resolution) requiring all members to support the Union. It was a very injudicious and arrogant move rammed through by the majority. This led to the withdrawal of the Southern commissioners to form the Presbyterian Church of the Confederate States of America (PCCSA). Memories of the Gardiner Spring Resolutions rankled and remained a festering wound for over a century. In every mention of the separation of Southern and Northern churches in my childhood home, the Gardner Springs Resolution was always offered as the only reason advanced for the schism. Slavery was, of course, the "elephant in the living room" that nobody wanted to acknowledge, but support for slavery played a significant role in establishing the character of the Presbyterian Church (CSA), which named itself the Presbyterian Church (US) after the war.

Leading theologians aggressively had used Bible teachings to justify slavery. After the war, they promoted what they called "the spirituality of the Church" in order to forestall action on social or political questions

---

[8]   When I take up the conditions and events of my wife Margaret and me in Japan, I will have occasion to mention the mission work of the Reformed Church in America. That church calls itself reformed because it developed over time from Christians emigrating from the Netherlands and was called the Dutch Reformed Church in its early years.

and confine faith and action to the sphere of individual salvation. During my years in seminary, some progressive-minded ministers started a church magazine with the purpose of moving away from the "spirituality" mind-set. They called it the *Presbyterian Outlook*. One of my rather conservative schoolmates warned, "Lookout, Presbyterians!"

When early in 1921 I was baptized as an infant in the First Presbyterian Church of Charlotte, North Carolina, I was imbued with Southern culture. It was totally segregated, white supremacist, male superordinate, and prejudiced against Jews, Catholics, foreigners, divorcees, and homosexuals. More than once, I heard my father extol North Carolina as the best state in the Union, for it had fewer Jews, Catholics, and foreigners than any other state.

Once, Dad and I stood in line for the father-and-son banquet at the local YMCA, featuring ham on the menu. Next to us were Abe Cohen and his son, and Dad teased Abe about eating ham. He responded by saying that Jewishness was a matter of here (touching his breast) rather than here (touching his stomach). Abe Jr. was a school classmate of mine, but he insisted on calling himself Bob. Given the mild (but pervasive), general anti-Jewish atmosphere, he probably wished to reduce somewhat the obvious Jewishness of his name. Dad was anti-Jewish, but not aggressively so. He loved to read political comments by columnist Harry Golden, a Jew who never dealt specifically with that issue. Dad praised the services of Judah Benjamin, secretary of the treasury of the Confederacy under President Jeff Davis.

The doctrine of the spirituality of the church and objection to more progressive policies of the "Northern Church" delayed the accomplishment of church reunion until 1983. My wife Margaret and I were on home assignment as missionaries from Japan at the time, and my presbytery sent me as a commissioner to the General Assembly in Atlanta that voted for reunion. (For greater detail, see the biographical sketch of Margaret in this book.)

4. Taylor Bros. in Winston, North Carolina

I never heard what became of the Taylor property after the Civil War. Apparently, W. B. Taylor's early business experience had to do with tobacco; and by 1879, he had worked his way up to manager of the Cameron & Cameron tobacco factory in Richmond, Virginia. In 1880, he voyaged to Australia, where he was recruited to manage a tobacco factory. Before he accepted that offer definitively, he returned to the USA where he married Elizabeth McCaw Boggs and settled down. W. B. Taylor became a senior partner in the firm of Taylor and Gish manufacturing plug tobacco in Lynchburg, Virginia. He invested his profits in leaf tobacco, which he lost when the plant was completely destroyed by fire.

He borrowed $10,000 and bought a small tobacco factory in Winston, North Carolina, and started his own business in 1883. Winston grew up on the railroad, and like other entrepreneurs, Taylor saw the advantages of the piedmont area for growing leaf tobacco. The railroad bypassed the nearby town of Salem, which was much older and had been settled by Moravians, devout Christians who descended from the early Czech reformer John Huss (1369-1450) who had been martyred. In 1885, William's younger brother, Jack, joined him, and they established the Taylor Bros. Plug and Twist Chewing Tobacco business. W. B. was thirty-two years old at the time and Jack twenty-eight. The facility eventually combined two other small adjoining buildings bought by the Taylors as their business grew. They connected the three structures by adding stairways and installing elevators in between. That improvisation was complicated by the fact that the floors of the buildings were not on the same level throughout.

The majority of the labor force was black, referred to as hands. William was the head of the establishment, and they called him Mr. Bill. Mr. Bill was reputed to know all employees by name and to have some knowledge of their personal circumstances. The loyalty of the Taylor Bros employees was well known in the community.

At first, the Taylors lived in the neighbor town of Salem, where my father, Archibald Boggs Taylor, was born on January 10, 1892. Mr. Bill bought half a block of property in the adjoining town of Winston between West Fourth and West Fifth streets. (The other half block was a small city park. Winston and Salem eventually merged.) Mr. Bill built a large house for himself facing Fourth Street, and later, he built on the back half facing Fifth Street homes for his three sons, Harry (Henry Porterfield), William Barrett Jr., and Archibald Boggs. Dad says the brothers never got along. Only Harry lived in his house. The others rented theirs out and lived elsewhere.

When Taylor Bros. opened in Winston, there were many small tobacco factories. But one by one, they were bought out or run out of

business by either R. J. "Dick" Reynolds or W. B. "Buck" Duke. Dad said
Mr. Bill told him once that Dick Reynolds had offered him a good price
for Taylor Bros., but he refused to sell. Had he accepted the offer, he said,
by that time, the family would have been worth millions. Asked what
he thought of that, Dad said, "I think you would have raised five of the
biggest damn fools in town."

Sad to say, the Reynolds children gave evidence to the dangers
that often accompany the possession of great wealth. R. J. Reynolds Jr.
married Elizabeth McCaw (Blitz) Dillard, only child of Dad's older sister,
Mary (Aunt Mame) Taylor, who had married John Dillard. Blitz bore
R. J. Reynolds Jr. four sons before he divorced her for the first of several
trophy wives. Patrick, a half brother of Blitz's sons, wrote a book, *Gilded
Leaf*, describing some of the effects of money on three generations of the
family. Dick Reynolds Jr.'s younger brother, Zachary Smith Reynolds, a
skillful and enthusiastic airman, zealously promoted commercial flight
and the airport in Winston-Salem. In a scandal apparently arising out of
a wild party that somehow involved his wife, Hollywood starlet Libby
Holman, Smith Reynolds was shot to death in their home outside of
Winston-Salem under suspicious circumstances that were never resolved.
One of Blitz's sons, John Dillard Reynolds, who had married three times,
died an apparent suicide in a fall from a hotel balcony in Florida. One
may see other details in the book.

5.   W. B. Taylor, Presbyterian Elder and Christian Businessman

Mr. Bill was a faithful member and a ruling elder of the First Presbyterian
Church, and he tried to apply Christian principles to his business.

5a.   Prayer Meeting at Taylor Bros.

Every day, ten minutes before noon, the factory whistle blew, and all
hands who wished to do so gathered in one big room for prayer meeting.
They were being paid by the hour, but attendance on prayer meeting did
not cost them any wages. Several of the hands were local pastors who
got their main income from factory work. They could preach rousing
sermons, and there was usually very inspiring singing. Freedom of speech

was permitted, though Dad passed on an anecdote to the effect that Mr. Bill once interrupted a prayer beseeching the Lord to move the boss to raise wages. Uncle Jack was seriously injured when his horse fell on him, and special prayer meetings at the factory were credited with helping him recover. As a young child, my second sister Katharine (Kass) had whooping cough and lapsed into a coma. Dr. Pfohl said he thought it must have resulted from the swelling of a blood vessel in her brain caused by severe coughing, though he could not be sure. Kass was also made the subject of intercessory prayer at Taylor Bros. After her recovery, she was brought to the factory so everybody could see the answer to their prayers.

Dad told me that Mr. Bill once ran for governor of North Carolina on the Socialist ticket, but at the time, I was too young and not curious enough to ask for more detail. In some of the recent documents concerning our family history, Uncle Jack Taylor is incidentally mentioned as a Socialist. In my subsequent inquiries, somebody said it might have been Uncle Jack who ran for governor, but I'm not sure.

Certainly, the Bible encourages principles that characterize what came to be called Christian Socialism at its best. In the Old Testament, from the king on down, people are required to care for the disadvantaged, such as the poor, widows, orphans, and alien residents (see Exodus 22:21-22, instructions for ordinary folks, and Psalm 72 "for Solomon"). In the post-resurrection Jerusalem church, all the members shared everything in common so that no one lacked anything, and some actually sold property and contributed capital assets (Acts 4:32-37). As a Jew, Karl Marx gave evidence in his writings of the influence of Old Testament prophetic teaching, and he incorporated some aspects of European Christian Socialism, though he attacked it from an opposing nonreligious viewpoint.

Some Christians who took biblical principles seriously responded favorably to early Marxism before it became obvious that Russian style communism was based on totalitarian compulsion, not the voluntary sharing based on mutual love that characterized the early Christians. In time, that Christian communal style of life disappeared. The explanation for that that I am inclined to accept is that the earliest Christians really believed Jesus was going to return to earth in the near future so that all materialistic aspects of life would cease. As Christ's coming was delayed, they had to adjust to real-life conditions, which made such communal social arrangements very difficult. Jesus's earthly ministry had appealed especially to the masses of poor and indigent people suffering under double exploitation by Roman imperial wealth extraction and Jewish elites who were responsible for keeping the masses under control.

Many early Christians were slaves or lower-class workers, who had no real power over the government or the economy or even their own personal lives. After the beginning of the Constantinian era when Christians gained control over the Roman political structure, they gave way to the temptations of power and helped create and perpetuate a socioeconomic structure based on inequality and supported by church authority and religious arguments. We haven't gotten past that yet, particularly after the U. S. Supreme Court accorded to corporations the rights that properly belonged only to human beings. Theologian Harvey Cox likened the market to a god (i.e., an idol) who acts according to what does and doesn't suit Wall Street, distributing rewards and punishments based on material success or failure. The Market tends to value profit above people, money above humanity. That's what I understand to be at least a part of the meaning of Jesus's condemnation of serving Mammon (wealth) rather than God (Matthew 6:24).

American public opinion has been so powerfully pushed in opposition to "godless communism" that there are not a few who are quick to charge "socialism!" if not even "communism!" to condemn any and all sociopolitical programs to produce and maintain an adequate safety net for the benefit of people in need. Some of those people may even be Christians in both name and deed yet still recoil at the cry of "socialist."

The general principle of the separation of government and religion that the founding fathers proposed and the Bill of Rights in the constitution requires is constantly under attack and must be carefully defended. The Presbyterian Church from colonial times through independence supported freedom of religion and advocated public education for all children. Robbing public funds for education to support private schools is contrary to my personal view, which I believe is firmly based on Presbyterian policy and biblical teaching, as well as consistent with our federal constitutional form of government.

W. B. Taylor did his best to conduct his business in what he understood was consistent with his Christian faith. On his gravestone in the family cemetery plot, there is inscribed "I hate every false way," a statement that occurs twice in Psalm 119 at verses 104 and 128. Evidently, the psalm was one of my grandfather's favorite scripture passages. Psalm 119 is the longest chapter in the Bible, and it extols God for giving guidance for upright human life and expresses the psalmist's joyful response. Its structure is somewhat contrived. It is a poem of twenty-two stanzas, there being twenty-two letters in the Hebrew alphabet. Each stanza has eight verses, and the first word of each verse begins with the appropriate Hebrew letter. The poem is somewhat stilted and repetitive, but nonetheless effective for anyone who sincerely loves and desires to please God. Dad told me that when he was a boy, he memorized and recited Psalm 119 for his father, who rewarded him with $5, a munificent sum in those days.

5b. A Problem at First Presbyterian Church

Bill and Jack Taylor were both ruling elders in the First Presbyterian Church of Winston-Salem. Each Taylor family, parents and children, occupied their own pew every Sunday.[9] First Presbyterian sponsored an outpost Sunday school in East Winston, a nonaffluent section of town, and the Taylor brothers actively supported this outpost. The general expectation was that eventually, the Sunday school would develop into the East Winston Presbyterian congregation; and to that end, First Church was gradually accumulating funds for a building.

The pastor at First Presbyterian became ambitious to enlarge that facility by adding an annex, and he proposed using the funds that were being accumulated for East Winston. The issue began to heat up, for the session sought to protect the East Winston project and lined up in opposition to the pastor. One of the Taylors had a spavined horse that he named Annex as a gesture to ridicule the pastor's plan, but the latter reacted even more vigorously, and he evidently had some support in the congregation.

The controversy dragged on for a while till the session took action to call for the pastor's resignation, and they commissioned the Taylor brothers to convey the decision to the pastor. In my opinion, that was done irregularly, for the session has no authority to meet without the pastor. At any rate, while all this was going on, the pastor's wife had become ill; and after the call for the pastor's resignation was announced, her illness grew more serious, and she subsequently died. Thereafter,

---

[9]   In what follows, I have only the information given me by my father.

general sympathy for the pastor grew, along with antipathy for the Taylors. The upshot of all this was that a majority of the session (probably with approval of a proportion of the members) voted to expel Bill and Jack Taylor from First Presbyterian Church.

The Taylors refused to obey that decision. Every Sunday as usual, each family came to the worship service and marched into its pew. Not only that, they filed an appeal to the presbytery against the decision. When the presbytery voted to sustain First Church, the Taylors appealed to the synod, or the next higher judicatory level, where the Taylors were vindicated. Bill attended a different Presbyterian congregation for a while. When my family moved to Winston-Salem he sat with us at First Presbyterian (Mother Bess had died meanwhile). I think the Jack Taylor family left. By the time I was old enough to know anything about it, Uncle Jack and his wife had died, and his children were no longer active in First Presbyterian.

6. My Father Goes to War

Dad attended Davidson College at a rather young age, graduating in the class of 1911. He used to tell stories of pranks the students played, as the school was in a rural setting north of Charlotte, North Carolina, and there was little in the way of entertainment. Once, a man left a wagonload of firewood overnight on the street near the college. The students dismantled the wagon, reassembled it on the roof of Chambers Hall, the main building, and reloaded it with the firewood.

After graduation, Dad returned home and worked in the Taylor Bros. factory. When the war came and President Woodrow Wilson led the U. S. to help "make the world safe for democracy," Dad was eager to go "teach the kaiser a lesson." He wanted to join the fledgling Army Air Force but was not successful. He said that after the war, he learned that Mr. Bill had been pulling strings with authorities to prevent that. There was a local physician in town, a Dr. Darling, who said that he would gain a colonelcy in the Medical Corps if he could recruit enough volunteers. He persuaded Dad to join his group. He promised that once they got to France, Dad could transfer to a combat division if he desired. That too proved impossible, and Dad ended up in a base hospital at Bordeaux, France, about as far from the front as possible.

Dad achieved the rank of sergeant. He told about some of the most severely injured soldiers who came there and his responsibilities for supervising "make work" jobs for them to aid their physical rehabilitation. One job he devised was to dig a ditch along one of the roads within the hospital grounds, and when that was done, he had the men fill it up again. He used to fascinate us children by telling about "the war," but most of his anecdotes had to do with tricks they played on some of the French people outside the base. Dad had a low opinion of them, and he referred to them as frogs. He did admire their spirit of frugality, saying that the only things they threw away were eggshells and coffee grounds. Dad and his buddies engaged in "liberating" various army supplies and equipment for their personal use. "After all, it belonged to us—it was a property of the people of the U. S.," they asserted.

After the armistice was signed, U. S. soldiers began to return home, and Dad was among a bunch that landed in New York and had to spend some time in quarantine. Mr. Bill decided to go up to the big city to welcome his son Archie, and Dad and a few friends got leave to go into town for dinner at a nice restaurant and a show. Dad acted as host through it all, and everybody thoroughly enjoyed this welcome break from the monotony of army chow. The waiter brought Dad the bill afterward, which he passed on to his father. Dad said when the old man looked at the reckoning, his eyebrows shot up almost two inches. Mr. Bill unbuttoned his coat and then his vest, inside which was a pocket closed with a large safety pin. He undid that and pulled out a purse that was attached to a cord secured to the inside, opened the purse, and took out the cash needed to pay the bill. Then he repeated the whole process in reverse.

After dinner, Dad's party went to see a play on Broadway, and they all sat on the first row in the balcony. The play was a bedroom farce. Friend husband suspected that his wife was playing him false, so he pretended he had to go out of town on business. When he returned unexpectedly, the other fellow was already there, and he began suspiciously snooping around the bedroom. Loverboy was behind a curtain, but wifey distracted hubby enough that he could slip into the closet. Whenever hubby was on the point of opening the closet door, wifey would draw his attention elsewhere, and this was repeated several times. During all this, Mr. Bill, a very morally upright gentleman, was getting more and more excited, inching forward on his seat. Finally, he stood up and shouted, "He's in the closet, the son of a gun!" The whole house broke into uproarious laughter, and the cast on the stage broke down laughing too. Things finally quieted down, but whenever the actors tried to resume the play where it had been interrupted, somebody else would shout, "He's in the closet, the son of a gun!" and the laughter would break out again.

The incident was said to have been reported in one of the newspapers the next day. I had a notion that the play was *Up in Mabel's Room*, and I tried to see if I could locate the newspaper account in the archive of the Louisville Public Library, but without success. There was indeed a play of that name, but it was several years later than the Mr. Bill Taylor episode.

As a World War veteran, my father was a member of the American Legion, and I used to look at its magazine that came regularly to the house. I think Dad also was for at least a short time a member of the organization called the Forty and Eight, named after the narrow gauge freight cars of the French railroad system that could transport forty men or eight horses. On one occasion when I was a boy, Dad took me to a sham battle. That was a rather primitive and early example of what by now has become a really "big business"—hundreds of men in period uniforms with authentic weapons reenacting a Civil War battle. Dad and I relaxed on a hill overlooking the sham battle below, but it meant nothing to me.

Although I heard my father express critical opinions about the Wilson War, it is clear that he was not opposed to the war as such. In fact, his initial desire was to join the air force; and failing that, at least to want to go into battle on the front is indicative of his mind-set. I can only express thanks that he was thwarted from actually ending up in one of the trenches in France.

Dad was a great admirer of Sergeant York and evidently had read a good deal about him. Long before I saw the movie in which Gary Cooper portrayed the war hero, I had already heard about Sergeant York from my father. As a mountaineer, woodsman, and hunter, Alvin York had had considerable experience in the use of firearms. He taught the men in his squad how he would shoot geese or ducks: if he saw a flock approaching in its V formation, he would first shoot at the last bird in line, for hitting the closest, the one in front, would cause the flock to scatter, losing the opportunity to bag more than one. In France, York and his men applied the same principle to killing a large number of Germans. York had also single-handedly captured quite a number of the enemy.

Dad took me to several war movies, which he evidently enjoyed. Two in particular stand out in my memory. *Hell's Angels* must have revived Dad's interest in the air war and his personal ambition to be a fighter pilot. I recall severe discomfort of my eyes to such an extent that we had to leave the theater early. A visit to an eye doctor revealed some abnormality that seemed to involve a muscular dysfunction. The doctor tried to correct that by giving me exercises designed to cause one eye to move while the other remained fixed. I never understood the exact condition, and apparently, the exercises were not effective, for they didn't last very long. I did have to start wearing glasses because of nearsightedness. At this late date, I don't know whether I suffered an actual eye discomfort or whether I was having a psychosomatic reaction to basic dislike of the movie. I certainly was not enjoying myself, and this may have been an unconscious means of escape.

All Quiet on the Western Front was another movie I saw with Dad all the way to the end. The film was based on the novel by the German author Erich Maria Remarque, and the story was told from the point of view of men who were all soldiers in the German army. The movie closed with the camera focused on the principal character wearing his helmet and standing in a trench with only his head on view. He holds a pair of binoculars to his eyes, and evidently, he is looking out over a no-man's-land. I have no recollection whether I heard the sound of a shot when he lowers the glass from his eyes, but a bullet hole appears in the center of the soldier's forehead, and he slumps forward. The end.

This closing scene, together with a brief incident earlier in the movie, left an indelible antiwar impression on my young mind. The scene involves several soldiers sitting around somewhere behind the lines, relaxing and shooting the breeze. One soldier, older and more mature than the others, is holding forth. He says, "I don't know what we're doing here anyhow. They say the kaiser and the king of England have some sort of a quarrel. What does that have to do with us? Why don't they put the kaiser and the king inside a fence and give them each a club and let them settle it by themselves? Why do we and the other blokes have to get involved in it and try to kill each other?"

In retrospect, I don't think that my father was making an effort to indoctrinate me as it were. He enjoyed himself, and he was taking his son along for a good time as fathers and sons should do. Still, I look back on these childhood experiences as the seed planted in my mind that has grown into my antiwar, nonviolent worldview. My refusal to take the Reserve Officers Training Corps (ROTC) in college was another step along the way.

7. My Father and Mother's Marriage

My mother was Margaret Louise Webb, who was born in Tacoma Park, Maryland, and grew up in Portsmouth, Virginia. There her mother, the former Katharine Strudwick Pratt, operated a boardinghouse mainly for people with navy connections.

After finishing high school, Mother attended Harrisonburg Teachers College (now James Madison University) in Virginia for two years, and she used to tell us stories of her experiences there and of the strange speech of the native people in the area who spoke Pennsylvania Dutch. They called baby chickens peepies, and the door on one house had a sign that read, "Bump. The bell don't." Doing practice teaching in the local school, Mother was giving illustrations about fractions. "What do you call the pieces if you cut an apple in two?" Halves! "What do you get when you cut the halves in two?" Quarters! "And what do you get when you cut the quarters in two?" Schnitz! Evidently, stewed apples cut up that small were a familiar local dish that they called schnitz. So at our house, whenever we had apples cut so and stewed, we referred to them as schnitz.

Mother had kinfolks in Winston-Salem, and it was while she was visiting them that she and Dad became acquainted. They were attracted to each other, but the war came along, and Dad wanted to go to France. He told Mother she had no obligation to him during his absence, but she remained loyal. Dad had let it be known that he disapproved of women becoming schoolteachers because that tended to give women too great a sense of authority. While Dad was in France, Mother became a yeomanette, an official rank for women in the navy, and she worked in a laboratory testing the efficiency of different types of coal used to fuel navy ships. She and Dad were married May 20, 1919, soon after he was demobilized.

2

My Taylor Family Life

Before I take up the next part of my personal family history, I'll give a brief introduction to my mother's family. I mentioned above that her mother was Katharine Pratt Webb, whom I knew as Mother Kate. Mother Kate's parents, the Reverend and Mrs. Henry Barrington Pratt, had been missionaries in Colombia, South America. Through their own family connections, the Pratts added more Presbyterian branches to my family tree.

1. Mother's Family: Pratts, Gildersleeves, and Lanneaus

Henry Barrington Pratt was from Roswell, Georgia, son of the Reverend Nathaniel Alpheus Pratt. As a young man of twenty-four and a graduate of Princeton Seminary and single, Henry B. Pratt went to Colombia, South America, as protestant chaplain in response to an appeal by a number of English and Scots businessmen who had emigrated there after Colombia gained independence from Spain. Pratt arrived in Bogota in June 1856 and began holding Protestant services in a hotel. Some of Colombia's political leaders and educated people who had fallen away from the rather obscurantist local version of Roman Catholicism were grateful to England for assistance in gaining independence from Spain. They also resisted the powerful hold of the church over domestic affairs and the uneducated masses of the people. In addition to expatriates, some Colombians attended his meetings, but Pratt said they seemed more interested in his incidental criticisms of the Catholics than his preaching the Gospel.

The arrival of A. J. Duffield sent by the London Bible Society provided a spiritual companion and fellow worker for Pratt. The difficulty of obtaining printed Bibles from England spurred the partners to set up a press and print the New Testament in colloquial Spanish, the first such effort of its kind in South America. The first printing of five thousand attracted both customers and severe criticism by the local archbishop. He threatened to excommunicate anyone who attended the heretics' meetings or bought one of their Bibles. He announced a day on which he would have a bonfire to burn collected copies of this work, but the only two books that were brought for burning were copies of the outdated Catholic version of Father Scio de San Miguel.

In 1859, Pratt returned home to work with the American Bible Society on an edition of the entire Bible in Spanish, which he eventually completed, *La Version Moderna*. While at home, he married Joanna Frances Gildersleeve shortly before the outbreak of the Civil War. Her father, the Reverend Benjamin Gildersleeve, during his lifetime, participated in editing and publishing several Presbyterian church-related newspapers, the *Missionary*, the *Georgia Reporter*, the *Charleston Observer*, and *Watchman and Observer*. The Gildersleeve family had first come to Hempstead, Long Island, in the early 1600s from Suffolk County, England. Through Pratt's wife, Joanna Frances Gildersleeve, another branch was added to our family tree, for her mother, Emma Louisa Lanneau, was descended from French Huguenots who had fled to Charleston, South Carolina. On a visit to Charleston once with my second wife Wanda to visit her daughter Marsha and family, I saw the old Huguenot Church, and I found a gravestone marked Lanneau in the cemetery.

The family was all of Southern culture. Henry Barrington Pratt served for a time as a chaplain in the Confederate army, and later, he was pastor of the Sugar Creek Church, a fairly large Presbyterian congregation in Mecklenburg County outside Charlotte, North Carolina. (By the late twentieth century, the metropolis had expanded to surround the church.) When I was a child in Charlotte, we used to drive past the Sugar Creek Church once in a while. My mother told this story: On one occasion while H. B. Pratt was preaching, his young daughter Katharine (my mother's mother, my Mother Kate then a little girl) had misbehaved such that she had to be taken outside to the woodshed.

Joanna Gildersleeve Pratt's older brother, Basil Lanneau Gildersleeve, became a well-known classical scholar, first at the University of Virginia, whence he spent three years in Germany gaining a doctorate. After returning to UVA for a while, he was called to Johns Hopkins University in Baltimore, where he had a distinguished career as an authority on Greek and Latin language and literature. In his younger days, he fought for the Confederacy and was wounded in the leg. He explained the Civil War—the War between the States—as a conflict to determine the true name of the republic: was it "*these* United States" or "*the* United States"?

H. B. Pratt, his wife, Joanna, and several children, including my grandmother Katharine born in the United States, returned to Colombia, which was then a mission field of the Presbyterian Church (USA, northern). At that time, the postwar Presbyterian Church (US, southern) sent missionaries only to China or to the Belgian Congo. Living conditions for the Pratts were difficult at best, and the reactionary Catholics made it all the more difficult. Early on, I absorbed an anti-papist prejudice from hearing Mother Kate tell about experiences of her and her young siblings sometimes when children in the streets, egged on by a priest, would shout insults or even throw stones at them.

In time, Joanna's health was so seriously affected that they had to return home, and one daughter became so ill that she died soon after their arrival back in the U. S. Henry B. Pratt continued to work on his Spanish translation of the Bible, a labor that necessitated his spending some years in Mexico. The American Bible Society even now publishes *La Santa Biblia*. On the title page of a revision of 1960, the dates of revisions of 1862 and 1909 noted on the title page were evidently the fruit of Great-Grandpa Pratt's faithful work. He also wrote commentaries on Genesis and Exodus in Spanish, and I have a copy of the English version of the volume on Genesis. It is inscribed, "To Katie and John, from their aft father H. B. Pratt, Sept 1, 1906."

Mother's father was John Norwood Webb (Grandpa John) originally from Hillsborough, North Carolina. He was interested in homeopathic medicine and invented various home remedies, with which he had only modest success. Grandpa John took his family to England for a brief stay, where he had a more positive response. In my home, we regularly used a device he invented called the electropoise, which we referred to as the poise. It consisted of a tubular metal container about four inches long and perhaps an inch in diameter (I have no idea what was inside). Attached to one end something like an electric cord about three feet long ended with a small metal disk that was secured to one's ankle by a strap. Whenever one of us had a cold or complained of any ill feeling, we would go to bed with the poise immersed in cold water and attached to our ankle.

Mother said Grandpa John lost out when the federal government began to regulate all private nostrums, some others of which were truly harmful. When I knew him, Grandpa John had no outside job but lived at Mother Kate's residential Heart O' Ghent Hotel on Redgate Avenue, Norfolk, Virginia where he did a variety of jobs. He rode a bike to get around.

2.   Taylor Family Life in Charlotte, North Carolina

After my father and mother married, they lived in Charlotte, North Carolina, where I was born on December 23, 1920, and named Archibald Boggs Taylor Jr. My parents presented me as an infant child of the covenant for baptism by Dr. Albert Sidney Johnson, pastor of the First Presbyterian Church of Charlotte, where my parents were faithful members. Twenty months later, my first sister was also born in Charlotte on August 20, 1922. She was named Elizabeth McCaw Taylor in memory of Mr. Bill's wife, "Mother Bess" who died about that time.

2a.   Taylor Long Bottling Company

Dad formed a partnership, the Taylor Long Bottling Company, with his brother-in-law Ralph Long (Uncle Shorty), a squat little guy who married Dad's younger sister, Cornelia. They lived in the big house with Mr. Bill. I assume Mr. Bill provided financial backing for their business. They produced soft drinks because prohibition had stopped the production of hard liquor. Dad and Mother lived at 309 East Ninth Street, next door to the bottling plant that Dad operated and where he had his office. Dad had majored in chemistry in Davidson College. He originated the formulas for the drinks such as grape, orange, and root beer, and he sold the flavors to several franchisees. The most popular drink was Chero-Cola, and originally, I thought that was Dad's formula. Dad had big Mack Trucks to deliver the product all over the region in wooden crates of twenty-four bottles each. They brought the empties back to the plant to be run through the big washing machines for recycling—no cans left littering the landscape then. The brands never achieved wide distribution, and the business never really flourished.

I remember we were always careful about money. Dad brought his weekly pay home and turned it over to Mother. The first thing they did was set aside a tithe for "the church purse," and Mother was in charge of the rest. When we children received our allowances, we also tithed. Mother used to squirrel away small amounts in a special repository, and she would draw on that once in a while for something special for the family and never just for herself.

When I was in early teens, I told Dad I remembered as a child hearing him talk about a lawsuit—what was that all about? As I remember it, Dad said the Coca-Cola Co. had brought a suit claiming *cola* was their proprietary name and placed an injunction on Taylor Long using it for Chero-Cola. They then chose another name, Big Boy. Coca-Cola lost the suit, but Taylor Long never revived Chero-Cola. In an antique shop, I found a poster advertising Big Boy with a picture of a boy drinking through a straw from the bottle. I remember Dad telling me that the commercial artist who designed the ad used me as his model.

I have checked out this story, but I didn't get it quite right because I thought Dad had formulated Chero-Cola. According to the web history of Royal Crown Cola, the company was originally chartered in 1912 as the Chero-Cola Company, and that was the registered name of their first drink. Chero-Cola produced the syrup and sold it to franchisees such as Taylor Long. The lawsuit arose because of Coca-Cola's challenge to Chero-Cola, and that's how it affected Taylor Long to their great detriment—I think it must have been a serious blow to the business. In any case, it is certain that the suit determined there could be no exclusive claim to the cola name as we can see from the great number of cola drinks available now.

2b. Affectionate and Frugal Family Life

With all the inevitable ups and downs, my parents were happily married and very affectionate. I remember seeing them embracing each other, and my sister Bess and I would rush in and hug their legs, and we would all sing, "Love in a bunch!" All of us children knew we were wanted and loved. We never lacked for anything, but we seldom got our wishes for mere luxuries.

We followed traditional Presbyterian practice: Sunday was the Christian Sabbath. We went regularly to Sunday school and church, no question. Sometimes when weather was nice in spring or fall, we might go for a car ride in the country. Mother usually planned some treat for Sunday afternoon. My fondest memory is a cake with a coconut topping, and we children were permitted to drink a demitasse of real coffee. Sometimes Dad would bring the "Sunday afternoon" home with him on Saturday afternoon. There was a stall in City Market where they sold peanuts roasted in the shell for five cents a sack and six sacks for a quarter, which exactly matched the number in our family. Mother played the piano, and when we got a piano, she often accompanied our Sunday afternoon family hymn sing. That practice proved a great blessing to me once when I was in a hospital in Japan. I lay awake at night in pain with a broken collarbone. I complained silently, "Nighttime is hell! Nighttime is *really* hell!" Altogether unbidden, a hymn tune entered my consciousness, and next came the words "Sun of my soul, Thou Savior dear / It is not night if Thou be near . . ." And then in my memory, I sang many other hymns that turned the misery of night into comfort and peace.

Our parents were rather strict about moral questions but never nagging. Their guidance was by example based on the principle "We Taylors do (or don't do) so-and-so." I remember once, mother scolded me for some untruth. "But, Momma," I objected, "I didn't tell a lie!" She replied, "No, but you *acted* a lie!"

Dad and Mother both punished us physically at times. Though I also used physical punishment on my sons Bill, John, and Sam, I now think that that sort of violent treatment of children tends to instill a mind-set that violence accomplishes good, which I now believe is a serious error. My recollection is that whenever we punished our youngest son, Sam, it only made him sullen and resentful. Once when sons John and Sam were home from Canadian Academy in Kobe, Margaret in another room overheard John ask, "Sam, do you remember when we used to think we had had a pretty good day if we had avoided getting spanked?" She was appalled to hear that, and so was I when she reported it to me. I have no recollection of our treating our boys in such a way, but maybe John can fill us in on the details.

In my mind, the Bible affirms the negative effect of violent punishment. God sent the flood because the imagination of the human heart was only evil, but after the flood dried up, there was no reformation in human character. Then God changed to a plan of mercy, vowed never again to destroy the earth with a flood, and made the rainbow the sign of the promise. One can identify all through scripture examples of the ineffectiveness of violent punishment in contrast to divine grace and forgiveness.

I now think the physical disciplinary regimen of my parents and of Margaret and me for our boys was mistaken. Discipline was not, however, so extreme as to cancel out my deep sense of being loved and valued in my home, and I hope that Margaret and I conveyed the same confidence to our own sons. At least Samuel once said he thought we had made a mistake in slackening up on discipline by the time he came along, the youngest of the three.

2c. The Value of Education

The Taylors have always greatly valued education. Henry Porterfield Taylor had been highly educated, but because of the Civil War, his son William Barrett Taylor's formal education ended when he was fourteen. He was very intelligent, and he sent his three sons to Davidson College. Both my parents were college graduates and read books to us from the earliest times. I particularly remember Dad reading Kipling's *The Jungle Book*. He smoked cigarettes, and I was fascinated to watch the smoke curl out of his mouth as he read.

Because I was born in late December, I could not enter public school in September before I was six, even though the First Ward School was on East Ninth Street in close walking distance from home. For that reason, I attended a private school run by Miss. Harriett Orr, one of the Sunday school teachers of First Presbyterian Church. I guess there were about twenty children of different ages all in one room.

Miss Harriett's school filled a great need to help children who didn't fit into the public school system at the time. I recall one of the girls seemed a bit strange, perhaps mildly mentally retarded. There was also one boy who had a severe injury to one arm. The public schools in those days were not into mainstreaming the handicapped. In our small, intimate class, we didn't develop prejudices against children different from ourselves. I got a good start, learning the multiplication tables, phonics, and cursive writing. I encountered a problem in writing. Miss Orr came by and wrote a line of *d* on my paper, but I didn't pay close attention—the *d* looked like an *a* with a loop on the top, so I made a line of *a* and added a loop on each one.

I was permitted to enter First Ward School for second grade, even though I was younger than the others. I remember standing in line to get registered as a transfer student. The children in front of me told which school they were transferring from, and the teacher would check them out. I felt a sense of shame for having gone to the private school, so when they asked me where I came from, I repeated "Fourth Ward," which had been the answer of the boy in front of me. The teacher checked her list and told me I was mistaken, which was not news to me. I can still feel the sense of heat moving up the back of my neck as I inwardly faced up to the big lie I had told, but I didn't admit it to the teacher.

2d. Black Helpers at Home

We were in very moderate circumstances economically, but Dad had enough income that Mother didn't have to work, and we had a Negro cook. She always had Thursday afternoon and all-day Sunday off, but she had made advanced preparation so Mother didn't have too big a job to set a very fine dinner on Sunday. When we got bigger, Bess and I did the dishes on the cook's day off and on Sunday. Every Saturday, Bess and I helped Mother change the sheets on all the beds. On Mondays, we had a wash lady to do our laundry.

I think the pay was about a dollar a day. There was, of course, no social security system for them, and I never had the least thought about the circumstances of their own home life, their children if they had any, and who took care of them while they worked for us. Mother used to keep a five-year diary in which she briefly noted the events of each day. I suppose those brief jottings were early examples of what nowadays is called tweeting. Over the years, the volumes accumulated. But before she died, Mother disposed of them. In going through her things afterward, my sister Bess came across one volume that she had overlooked when she disposed of the others. One entry mentioned that one of the helpers had quit, so Mother and Dad would have to go out "coon hunting." After we moved from Charlotte to Winston-Salem when I was eight, Dad would sometimes have one of the hands from the factory come to do work around the yard. I can still remember hearing my mother speaking to these helpers of ours in a rather condescending tone of voice. All this is symptomatic of the atmosphere in which I was brought up. We were Southern, and we were snobbish, no doubt about it. We haven't completely gotten over it yet.

2e. Our New Home in Charlotte

While we lived on East 9th Street my second sister Katharine (Kass) was born. The year I went to third grade, we moved from East Ninth Street to a newly built house at 9 Malvern Road (Telephone Jackson 536) on the edge of a new suburb of Charlotte. The street pavement ended not very far past our front yard, and it was an ideal place for children to play. We could go down to the end of the street and pick wild blackberries in season or to the woods across the street and play in the little creek and just have the best time in safe conditions. Mother warned us not to get too far away, and she kept a shiny police whistle, which she would blow to signal us to come home. *Wheet-to-wheeeee!* It always had an immediate effect. "Coming!" we would shout.

Malvern Road has long since been absorbed into metropolitan Charlotte and is prime real estate as being not too far from downtown, but when we moved there, it was on the edge of town, and new homes were going up all over. Dad set Bess and me up in business with the gift of a crate of soft drinks. We had a red wagon and a bucket of ice to deliver drinks to the house builders on their lunch break. Selling at five cents a bottle, we collected a dollar twenty. Then we bought another case at eighty cents wholesale, netting forty cents when we sold out.

Though Bess was not yet in first grade, she was too sharp to let any of the guys play tricks on her when making change. We started early saving our money, though I had the bad habit of collecting little toy cars, and I bought a red-colored cast-iron model of Lindbergh's plane, the Spirit of St. Louis.

3. Back to Winston-Salem

We lived only a few years in our new house when Mr. Bill called Dad to come back to Winston-Salem, so he naturally complied. We lived in a rented house down in the Salem part of town, but later, we rented a house on West Fourth Street, an easy walking distance a little farther down from Mr. Bill's house. While we lived in that house, my youngest sister Mary was born. There was a several-years time-lapse, making a noticeable gap between "the little girls" and Bess and me.

Bess and I improved our business experience a bit more. The public schools sponsored "Bank Day" once a week when they encouraged pupils to make deposits in individual savings accounts. After Bess and I had accumulated a tidy sum, Dad suggested that we borrow some more money from the bank, put it together with our nest egg, and each buy a share of R. J. Reynolds B stock. He said the dividends would accumulate a bit faster than it cost to repay the loan and would keep on building afterward. That proved true, and over time, I bought more Reynolds stock and war bonds later.

When I was a student in Louisville Presbyterian Seminary during the war years, Margaret Ruth Hopper, my wife-to-be, was also saving money and buying war bonds. Years later, after we had been married awhile, we had a nice account. On one year's home assignment from Japan, we visited Davidson College and decided to buy a waterfront building lot on Lake Norman, a newly developing project of Duke Power Company about twenty miles from the college by road. We thought it would someday make a nice place to retire, where children and grandchildren could visit and have fun on the lake. Eventually, it became clear that that was a vain hope. Later, when Margaret knew she was dying with cancer, she insisted that we sell the lot, which I did through a real estate agent in the Davidson community. Margaret was always more foresighted and a better manager than I, and it pleased her to know the deal was completed while she still lived.

3a. Good Health and the YMCA

Besides education and thrift, Taylors have valued good health. Mother always took care to provide nourishing food. Dad encouraged exercise. He joined the YMCA in Winston-Salem and played squash with Uncle Shorty and other friends. Dad entered me at an early age to the Y, where we played various games and ran around an indoor track. I learned to swim, and in that totally race- segregated and gender-segregated place, we didn't bother with bathing suits. Camp Hanes was a property of the Y about twenty-five miles northwest of Winston-Salem in mountain foothills, and when I was eight or nine, I spent a ten-day period at Camp Hanes. A big accomplishment was passing the water test to qualify to handle a canoe. I went hiking and did target shooting on the rifle range. Still, I was a skinny youngster, and some of the older ones teased me and called me puny.

I was a true greenhorn, and together with another boy very much like me with the same initials, André Tenille, the leaders chose us as one team for a snipe hunt. They equipped us with a kerosene lantern and a gunny sack, took us out in the woods after dark, and instructed one of us to swing the lantern while the other held the sack open, and we both whistled to attract our prey. We set about our task but had no success. After what seemed like literally hours to us, we decided to quit, so we rolled up the sack, took the lantern, went back to camp, and hit the bunk. Next morning, we learned that one of the other hunter pairs had wandered around lost in the woods, blown out the lantern, and fallen asleep on the ground before the counselors finally found them.

I have the dubious distinction of having gone snipe hunting twice. When I was fifteen years old, Camp Hanes decided to place a junior counselor in each cabin along with the senior counselor. We got our room and board plus a small cash pay, but the senior counselors dumped all the dirty work on us, such as keeping the campers in order and seeing that they made their bunks, kept their belongings orderly, and swept the cabin for daily inspection. There was a constant bickering between senior and junior counselors.

When snipe hunting time came, the counselors picked out another pair much like André and me of old. They led them out into the woods and stationed them with lantern and sack in a low place and assigned us junior counselors to spread out on rising ground in the dark and make appropriate noises to frighten the kids below, which we did with true gusto. In due time, we decided the hunters must have had enough, so we went down to rescue them, only to find that they had returned to camp in company with the counselors, and we had been whining and groaning at a mere lantern. We were so embarrassed that we hiked on up the mountain to a clearing overlooking the camp, where we waved the lantern and shouted to the campers below. Next day, we were a proper laughingstock.

3b. I Start Work at Taylor Bros.

The Camp Hanes experience led to my going to work at Taylor Bros. The summer I was eleven, I went up for a ten-day period, and I was all packed and ready to go home on the bus that brought the next batch of campers. The bus driver handed me a letter from Dad informing me that if I wished, I could stay another period, but he had a job lined up for me to make money and pay off the cost. I willingly accepted.

When I got back home, Mr. Bill put me to work in the sample department at Taylor Bros. from 7:30 a.m. to noon at fifteen cents an hour. I rode to work with Dad, and we came home for lunch. I was coworker with four other white guys. We cut plugs of chewing tobacco into smaller pieces, put each in an envelope, packed the pieces in one-pound cardboard boxes, and shipped them to salesmen on the field to give away as freebies. On each box, we had to affix an Internal Revenue stamp. We did this by hand with a dollop of wet paste in the palm of the left hand, slopping it on the stamp and affixing it across the closure so it would be destroyed when the box was opened. There was always competition as to who could do the fastest, neatest stamp job. I got pretty good, but I never won. I did learn to pack and wrap packages neatly.

Charlie Myers taught me how to chew tobacco without getting sick. Taylor Made was a mild brand without much flavoring, and he said I should be careful not to swallow the spit and to get rid of it completely and wash my mouth out if I started to feel queasy. I followed his instructions successfully, and for many years, I enjoyed the pleasures of chewing tobacco, being supplied gratis. Long indulgence can cause terrible damage to the lips, tongue, or throat by cancer, so I gave it up eventually, but not till I had used up what I had on hand.

During my time, the sample department grew and was mechanized to cut and wrap smaller pieces for sale in cardboard boxes, whereas up till then, tobacco was sold in bulk in wooden boxes and the clerk at the retail store had to cut the plugs in smaller pieces for sale. A machine cut the plug and pushed the "cuts" onto a track, where they were wrapped in cellophane and dumped off to be boxed. A few women joined the team. None of these fellow workers had much education, and several of them had friends or family members who had served jail time—nothing serious, but to me a novel life experience. Most of them lived out in the country on small farms and drove in to Taylor Bros. to supplement the meager income they got from working the land. Though we never got really intimate, I considered them my friends and came to sympathize a great deal with their hard lot. I learned a few country songs from them, some of which I still remember.

For several years, I was a senior counselor at Camp Hanes instead of working at the factory. Then Dad asked me to come back to the factory one summer, and I agreed. By then, I had no proper work clothes, so I went out and bought a couple of blue denim shirts and pants. My assignment was with a group of three black fellows, and we had a specific assignment calling for good teamwork. They soon forgot that I was the boss's son and included me in all their banter. One of the three was very light colored, and the others teased him and said his daddy was the insurance agent who came to his home regularly to collect the small premiums on burial insurance that so many black people bought those days.

Those three fellows could really sing. One of them was named Chamins Graham, whom everybody called Kid. Kid lived on credit every week, paid off his debts after payday Friday, and lived on credit the next week. One day, Kid told us, "You know, I'd rather be a rich man's bulldog than a n----- any day." We all chimed in, "Aw, come on, Kid, you know that ain't so!" "Naw, I really mean it," he said. "A rich man's bulldog gets the best steak to eat. He can ride the front seat of the bus with his master. Aw, naw! He wouldn't be riding no bus. He'd ride on the front seat of the rich man's car. They'd match him up with the finest bitch in town." Kid went on to comment more explicitly on that theme. Not many days later, I saw in the local newspaper in the column devoted to miscellaneous high society or movie star items a photo of one of the rich department store heiresses showing off her dog wearing a diamond bracelet. These two incidents occurring together so quickly left a deep impression on me.

One day, during lunch hour, I was walking down a hall in the factory, and two old friends from the sample room passed me going the opposite direction, and of course we howdied each other. As they passed on, I overheard one of them say, "Did you notice Archie is wearing the same clothes as the n-----s?" At once, I became conscious for the first time that all the white employees had taken to wearing tan-colored shirts and pants while the blacks wore blue. Totally without being aware of it, my choice of clothing had put me on the "other side." I wonder today whether Kid and the others of our team noticed and whether it made any difference in their attitude to me.

3c. Embarrassing Racist Attitudes

My father strenuously opposed school integration, and he advocated separating the genders in schools if the races were to be integrated. In one sense, this opinion arose from his deep respect for women and his desire for a high level of sexual morality on all levels. I am convinced that Dad was never promiscuous as a young male and that he was totally faithful to my mother. Dad took seriously his responsibility for his three daughters, Bess, Kass, and Mary, and he always took the initiative in addressing any young men that might come calling to let them know his expectations about how they should relate to his girls. The three brothers-in-law all had stories to tell about that.

On the other hand, Dad was captive to the superstition that all black men were very highly sexed and lusted to sleep with white women. He believed mixing the races would result in general inferiority. In this, he was a child of his times, accepting without question an almost-universal cultural presupposition of white Southerners. The earliest legal imposition of this ancient taboo in America occurred in 1662 when the Virginia legislature decreed, "Children got by an Englishman upon a Negro woman shall be bond or free according to the condition of the mother." Some states by law decreed that even one drop of Negro blood made one legally a Negro. A story in our family concerned a seriously wounded white Confederate soldier who was nursed back to health by a Negro woman. In order to qualify to marry her, he arranged to have several drops of her blood mingled with his. Even today, not only in informal conversation but also in public discussion, some white men might demand, "Would you want your daughter to marry one?" African American author James Baldwin, debating with racist newspaper columnist James Kilpatrick, countered, "Man, it's just *your wife's* daughters you don't want us to marry. We been marrying *your* daughters for years."

Throughout human cultural history, fears and taboos about sex have always complicated relations among ethnic and class groups, especially when one society gains supremacy over another. During the recent warfare following the breakup of Yugoslavia, victorious Serbs routinely raped Muslim men as well as women, and they castrated hundreds of the men and boys. A problem at issue between Japan and Korea in the late twentieth century was the demand for justice from elderly Korean women who earlier had been forced into prostitution for Japanese soldiers during the Pacific War. During their imperial expansion, the Japanese exploited Koreans for cheap labor, and they still consider resident Koreans as a potential criminal class. The Japanese exploit numbers of Korean women in the sex trade and take them as mistresses, but they get extremely upset if Japanese women want to marry Korean men.

The ancient Israelites propagated sexual taboos against the Canaanites, but many of them took Canaanite concubines. When the kingdom of Judah was in decline in the sixth century BCE, the prophet Ezekiel railed against Judahite women for lusting after Chaldeans, Assyrians, and Egyptians, "whose members were like those of donkeys and whose emission was like that of stallions" (Ezekiel 23:20). Among the Judeans who returned from exile to reestablish Jerusalem, the leaders forced Judahite men to divorce foreign wives and send them and their children away (Ezra 10:6-43). I assume the men complied because they had Jewish wives already.

Given all this cultural background reinforced by biblical texts used to support exclusiveness, I don't totally condemn my father for his opinions, but I have to say that the way in which he expressed his prejudices left a lasting negative impression on my mind and heart that has impelled me in a different direction.

I still remember with appreciation Miss Gladys Moore, my high school history teacher, who taught us how to do library research and prepare a documented essay. Under her guidance, I wrote a paper on the causes of international war, which helped mold my leanings toward peace. I can't remember how the invitation originated, but Miss Moore took our class down to Taylor Bros., and Dad gave us all a tour of the factory. At the end, we gathered around him while he entertained us with stories of the early days in Winston and Salem. I don't remember the date of one incident he related, but I think it must have been back near the end of the nineteenth century before the full onset of Jim Crow, before Negroes were legally deprived of the vote. Early one election day, several blacks showed up to cast their ballots, and the white poll watchers were outraged. Several whites set off to round up others. They got their guns and spread out to every polling place in town, with the declaration (as Dad stated it) "Ain't another n----- gonna vote today." I was terribly humiliated and felt a deep sense of shame on behalf of my father, who at the moment seemed to me to be basking in self-approval.

During my childhood, blacks didn't vote in my hometown. There was no possibility of a bus strike either, like the one in Montgomery, Alabama. In Winston-Salem, the streetcars took only whites. Blacks rode on the separate Safe Bus Line, which we used to ridicule as "safe in name only."

The general attitude of my father was almost universally held throughout the South where I grew up. After I graduated from the seminary in 1945, I was a pastor in Buffalo Valley and Silver Point, Tennessee, an area where there were very few blacks. Hence, there were little or no face-to-face encounters between the different races. I led a group of our young people to a youth conference in Nashville. One of the speakers was an older minister from Memphis, who struggled to lead all of us to a more Christ-like attitude on the race question. He said that in Memphis, young whites went out "coon conking" on Saturday nights— riding in an open convertible car through the Negro part of town and bopping blacks on the head with a long stick. He said the ministerial association was calling attention to the issue, but the police never did anything to stop it. During Black History Month in 2007, journalist William Fisher recalled his apprenticeship as a reporter in Central Florida in the 1950s. He was assigned to the police beat, and he routinely rode Saturday nights with the cops as they indiscriminately rounded up men, women, and even children in "n—town" and brought them to court, where they had to pay small fines mostly on trumped-up charges before being let go.

Nowadays, nobody would dare speak as my father did in a public place; and since our first African American president is in his second term, many people think the race question is past history, but it persists in a subtler form. It's seen in the persistence of those "birthers" who refuse to accept President Obama's birth certificate, those who made it their first priority to assure that he would end up as a one-term president, and those who still strive mightily to frustrate his every effort, even with the result of a general loss to the common good. Former President Jimmy Carter was severely assailed when he accused the early Tea Party folks of being racist, and they themselves strongly denied the charge. But Jimmy Carter knows racism and racists. He was one himself. He could never have been elected governor of Georgia otherwise. Make no mistake: Jimmy Carter knows racism. I know racism, for it was the very atmosphere in which I grew up in the South. Every once in a while, I'm surprised to sense a twinge of racism rising out of my deepest subconscious. I suspect that even now, Jimmy Carter does too.

Without in any sense being apologetic, as a typical white Southern male, I wish to bear witness to having grown through childhood and youth at the height of Jim Crow. Certainly, much of our culture was openly and crassly racist, but there were also subtle and unrecognized influences that formed my inner being. Even after I gradually matured and "knew better," I would lapse into racist ways of speech and thought.

Reflecting on my own case, I can understand now that what we call racism was, for my father, so much deeper, more pervasive, more "natural," and more difficult to recognize and confront. I want to assert that for me, his failure to recognize and confront his racism did not deny or negate his genuine deep Christian faith, his general good will toward the Negroes who worked for him. My father's love for me and the aid and encouragement he gave me in my Christian faith, growth, and expression never failed, even when it was gradually revealed how different my attitude was from his.

Dad's generosity was undeniable. I know of cases in which Dad gave jobs at Taylor Bros. to several friends who were genuinely in need, even though the result was probably not in the best interests of Taylor Bros. as a business. I think one reason Dad disliked the New Deal so much was that it imposed regulations and conditions on his business that he thought made it almost impossible for him to do such generous acts of kindness.

3d. The Taylors and the Church

As I have indicated above, Christian faith and church life were very important to the Taylors. There was never any question whether we went to Sunday school and church. "That's what we Taylors do." While we were still in Charlotte, a lady missionary to China who was some distant kin (Mother called her Cousin Augusta White) came to speak at First Presbyterian, and she stayed in our home. She fascinated me with small figures representing a Chinese festival parade, and besides her programs at church, I had friendly talks with her at home. From that time, I used to say that I would be a missionary to China some day.

Dad had an older friend from Davidson College, Mac Long, who became a Presbyterian minister and got carried away with dispensationalism, which he passed on to Dad. Dispensationalism is a system of Bible interpretation originated by an Englishman named Darby. A man named Scofield popularized Darby in the U.S. by preparing notes that were printed together with the text of the King James Version in the Scofield Reference Bible.

The Scofield system presupposes that Jesus came to set up the Kingdom of God on earth for the Jews, but they rejected and killed him. Therefore, God rejected the Jews and started the Christian church and opened it to anybody who believed in Jesus as Savior. The Church is the Kingdom of Heaven and in a sense doesn't really belong on earth. Membership in this Kingdom of Heaven seen in the Church is open to all who believe in Jesus and get baptized, whether Gentiles or Jews. The church has superseded or replaced the Jews as the true people of God.

Dispensationalism anticipates a literal fulfillment of every prophetic statement in the Old Testament and especially the prophecies of Jesus's second coming when he finally will set up the Kingdom of God for the Jews on earth for a thousand years. That will be preceded by the Great Tribulation, that is, the onslaught of wars, earthquakes, famines, and other horrible catastrophes that are expected to come before Jesus finally returns to impose peace.

Darby and Scofield's scheme builds on this scenario with great detail and with a special improvement. Traditionally, people had believed that everybody who still lived at the end time (the apostle Paul thought he would be one of them; see 1 Thessalonians 4:15-18) would have to go through the Great Tribulation, but faithful believers would be saved because believers who belonged to the Church as the Kingdom of Heaven would be raptured up to meet Jesus in the air when he came. Darby's innovation was to assure true believers that they will *not* go through the Great Tribulation but will be raptured *out* of earth *before* the tribulation, a wonderful privilege that makes the system very appealing.

A typical feature of this method is a literal interpretation of the many exotic visions in the Bible. In the Old Testament, the book of Daniel describes among others the giant statue with a head of gold, chest of silver, loins of bronze, and legs of mixed iron and clay and three fierce beasts rising out of the sea. Revelation in the New Testament has many such visions, including the beast with ten horns and seven heads and a scarlet woman riding on a beast. Mac Long lent Dad several volumes on the subject, and I remember being fascinated by all the pictures and the charts.

Dad's friend Mac Long as pastor managed to split two Presbyterian congregations by his zealous promotion of dispensationalism, and finally, he left the Presbyterian church completely. As Dad studied the books lent by Mac Long and observed the divisive results of Mac's ministry in two Presbyterian congregations, he concluded that if that was what resulted from the doctrine, there was something seriously wrong with it, so he and Mother abandoned dispensationalism. It became such a problem in the south that the General Assembly of the Southern Presbyterian Church appointed a study committee chaired by Dr. Felix Gear of Columbia Theological Seminary in Decatur, Georgia, that examined the whole system and concluded that it was not an acceptable method of biblical interpretation.

Little by little, dispensationalism disappeared from among Presbyterians, as those who held it either changed or left. The name Scofield is not so prominent nowadays, but the system is very popular among independent churches and underlies the popular series of *Left Behind* novels.

One striking feature of dispensationalism's New Testament interpretation holds that Jesus's familiar "Sermon on the Mount" (Matthew 5-7) does not apply to our present life. It is really the law for the Kingdom that will prevail only after Jesus comes again. Therefore it is easy for believers to ignore the problems of poverty and war that go on continually.

Mac Long became a prolific primitive artist and painted a number of very graphic pictures to illustrate the exotic visions in the Bible. One issue of the quarterly *Alumni Journal* published by Davidson College featured Mac Long's paintings, which his heirs had donated to the college.

As soon as we children could read, we each received our own Bible; and after supper every night, we had family prayers, reading pretty straight through the narrative portions of the Bible, Old Testament and New. Mother read one verse, then Dad, then I, and the three sisters in order of birth.

In Winston-Salem, we lived out our commitment by joining First Presbyterian there, where Mr. Bill sat with us in the same pew. Mother was very active in the Women's Auxiliary, and in the course of time, both Dad and Mother taught Sunday school classes. We had an active youth group meeting every Sunday evening, and I became one of the leaders. We had Presbytery Youth conferences locally and a synod-wide youth conference at Davidson College yearly.

3e. My Call to the Ministry

The summer after my junior year in high school, I went to the synod conference at Davidson College. The principal Bible teacher was Dr. Rachel Henderlite, professor at the General Assembly's Presbyterian School of Christian Education (PSCE) in Richmond, Virginia. Years later, she became the first woman ordained to the ministry in the Southern Presbyterian Church. At the youth conference, her theme was the account of God's call to Jeremiah to be a prophet to the nations as told in the early chapters of the book. I was deeply impressed how he had objected initially as being too young, only at last to submit to God's call. In the dorm one evening, several of us guys were discussing what sort of work we might eventually do. By that time, I had worked some years at Taylor Bros., and I was pointed toward being third generation in the family business. Recalling Dr. Henderlite's Bible lessons and my attraction to China from my cousin Augusta White, I told the group I was beginning to feel a call to the ministry, but I really didn't want that. I probably felt a subconscious influence from my mother. She by no means put pressure on me or made an issue of it, but I have a distinct memory that once when I was talking to her about the prospects of my going into Taylor Bros., she quietly asked what had happened to my early declaration that I was going to be a missionary to China.

The last session of the youth conference was an outdoor evening service, and the speaker, Dr. Samuel Glasgow, made an impassioned plea for young people to dedicate themselves to full-time Christian service. I felt a tremendous pull to respond, but I remained seated, and I could see the sweat on my upper legs seeping through my pants above the knees. I did not join those who went forward. After I got back home, the whole experience continued to weigh on me, and I finally concluded that I could no longer resist God's call.

One night, I came home from a date; and though Mother and Dad were already in bed, they heard me come in and called me to say good night. I decided that was the time to tell them about my call. There was a lengthy silence. Then Dad said, "Well, son, if you wanted to be a doctor or a lawyer or go into some other line of business, I would strongly object. But if the Lord is calling you to the ministry, I'll do everything I can to help you." And he did.

3f. My Father as a Presbyterian Churchman

Over the years, Dad's faithful devotion to the Presbyterian Church led to his becoming active at all levels. First, he was elected a deacon of the First Presbyterian of Winston-Salem. At that time, deacons were responsible for financial affairs and care of property, even though according to the

New Testament, deacons functioned in works of compassion and service. When Dad and other new deacons were elected, many members of the church had begun to feel that everything seemed to be going to seed. The new deacons studied the Book of Order to learn what was expected of them. They learned that at that time, the rules permitted congregations to elect officers on a rotating basis with limited terms. The honorable status of a ruling elder was for life (even if he might become inactive). In many congregations, the Session had neglected the reformed principle of keeping hearts and minds open to necessary change. Older men often became more conservative and set in their ways. Though deacons were subordinate to the elders, Dad and his fellow deacons availed themselves of the instructions of the Book of Order and gradually convinced the congregation to adopt the rotation of office for both elders and deacons. The result was a rejuvenation of the congregation's life.

Dad was always jealous to preserve the principle of the priesthood of all believers, to do his best to fulfill that responsibility himself, and to insist that the teaching elder or minister was actually a servant of the particular church. He loved to tell the story of meeting a well-known Presbyterian leader who asked which church he belonged to. Dad responded, "First Church of Winston-Salem." "Oh," said the other, "you belong to Dr. So-and-so's church!" In a dignified voice, Dad replied, "Dr. So-and-so is the pastor of *my* church."

In due course, Dad was elected a ruling elder; and after serving on various presbytery committees, he was elected a commissioner to the General Assembly. At that time, they finally decided to do something about the Negro question. Ever since the end of the Civil War, the minority blacks were organized into segregated presbyteries and the Snedecor Synod, where they were pretty much neglected. Dad took active part in the discussions at the General Assembly, and in the end, he was elected to the Executive Committee of Home Missions and its subcommittee on Negro work. For the first time in his life, I think, Dad became closely acquainted with African Americans who were more than mere factory hands. One of them was Dr. Lawrence Bottoms, who later became the first Negro moderator of the whole General Assembly of the Presbyterian Church (US).

It's very interesting to me that this same Dr. Bottoms at an earlier time had served a church in Louisville, Kentucky, and Margaret Hopper had come to know and admire him. At the time Margaret and I were planning our wedding, we naturally expected that her father would officiate. She did not discuss the matter with me, but she told me later that she had thought seriously about asking her father to ask Dr. Bottoms to assist him at our wedding, but she decided to let the matter drop. I think it was probably a wise decision. I'm not sure that I would have been sufficiently mature by then to feel comfortable with such an unusual act. Through Dad's new relationships, he began to moderate his views on race. The eventual outcome of the efforts begun by the Negro Work Committee was the abolition of Snedecor Synod and the full integration of the black churches.

4.   Further Developments at Taylor Bros.

When we first moved to Winston-Salem, Dad still ran Taylor Long Bottling. His main responsibility was designing the flavor formulas and producing the syrup for distribution to the bottlers. After a time in circumstances I don't know, Dad left the company with Uncle Shorty Long and moved over to Taylor Bros. with Mr. Bill and Uncle Harry. As far as my recollection goes, Taylor Long Bottling Co. dwindled away.

The summer I was twelve years old, I came home from a period at Camp Hanes, expecting to go back to the factory, but I had a high fever and had to go to bed. Dr. Pfohl diagnosed it as bronchial pneumonia. Mother made vests out of cotton muslin, slathered them with mustard paste, and wrapped them around my chest. I recall that Bess too was sick, though not so seriously as I. While we were still invalids, Mr. Bill died at age eighty-two. He suffered a ruptured appendix that caused intestinal peritonitis, and before the discovery of penicillin and sulfa drugs, the poison took his life after about ten days. Bess and I couldn't go to his funeral.

Uncle Harry succeeded Mr. Bill as president of Taylor Bros., and after he died, Dad took over. Somewhere along the line, Bohannon Company, the only other surviving independent tobacco company in Winston-Salem, went out of business. They had no member of the current generation willing or prepared to take over a precarious operation. Taylor Bros. bought some of their brands and goodwill. By then, it was clear there would be no third generation Taylor in our business. Uncle Harry's only son Harry Jr. was brain injured at birth. Uncle Barrett had long since gone into another line in a different city, and his only son,

William Barrett Taylor III, had remained in the professional military after the war. I was committed to the Christian ministry.

Dad recruited several people in succession to join the business and understudy him to be able to take over eventually, but it never worked out. Taylor Bros. was too small to be able to pay the kind of salary needed to attract a truly capable person. So the board of directors and the Taylor family members who owned stock responded positively to a proposal from American Snuff Company of Memphis, Tennessee, to buy the business.

That all came about while I was in Japan. As I understood it, it was a stock swap deal. Taylor Bros. stayed in Winston-Salem, and Dad remained president, though subordinate to the Board of American Snuff, and he was an active member of that board of directors. Many years later, my cousin William Barrett Taylor III told me his account of the deal. Evidently, through his father, Barrett had voting rights of some shares of stock and was present in the negotiations. Dad told me once that Mr. Bill knew his children didn't get along too well, and he had designated a large block of stock to be administered by the Wachovia Bank under the authority of Mr. Charlie Norfleet so as to prevent a stalemate on a serious issue if the siblings couldn't agree. According to cousin Barrett, Dad at first opposed the merger though the other family members wanted it. Finally, Mr. Norfleet mediated the arrangement that kept Dad president of Taylor Bros. and a member of the board of American Snuff. On those terms, Dad agreed.

American Snuff sent Donald Soefker to understudy Dad, and he was an excellent choice, a quick learner, and an able successor to Dad. Donald was a Catholic (many of Snuff's senior officers were), and he was very active in building a new Catholic church in Winston-Salem. He and Dad had a very warm, mutually admiring relationship. Dad had expected to follow his father's example and continue active at Taylor Bros. as long as he was physically able, but when he reached American Snuff's mandatory retirement age of sixty-five, he had to quit.

Donald Soefker was made the next president, and he completed plans to abandon the rickety old buildings at the end of First Street and build a modern, up-to-date factory on Stratford Road. Donald told me that American Snuff had wanted to build the new Taylor Bros. factory in Memphis, but he had firmly put his foot down and refused. "The Taylor family and Taylor Bros. have been important parts of the whole history and development of Winston-Salem, and you can't take this away."

Donald fought and won that battle out of appreciation of the Taylors and his loyal admiration of Dad.

4a. Dad's Last Years

Affiliation with American Snuff made things financially much more comfortable for Dad in his later years. He and Mother made a good long visit to Japan to visit Margaret and me and the boys at Shikoku Christian College. They stayed in the apartment of Lardner and Grace Moore since they were away on home assignment at the time. Back at home, Dad was active in the Kiwanis Club. He said the Rotarians owned the town, the Lions ran the town, and the Kiwanians enjoyed the town. Dad also enjoyed driving one of the early Volkswagen Beetles, and he and Mother did a good deal of traveling. He was not feeling very well when they returned home one Saturday evening from an extended trip up to New England.

The next day at church, a friend and fellow elder who was a medical doctor recognized signs of jaundice and insisted Dad see him the next day for an examination. Various tests indicated cancer of the liver, which apparently had made some progress before Dad felt it and the signs had become recognizable. The operation was too late to be effective, and that was before the days of chemotherapy and radiation. The prognosis was that Dad might survive as much as six months. Though he considered another trip to Japan to see his son Archie, he died five weeks to the day after surgery.

While Dad was in his terminal illness, Donald wrote to me in Japan to tell how Dad was taking it. "He is very comforted by his Presbyterian faith," Donald said. Dad had no fears of death or of having to go through purgatory. As the Westminster Shorter Catechism states, "The souls of believers are, at their death, made perfect in holiness, and do immediately pass into glory; and their bodies, being still united to Christ, do rest in their graves till the resurrection" (Question 37). Dad's funeral took place at First Presbyterian. He insisted on a plain coffin, but wanted one with handles comfortable for the pallbearers. Instead of cut flowers, he wanted a couple of potted trees. As a hymn, he chose "The Church's One Foundation." American Snuff big shots (all backslid Catholics according to Dad) attended the service. They expressed their amazed appreciation for the note of total joy and hopefulness of the service.

The Kiwanis club published an obituary of Dad in their newsletter, including the following:

> Arch Taylor was always ARCH TAYLOR. In whatever he did, he was himself. In a way, he was a nonconforming conformist. He spoke out but stayed in and kept his sense of humor. Like the community at large, Kiwanis has lost a thoroughly fascinating, refreshing, useful, individualistic member—kind, friendly, firm, and true.

This tribute to my father lingers in my memory and in a way serves as an example for me. As a Taylor, as a Christian, as a Presbyterian, and as a citizen of the United States, I try to be a nonconforming conformist to speak out but stay in and always keep my sense of humor.

Dad was very generous and shared his good fortune. He planned his estate based on American Snuff stock. While he still lived, he set up a trust for each of us four children. During our lifetime, we can use the income from the trusts, but not until our individual death can the principal of each trust be touched, at which time each of our several children per stirpes is to get equal shares. I think all of us beneficiaries of the trusts used some of the money to buy homes. Certainly, the income from my trust made it possible for Margaret and I me to build our home in Tadotsu, Japan. This was entirely Margaret's idea. She observed that older missionaries, such as Lardner and Grace Moore, who had always lived in housing supplied by the mission, had no equity in a home when they retired back to the U.S. Together, Margaret and I worked it out with the Japan mission to allow us to build our own home and to pay us the equivalent of mission housing allowance since the mission already housed some of our colleagues in rented homes. This was one of the many examples of Margaret's wise ways.

At first, the Wachovia Bank administered the Taylor trusts very efficiently. But eventually, they informed us that American Snuff was not important enough for them to track its stock regularly. Either we would have to pay them extra to do that or we would have to let them sell that stock and replace it with some of the stocks they regularly tracked. That possibility is in fact included in the original trust document. Thus, our material connection with Taylor Bros. has long since ended.

American Snuff changed its name to Conwood Corp. and diversified. They took on Hot Shot insect spray and Griffin shoe polish among others. Diversification didn't pay off as expected, and for a while, Taylor Bros. was the best moneymaker for Conwood. Later, the Pritzker family bought Conwood and concentrated on tobacco products. In 2006, Pritzker sold out to Reynolds American, the latest manifestation of the old R. J. Reynolds Tobacco. My sister Bess sent me the notice of this sale, which she saw in the *Wall Street Journal* on May 26, 2006, "Smokeless-Tobacco Deal is Struck," in which it says Reynolds bought Conwood for 3.5 billion dollars in cash. Bess commented, "Wow! And to think, Wachovia in its wisdom sold off all the Conwood stock in our trusts and replaced them with their own lethargic Wachovia (now Evergreen) units!" Thus, Reynolds finally gained control over the survivor of the old Taylor Bros. Inc. that Dick Reynolds could neither buy from Mr. Bill Taylor nor drive into bankruptcy. At least, we Taylor heirs were spared the temptation of having too much money.

5. Mother's Second Marriage

Some time after Dad died, Mother visited my sister Bess and her husband, Colonel Karl Zipf, who were living in Arlington, Virginia. Dr. Clem Williams, who was a dentist living in Washington, DC, knew of the circumstances of Mother's visit, and he called Bess to inquire if it was appropriate for him to visit. Mother and Dr. Williams's first wife, Mae, had been close girlhood friends, and Mother had been one of the bridesmaids in their wedding. Mae had been killed in an auto accident some years previously. With Bess's approval, Dr. Clem came to visit; and in a short time, he proposed that they marry. Mother insisted that they delay at least a year, but then they married, and she moved to Dr. Clem's home in Washington, where his dental office was in his residence. Though officially retired, he still cared for a few longtime patients. Dr. Clem had two sisters, one of whom was a retired secretary with a skill at bookkeeping, and she managed their affairs, including filling out income taxes. She also took charge of arrangements when the whole group decided it was time to move to a retirement facility, which they did to Tampa, Florida.

After some years, Dr. Clem became a partial invalid, alternating between their apartment and the health wing of the facility. One day, while Mother was alone at home, she didn't show up next day as usual; and upon investigation, she was discovered lying half dressed in her bedroom. Apparently, she had had a sudden stroke or heart failure while preparing for bed in the evening or getting dressed first thing in the morning. Dr. Clem himself passed on a few days later.

In writing her will, Mother set aside a sum of money to provide for a memorial service at First Presbyterian in Winston-Salem, and she wanted the date set at a reasonable time after her death to allow all family members, including Margaret and me and our boys from Japan, to gather for a family reunion of several days. In the family, we took to referring to this event as her wake, but Mother called it her houseparty. Bess was the executor of Mother's estate, so she was in charge of this and all other details, and she carried it all off in a very efficient manner. It was a good opportunity for all the immediate family to get together, and it actually became the first of a series of reunions about every two or three years thereafter for quite some time.

By now, the direct descendants of Archibald Boggs Sr. and Margaret Webb Taylor have multiplied numerically and scattered geographically to the extent that it is no longer practicable for the whole Taylor tribe to hold a full family reunion. We try to keep in touch as well as we can, and from time to time here and there, a small group of us may get together for personal connection and reacquaintance.

PART TWO

Education, Marriage, Early Ministry

3

Education, Marriage, Early Ministry

1. High School

During our first years in Winston-Salem, we lived in Old Salem, close enough to walk to Wiley School. When we moved to Fourth Street, I could walk to the elementary school adjacent to R. J. Reynolds High School, where I went after that. When I had gone to the Y as a boy, Mr. Charlie Grimes the athletic director told Dad that I was a natural runner, so I went out for cross-country in the fall of my first year at Reynolds High. It didn't take me long to realize I wasn't meant for long-distance running, so in the spring, I tried other events. I had pretty good speed for the dashes, but somehow or other hurdles ended up being my event—110 yards high hurdles and 220 yards low hurdles. By the time I graduated, I had set the record for those events in the statewide track meet.

I didn't have any trouble in schoolwork, except in geometry. The teacher was Mr. Ralph Sullivan, who was a prissy old fellow who couldn't keep discipline in his class. There was a lot of whispering and note passing going on. During the year, Dad took me on a business trip to New Orleans. On my next report card, my geometry grade was the first C I had ever gotten, and Dad wanted to know how come. On inquiry, Mr. Sullivan said I had missed a test while I was on the trip, and that's what pulled my grade down. He would give me a makeup test so I could pull my grade back up. I took the test and thought I did OK, but on the next report, that C remained. Mother and I were afraid Dad would blow the roof off if he saw it, so we surreptitiously altered the grade to B before we showed it to Dad.

World history was another pitfall for me, but that was because I thought I knew more than the teacher. He was Mr. Joby Hawn, who was also (or primarily) the football coach. He was heard to yell at the football squad in practice, criticizing them for a poor defensive play. "You coulda drove a wagon through that hole!" I thought Mr. Hawn misinterpreted what was written in the textbook a time or two, and I didn't hesitate to let him know. I also undertook to correct his pronunciation of *Chaldea*, the name of one of the ancient Mesopotamian lands I knew from family Bible reading. On that period's report card, I got a C in deportment, and I couldn't help thinking he must have given me a low enough rating to pull the average grade down to C. In any case, when the time came for inducting students into the honor society, I was passed over and had to wait till the next semester to get in. The motto for the honor society was "Noblesse oblige." On one occasion, I was asked to give a brief talk on the theme, which I did. As I look back on it now, the whole idea of the motto gives the impression of being self-congratulating and condescending. I think my remarks probably gave that impression, but I didn't realize it at the time.

1a. High School Girlfriend

In high school, I never took any special interest in girls. We used to refer to the most aggressive guys as wolves. I certainly was not a wolf. However, one of my classmates, Jessie Evans Brunt, set her cap for me, as the old saying has it. Whether it was by her instigation, I don't know. But the first I knew of it was one day, I was headed back to class from recess when several people walking behind me spoke loudly enough for me to overhear. "Jessie is sweet on old duffle britches." I walked on as though I hadn't heard it, but I knew they must be referring to me because I was the last one still wearing knickers and I let them flop down around my lower legs. My mother, ever frugal, had found a bargain and bought me two perfectly good pairs of corduroy knickers at a very reasonable price. Not long after that incident, the gossip column in the school newspaper had an item that read, "*Jebat* is a special word that describes Jessie Evans Brunt and Arch Taylor." She had made up that word by combining our initials and had shared it with some of her friends, but that was the first I knew of it.

I didn't take any initiative in this thing, but Jessie's stratagem succeeded. I have no recollection how we actually got together for our first date, but summer vacation started soon, and I used to ride my bike over to her house, and we played tennis at a park in her neighborhood. I had a workshop in the basement of our house where I used to make model planes and ships. I was working down there one day when my mother's laundry lady had come to do the wash. I went upstairs to phone Jessie to set up a tennis date, and evidently, the wash lady had somehow listened in and knew what I had done. When I came back downstairs, she teased me about it and pointed out that the pencil protruding from my left shirt pocket was pulsing noticeably.

Jessie and I went swimming several times out to Crystal Lake. Once when we were in the water, the sky clouded over, and the breeze quickened, and next thing I knew, I was shivering. Jessie didn't seem to be bothered, and I didn't say anything, but she noticed my discomfort and suggested we leave. I had a similar experience later in midwinter at one of our high school football games. I had a nice leather jacket that I thought was comfortable as well as pretty neat looking, but evidently, I didn't put on enough layers underneath. By halftime, I was thoroughly chilled, so we left early again.

Winston-Salem was the site of the Forsyth County Fair about the end of August every year, and since school didn't start till after Labor Day, children could freely go to the fair. As the big brother, I had the privilege of accompanying my three sisters to the fair one day. As we strolled down the midway, we saw a booth where a man was selling triangular felt pennants on which he would stitch your name or some expression of your choice, so we decided we would each get one. I was first, of course, and I asked for JEBAT. "What? What's that?" the man asked, and I explained so he could spell it correctly. BESS was next, but he mistook her name and sewed MESS. We objected, of course, and he reluctantly ripped out the stitching and redid BESS. Next was KASS, and he acted as though he never heard of such a name, so we carefully spelled it for him. So far, so good. Last was my youngest sister, who was hardly as tall as the edge of the table where he worked. He leaned over, glared down at her, and snarled, "And what's *your* name?" In a meek little voice, she replied, "Mary."

I never got really serious about Jessie, but I never dated anybody else. We ate lunch together at school and went to movies once in a while. We were a natural couple at school events. One of my friends whose family had a summerhouse up in the mountains at Blowing Rock hosted a house party one weekend, and Jessie and I were among the dozen boys and girls who were invited. Somewhere around I still have a photo of that group.

After graduation, Jessie went to North Carolina Women's College in Greensboro, and I went to Davidson College near Charlotte. I joined a fraternity, and on one of the dance weekends, I invited Jessie to come as my date. In those days, Davidson didn't permit dancing on campus, so we had to go to Charlotte for the dances. The girls stayed in various rooming houses in Davidson, and the boys, of course, stayed in the dorms. For me, it was a so-so event, not bad, but not particularly thrilling. Jessie wrote me a thank-you note afterward, but I let the correspondence sort of lapse after that. Sometime later, Jessie wrote and suggested that maybe it was time for us to end our relationship. Reading that gave me a genuine sense of relief, as I had long since felt the same way and I didn't know how to let her know. I simply replied that I agreed with her and thanked her for our times together in the past.

During summer vacation, I expected to be a counselor at Camp Hanes most of the time, but I was at home for a little while before camp started. I went downtown for some errands one day, and as I crossed a street one direction, I saw Jessie on the other side coming toward me. As we approached, I smiled and spoke up very cordially. "Well, hello, Jessie!" Without so much as a glance, she passed me by in stolid silence. That was the last time I saw Jessie for many years.

After I retired from Japan and was living in Louisville, Kentucky (my wife Margaret had died several years previously), I received a letter from a Chris Nichols in Winston-Salem, who was totally unknown to me. I opened the letter, and the writer introduced himself as the husband of Jessie. He said she had often spoken of me, and he was curious to meet me. That struck me as an intriguing idea, so I replied that perhaps we could get together some time.

In early summer 1990, our family had one of our biennial reunions, this one at Montreat, North Carolina, the principal summer conference center of the Southern Presbyterian Church. Wayne Todd, husband of my sister Mary, planned the event. The reunion was in conjunction with the wedding of their second daughter, Martha, to Ross Sloan. Montreat was special to them, for as young people, they had participated in summer youth events there. I thought that since I had to go so far as Montreat, I might as well go on to Winston-Salem to meet Chris and Jessie. I informed them of the date, and I offered them dinner at the hotel where my son Samuel and I had made reservations. He was single and was coming from New York for the reunion and Martha and Ross's wedding.

After the reunion, Samuel and I drove east on the interstate and turned in to a rest stop. As we were on the way back to our car, we overheard a woman's voice calling, "Jared! Jared!" It was Evelyn Rich addressing Samuel by the name he used professionally. She had come from her home in England to do graduate work at Boston University, and she was researching right-wing political groups in the U.S. for her thesis. She had gotten acquainted with Samuel that way. She had been in Winston-Salem earlier to attend some such meeting and after that had gone west to Asheville, beyond Montreat, to interview one of the big shots. She too was now headed east, so she booked in at the same hotel.

Jessie and Chris arrived in due time, and Jessie had thoughtfully brought along the Reynolds High School yearbook of 1937 to rekindle memories with me and to share with Samuel. She also had clippings from the Winston-Salem newspaper, some of which featured Taylor Bros. Jessie and I swapped information about our respective families. She and Chris had no children of their own, but they had adopted a daughter, who had showed resentment and rebelliousness and given them a lot of trouble before she finally left home. Chris was a retired Episcopal minister, and he and Jessie had been active in many worthwhile peace and justice activities.

When I wrote them afterward, I enclosed a clipping from the Louisville paper telling about a group called the Giraffe Society—featuring and celebrating people who were willing to stick their neck out. I said I thought Chris was a suitable candidate for that honor. We exchanged Christmas greetings for a few years. Jessie died first, and Chris went to live in an Episcopal retirement facility in Eastern North Carolina, where he passed away later.

2. Davidson College and Louisville Seminary

Dad and his brothers and two cousins had attended Davidson, a well-known Presbyterian-related men's college, and I never had any desire to go elsewhere. When I entered, the student body numbered only about four hundred and reached perhaps 650 by the time I graduated. In those days, only applicants for prestigious northeastern universities had to take entrance exams, so I was admitted to Davidson on the basis of my high school record. All students were required to attend chapel every day and take four consecutive semesters of Bible. The daily Bible readings at home during my childhood gave me a good grounding, and I won the gold medal awarded to the freshman student with the highest grade in Bible. I was a candidate for the ministry, having already been examined and approved by Winston-Salem Presbytery. During that examination, one of the ministers pressed me rather insistently, wanting to know when I had my first experience of being saved. I replied that I had never known a time when I wasn't saved and that I always knew God loved me and Jesus was my Savior. Dad told me that that particular minister was always trying to insist that everybody had to be able to relate an experience of being born again. The best I could do was to tell my experience of being called into the ministry at the Synod Youth Conference.

During my four years in college, I was a regular on the track team, running hurdles as I had in high school. The high hurdles at college were three inches higher than those for high schools, so it took me some time to improve my high school record of 15.2 seconds to 14.9, a new record for Davidson. (It has since been lowered.) For three years, I sang second tenor in the men's glee club, and I was also a member of Le Cercle Français. Both of these groups made trips to other schools, and we always seemed to make a big hit whenever we visited a school for women. As we entered one such school, a girl came up to me, licked her finger, and placed it on my chest, exclaiming, "A man!"

One of my most enjoyable activities was membership in the honorary fraternity *Sigma Upsilon* dedicated to the practice of writing. At every monthly meeting, we heard a poem, an essay, and a short story presented by members. One year, we undertook a narrative poem in blank verse, a different member adding a new chapter each month. At daily chapel services with everybody required to be present, the student body president usually made various announcements. He had to weed out numerous attempts to slip in a bogus announcement to get a laugh. Once in a great while, somebody would succeed in slipping in something connected to *Sigma Upsilon*, which always resulted in everybody shouting, "Oop! Oop! Oop!" Once in a while, some student who had done something notable (good or bad) might be picked up from his seat and passed down to the front. It was a great honor for anybody who was passed down.

Present-day students or readers who have attended much larger and much more impersonal schools may think this all sounds rather juvenile, but actually, Davidson was a very rigorous college, and I look back on it with deep appreciation for having given me a sound liberal arts foundation. I took full advantage of all my opportunities, and I was elected to Phi Beta Kappa and to the student leader honorary society Omicron Delta Kappa.

One of the most impressive traditions at Davidson is the honor system, which has existed since before Dad's time and still today is in full force. At freshman orientation, we were made familiar with the honor system, along with other rules and regulations. I remember Dean Sentelle emphasizing the importance of the "little red book," which he held up and waved significantly as he advised us to become familiar with its contents. "Remember," he warned, "ignorance of the law is no excuse." During the orientation, the freshmen were divided into groups, and an upper-class adviser instructed each group, explaining the rules and placing special emphasis on the honor system.

In actual operation, the student honor council, representatives elected by the student body, took full responsibility for enforcing the honor code, and the faculty and school administration accepted their decision in every case. At the end of every test or exam, students would write and sign, "I have neither given nor received help on this test." Not only did we pledge not to cheat but also to inform members of the honor council of any infractions we might have witnessed.

Davidson is still considered one of the best liberal arts colleges in the country. Its student body, around twelve hundred, consists of about half-and-half women and men, and its physical plant is constantly improving. For some decades, Davidson has awarded scholarships for athletes, but it has adhered strictly to high academic standards and is well-known for outstanding athletes who maintain top-level grades, including Phi Beta Kappa. An early impression I got was the striking difference between the atmosphere at Davidson and Mr. Sullivan's high school geometry class. In his, it was easy to cheat because everybody did it and nobody was punished, whereas at Davidson, the whole system and general atmosphere made it easy *not* to cheat.

Near the end of my sophomore year, I saw a notice offering Patterson scholarships to Louisville Presbyterian Theological Seminary that provided full tuition and board for three years, plus the possibility of aid for further graduate work after seminary. Qualifying for a Patterson scholarship required superior grade average, but also three full years of both Greek and Latin beyond the introductory level. As a ministerial candidate, I was finishing my second year of Greek, so two more years would qualify me for that. In high school, I had had Latin for four years, which covered the introductory requirement, but I would have to get three years of Latin in my next two years at Davidson. Professor Ernest Beaty was very accommodating and allowed me to take those courses, though I was the only student at that level.

Another advantage of the Patterson Scholarship program was that it provided aid during college years also if one applied early enough. Watson Street was a later Presbyterian leader who grew up in an orphanage, went to Davidson, and qualified early for the Patterson. After going to Louisville Seminary, he did graduate work at Union Seminary in New York under the renowned scholar Reinhold Niebuhr. Watson Street was the executive secretary of the Foreign Mission executive Committee during the time the future of Shikoku Christian College was being debated (see below chapter 7, Shikoku Christian College).

One subject I avoided at Davidson was ROTC (Reserve Officers Training Corps). In addition to class work, the course involved a certain amount of physical exercise and marching, and that was counted as the equivalent of a physical education course. Those of us who opted out of ROTC were required to spend several hours a week at the gym engaging in some sort of physical exercise, and I did that during the off-season from track. Some students continued with two advanced years of ROTC training, which, with summer camp at an army post elsewhere, qualified them for second lieutenant rank in the Army Reserve at graduation.

The Pearl Harbor attack occurred in December of my senior year in college, and we students had to register for the draft. As I recall, only about one or two Davidson seniors were drafted immediately and didn't graduate. All those who had taken the advanced ROTC courses were automatically required to go straight into the army after commencement. I was deferred from the draft as a ministerial candidate, so I went on to Louisville Presbyterian Theological Seminary (LPTS) after I graduated in June 1942.

Above, I mentioned going with my dad to a sham battle and to war movies when I was a child and how at that very young age I picked up a sense of dislike for the very concept of war. That general attitude was further strengthened by my avoidance of the ROTC course at Davidson and my deferment from the draft by reason of being a formal candidate for the Christian ministry. I had also qualified for the Patterson Scholarship while at Davidson College, so in the fall after my graduation in 1942, I rode the train from Winston-Salem to Louisville, Kentucky, and entered Louisville Presbyterian Theological Seminary at 109 East Broadway, very near the center of town.

3.   Margaret Ruth Hopper

About the middle of October, in my first year in seminary, Dr. Lewis J. Sherrill, my professor of Christian education, invited me and two other students to his home for dessert after our evening meal in the seminary dining hall. Dr. and Mrs. Sherrill lived out in the East End, and the seminary was still in the old location at First and Broadway downtown, so Dr. Sherrill took us to his home in his car. Shortly after we arrived, Mrs. Sherrill came home, bringing two young women with her. The Sherrills' two children were away at college. In fact, their son John was a freshman at Davidson during my senior year there. Mrs. Sherrill had taken that opportunity to get an advanced degree at the Kent School of Social Work at the University of Louisville. The two young women were members of some of her classes.

We had a very pleasant evening with a simple, but delicious dessert and lots of good conversation. I was particularly impressed with one of the young women, Margaret Hopper. When the evening ended, we men had to see the women home by public transportation. Margaret lived at quite a distance in the West End, involving several transfers to get there and then return to the seminary. One of the other seminary students was in his second year, and he was familiar with the trolley bus system, so it was logical for him to see her home. Besides, he had been acquainted with Margaret previously during their participation in Presbyterian youth activities in college days. As for me, I was unfamiliar with the bus system, but the other young woman's home was much easier to reach and less complicated for me to get back to the seminary afterward, so I saw her home. I never saw her again. I don't remember her name. I didn't wait many days to call Margaret for a date.

A senior at the seminary was Bill Laws, also a graduate of Davidson, who had befriended me when I first arrived. He had a car, which was of particular importance since it was wartime. I told Bill about having met Margaret Hopper and asked her for a date. He said he would call his friend Ellen Davis and we would double date to a musical concert at the U of L School of Music. That was an excellent plan, so I called Margaret with the suggestion, which she accepted. Her schedule included an evening class at the General Hospital just a few blocks away from the seminary, so it would be easy for us to pick her up. She would meet me in the lobby of the hospital at an appointed time.

In the event, it turned out that Ellen Davis was not well that evening and couldn't join us, but Bill had made the commitment, so he used his car and went along on the date with Margaret and me. The concert was a string quartet, about which I knew very little, but it turned out Margaret played cello, and she enjoyed it a great deal. Afterward, she invited us to come into her home for a snack, and we sat in the living room for a while. When we got up to go, the arm of the chair in which Bill was sitting came off in his hand, a rather embarrassing moment. We went into the hall to retrieve our coats. For some reason, the basement door was ajar; and when Bill took his coat off the coat tree, it fell over into the basement entrance. Another embarrassing moment! Margaret didn't hold the incident against us. I was not at all deterred, and I kept on dating her.

Later on, she told me about another detail of that first date which had been hitherto unrevealed. She said that when we first met at the Sherrills' home, she was not wearing her glasses, for she was nearsighted and the lenses were rather thick. This was before the day of contact lenses, and she had left her glasses off for appearance's sake, so she had not gotten a clear picture of what I really looked like. Therefore, for our first date, she had asked Mrs. Sherrill to stand with her in the hospital lobby to identify me when I showed up.

We dated pretty regularly during the next months, and I invited her to some of the events at the seminary. Unaggressive as usual, I had not embraced her or tried to kiss her. But after a date one evening, I told her I loved her and wanted to marry her. She then informed me that another seminary student was also dating her. He had met her when I brought her to one of the seminary functions, and totally unbeknownst to me, he had been cutting in on me. At that point, Margaret could only decline my proposal. I later came to know that she was a very popular young lady who had several suitors, including one in the army who dated her whenever he got leave and wanted to dance all night. She was an excellent dance partner, which I was not. Margaret's younger brother Bill, who was a student at Centre College at the time, liked to tell how he had to serve as a traffic manager at their home during summer vacation that year to avoid embarrassing encounters when more than one suitor showed up at the same time.

At the end of my first year at the seminary, I went to Charlestown, Indiana, where I was to be the student pastor of the Presbyterian Church there for the next two years. During the academic year, I would live in the dormitory and commute on Sunday. But during the summer months, I lived in Charlestown. Mrs. Kelly, who lived across the street from the church, had a washhouse in her backyard that had been furnished as a bachelor's apartment. That was to be my home during that summer and the next. A hot plate, a sink, and a small fridge made it possible for me to feed myself more or less adequately. There was a bus service between Louisville and Charlestown, and I had become familiar with the trolley bus system, so I visited Margaret often during the summer. The summer assignment of the other seminary student who had dated Margaret was far away in Eastern Kentucky, so I was spared that competition. Her house on West Burnett Avenue had a front porch with a glider where we spent many summer hours and talked about many things. One evening, as I stood up to leave, I took Margaret in my arms and placed my lips on hers. She did not resist. After several moments, she said (according to my memory), "I think we should get married."

I was eager to do the deed as soon as possible, but Margaret said that if she didn't complete her master's thesis, she would never get her degree. So at her insistence, we put off our wedding date for a year, that is, to September 5, 1944, after she got her degree and before the beginning of my third seminary year. That was a wise decision. We got better acquainted with each other and with each other's family. As a tobacco man, Dad had business in Kentucky sometimes, so he met Margaret, and over Thanksgiving holiday that year, she and I rode the train to Winston-Salem where she met some of my kinfolks. Margaret's thesis was a history of the New Deal's National Youth Administration program in Kentucky, and she was an admirer of Franklin D. Roosevelt and especially of Eleanor. Dad hated FDR, and he and Margaret would get in a hot discussion that I would have to interrupt. In this way, Margaret got some insights into my Southern family background. More information on this point is mentioned in the biographical sketch of Margaret included in this book.

3a. Margaret's Family: Hoppers and Terrys

My marriage to Margaret Hopper added more Presbyterian branches to the family tree of my sons, which I can briefly summarize here, thanks to the considerable research done by Margaret's brother Bill (William H. Hopper Jr.). The Hoppers apparently originated in the Netherlands, but Bill traced his line back as far as their early years in colonial America. The first of several named Blackgrove Hopper settled in what is now Fauquier County, Virginia, in 1715 on a grant of land from Catherine, Lady Fairfax of England. One of the Blackgrove Hoppers was a practicing lay Baptist preacher who moved through Tennessee into Kentucky and was officially ordained in 1812. A Major William Dunlap of Virginia fought in the Revolutionary War, and some of his descendants later came to Kentucky, where the Dunlap line was joined to the Hoppers: Mary Jane Dunlap married Joseph Hopper (the third of that name) on February 11, 1840, in Lancaster, Kentucky. Their son George Dunlap Hopper was the father of William Higgins Hopper, Margaret's father. By this time, the Hoppers were firmly Presbyterian. Father Hopper had a kinsman familiarly known as Uncle Joe Hopper, who was a well-known evangelist active for decades throughout Central Kentucky; and though he never attended seminary, he was ordained to the Presbyterian ministry at an advanced age.

Among George Dunlap Hopper's children, three entered full-time Christian service in the Presbyterian Church (US). His elder son William Higgins and his brother Joseph both graduated from Centre College and Louisville Presbyterian Theological Seminary and were ordained ministers. Joseph Hopper and their sister Margaret Higgins Hopper were missionaries in Korea. Older brother William had originally wanted to be a foreign missionary, but having to support his younger siblings due to the early death of his father, his own college and seminary education was delayed until he was considered too old for foreign mission service. Father Hopper was pastor of several churches outside of Louisville before being called to the Woodland Avenue church in Louisville. During those years, he married Ruth Eagleton Terry, and they had three daughters, of whom Margaret was the youngest. Father Hopper then was called to the Handley Memorial Church in Birmingham, Alabama, and William Jr. was born there.

Next, Father Hopper was called to serve on the Executive Committee of Christian Education and Ministerial Relief, which was located in

Louisville, so he and his wife and four children moved back to Louisville. A major accomplishment of William Sr. was the establishment of the Pension Plan of the Presbyterian Church (US), which is funded by contributions by the ministers themselves and the congregations they serve. This replaced the early system of "ministerial relief" according to which the care of retired or disabled ministers had depended on annual church-wide freewill offerings.

Margaret's mother was Ruth Eagleton Terry. The earliest of the Terry line in Bill's records was a Champness Terry in Louisa County, Virginia. Subsequent Terry generations included several more named Champness. Margaret's grandfather George Champ Terry, son of a medical doctor William Terry, was born in Peterstown, Virginia, near the state line with West Virginia. George Champ Terry was a businessman and settled in Murfreesboro, Tennessee, where he married Margaret Jane Knight (her mother was an Eagleton). Their daughter was Ruth Eagleton Terry, who married William Higgins Hopper. William and Ruth Hopper are the maternal grandparents of our three sons. William Archibald was named for his two grandfathers and our second son, John Eagleton, received names from families of his grandmothers. For our third son, Samuel Jared, we chose one biblical name and one from Mr. Wirt Jared and his wife, Miss. Leona, by far the most respected citizens of Buffalo Valley, Tennessee, and pillars of the Presbyterian Church of which I was a pastor for two years (see below chapter 4).

4. Student Pastor in Charlestown, Indiana

As I reported above, it was near the end of the summer of my first year in the seminary that Margaret and I became engaged to marry. I was still in my bachelor's quarters in Mrs. Kelly's backyard. My principal duties were as student pastor of the Charlestown Presbyterian Church, and I had considerable ministerial responsibility in addition to dating Margaret in Louisville. I moved my meager personal belongings into my "home" in Mrs. Kelly's backyard and gradually became accustomed to being a Hoosier.

The ministers of the local Methodist and Church of Christ (Disciples) churches were accustomed to inviting the Presbyterian minister to take turns with them preaching at the joint Sunday evening services on the town square during the summer. The first time it was my turn, I was going along pretty well in my sermon when, sitting near the front, a little old lady of the Methodist church spoke out, saying, "Ay-ay-ay-ay-*men*!" I was surprised by this response, an experience I had never had before, but I must say it stirred me up, and I think I did a better job as I continued my sermon, and she "aymened" me again before I finished.

4a. My First Funerals

One day, Mrs. Kelly came to tell me that she had word for me that a member of the church wanted me to conduct a funeral for her husband, who had just died. I went up to the church to get more details about this funeral. The deceased was the husband of a member of the church who lived almost up at Cincinnati, Ohio, on the Indiana side of the Ohio River. She had a teenaged son who was thought to be mentally retarded, and they had not actually attended the church for many years. Hardly anybody knew them. The husband, I was told, was not a professing Christian. The widow had telephoned the church to make her request and set a date. She informed us of the mortuary that would handle the casket and left all the other arrangements up to us.

The circumstances of this funeral put me in a situation of some disadvantage, with the facts that the family was totally unknown both to me and to most of the church people and the person who had died was not a Christian. To complicate things even more, my first year at the seminary had not included any instruction about conducting funerals; and during my entire young life, I had never so much as attended a funeral. Talk about a greenhorn!

Lucille Bare was a part-time secretary of the church who knew everybody and everything and also sang in the choir. I asked her to put together a trio or quartet, get the accompanist lined up, and pick out some hymns, which she did in her usual efficient manner. As for me, I got hold of the Presbyterian worship book and looked up the several orders of worship for funerals. We had only meager resources available, and I had no idea how to go about organizing anything elaborate, so I picked out the simplest order. Lucille and I and the pianist coordinated our various parts.

On the appointed day, the mortuary delivered the casket, and we placed it up front, but it remained closed. The widow and her son and a few friends and family members showed up in time for exchanging names and shaking hands before we started the service. A few members of the church also attended, including old Doctor Shelby, the irascible clerk of Session who played an important part in the education of student ministers like me. I followed the text of the service in a pretty literal manner, referring to the dear departed at appropriate points during the service.

As you can easily imagine, it was a pretty cut-and-dried affair. I don't remember the name of the family. I feel only a sense of failure that I did not offer any pastoral care or effective Christian comfort to this sister and her son in their time of bereavement, but they didn't seem to want anything like that and departed immediately after the service. When everybody else was gone, Doc Shelby said to me, "Don't they teach you all anything about funerals at that seminary? From anything you said, nobody would have known whether the body in the casket was a male or a female!"

A good many people from the hills of Kentucky moved to Southern Indiana to work at the Dupont Powder Plant nearby. Some found their way to local churches, but many seemed totally indifferent. The daughter of one of the latter families died, and somehow, the request for funeral service came to me. The service was held in the house where the family lived. The casket lay open at one side of the biggest room in the house, and the family and friends were crowded in. After the service, people filed by the casket to view the remains. When the father of the young woman came, he bent over the body and wept quite audibly. Somebody near me remarked, "Just listen at that old hypocrite! As long as she was alive, he used to treat her so mean. Just look at him now!"

4b. Margaret and I move to Charlestown

Margaret finished her thesis and got her master of science in social administration at the University of Louisville in 1944, and we were married on September 5. She expected to be a social case worker, which naturally involved a good deal of emotional pressure, and she let me know that she probably wouldn't be adding to that by going up to Charlestown every Sunday. That prospect didn't appeal to me, but there wasn't anything I could do about it, and we were looking for an apartment in the close neighborhood of the seminary and the

General Hospital. Dr. C. Morton Hanna, the seminary faculty member supervising the student ministers in a number of small churches in Southern Indiana, didn't like that idea either. He was able to get a part-time job for Margaret with the Presbyterian Church (USA) Board of Home Missions for home visitation in Charlestown, which had become the locus of incoming workers at the Dupont Powder Plant. He also arranged for us to rent an apartment in the Pleasant Ridge housing development in Charlestown that had been constructed for those workers.

We didn't ask any questions about how he managed all that, but we accepted the arrangement with gratitude. It necessitated our buying a car. Being wartime, no new cars were being made, and used cars weren't easy to get either. We both cashed in some of our war bonds and pooled our savings and bought an old Plymouth. It didn't even have a steel roof— only a fabric top that we had to keep patching at places along the edge to keep it from leaking. We were strictly limited by wartime conditions and had to have rationing coupons for gasoline and tires.

The Charlestown Presbyterian Church had a rather nice building plus a manse next door for a resident pastor, and Dr. Hanna, his wife, Margaret, and their two sons and two daughters lived there. Mrs. Hanna was a very able person herself. She was superintendent of the Sunday school and became an ideal role model for my Margaret. Besides doing her visitation, Marg, as I called her, also taught a class and accompanied the singing at Sunday school.

The seminary held classes Tuesday through Friday as the school placed special emphasis on students' getting real life pastoral experience, and many of us lived at a distance from Louisville, some considerably farther than I did. Several of us in Indiana, including one who attended the Southern Baptist Seminary, carpooled and took turns driving to Louisville for classes through the week.

During my third year in the seminary, one guest speaker at the daily chapel service was Miss Marian Wilcox, a China missionary of the Presbyterian Church (US) now back at home because of the war. She spoke of the rural ministry that had occupied her career and described in very vivid terms some of the hardships the Chinese people had to suffer because of the Japanese invasion. As I listened to her, my mind went back to my childhood when Cousin Augusta White had inspired me with the desire to go to China as a missionary. It seemed altogether as though there was nobody in the chapel except Miss Wilcox and me, and that through her, God was calling me to mission in China. In addition, I felt a connection to Miss Wilcox because I had heard my father mention her as the sister of one of his good friends during his Davidson College days.

Margaret was completely in accord with my call to China, as her Uncle Joe and Aunt Margaret Hopper were both in Korea and her father had originally wanted to enter foreign mission service. The war was still going on, so there was no possibility of our going to China soon, and besides, the Mission Executive Committee wanted us to have more experience at home before sending us overseas.

My calling into ministry had kept me from being drafted into the service, but Marg and I did our patriotic duty by recycling metal, paper, cardboard, etc., and buying savings bonds from our slender income. In addition, I signed up with the local Red Cross to make regular donations of blood. I received a small plastic pin for my lapel and got a special award when my cumulative donations exceeded a gallon. Dad was quite proud of my accomplishment. Given his own eagerness to volunteer in World War I, he may have felt some sense of dissatisfaction that I was not more directly involved in the war effort.

During my senior year in the seminary, Dad gave some indication that he thought I might inquire about becoming a chaplain in the military. Several of my fellow students were planning to look into the navy chaplaincy, so I decided to go along with them. Marg was upset when I told her and sort of criticized me for caving in to Dad, though I didn't feel that way. Three or four of us made our way to Memphis, Tennessee, where we met representatives of the Navy at the Coast Guard Station on the Mississippi River there. One of those officers interviewed me, asking various questions. He wanted to know to what church denomination I belonged. I replied "Presbyterian (US), that is, Southern." He looked through his data and informed me, "We've already got too many Southern Presbyterians. We don't need any more." For me, that settled the question. I considered it in a sense a divine answer to strengthen my pilgrimage on the path of nonviolence. Margaret was greatly relieved, and we began to take the next step in finding a pastorate for further preparation to go to China. Dad never said anything one way or another when I told him.

4

Pastorate in Tennessee

The Home Missions Committee of Nashville Presbytery, under the direction of its moderator Dr. Wilson, with supplementary funds from the presbytery and generous cooperation of the local Presbyterians, had accomplished some remarkable achievements despite wartime conditions. In Putnam County near the far eastern edge of Nashville Presbytery, there was a congregation in Buffalo Valley more than fifty years old that had never had a resident pastor but had been served mainly by retired ministers who supplied monthly or at most twice a month. They had built a manse next door to the church as a home for a pastor. Six miles away at Silver Point, Presbyterians had gathered enough members for a new congregation and built Mattie Smith Memorial Presbyterian. They hoped to attract a minister to come live in Buffalo Valley and serve this two-church parish. Dr. Wilson came to Louisville Seminary to try to recruit somebody for that post. Margaret and I were impressed at the initiative and generosity of the Presbyterians in the two communities and Nashville Presbytery, so we decided it was worth looking into.

On our visit to get acquainted, Margaret and I took the L & N Railroad from Louisville to Nashville, then transferred to a local line east to Buffalo Valley. Mr. Wirt Jared, a small spry man, neatly dressed and wearing a bow tie and a diamond stud in his shirt, met us and took us to his home where we were to stay. His wife, Miss Leona, confined to a wheelchair and much overweight, was waiting eagerly for us. When we walked in, she took one look at me and exclaimed, "Why, he's but a boy!" Then in flustered embarrassment, she flung her apron up over her head. I didn't look anything like the elderly supply pastors she was accustomed to. Dinner consisted of ham and chicken, all sorts of vegetables and fruits, biscuits and cornbread, and cake and pie. Miss Leona apologized for not offering us "light bread." The generous hospitality of the Jareds and the friendliness of the two congregations attracted us, and we felt a real sense of call to this ministry.

1. My Ordination into the Ministry

The congregations at Buffalo Valley and Silver Point issued me a call to be their pastor through the Committee on Home Missions of Nashville Presbytery, but I had to pass a written and an oral examination by Nashville Presbytery in order for the transaction to be official. I had to write essays on several subjects, one of which dealt with the question of the Second Coming of Christ and the other on baptism. I felt fairly well prepared on the Second Coming because of my early familiarity with dispensationalism and Darby-Scofield. These were no longer a problem within the Presbyterian Church, but the presbytery's committee on ministry knew that the general population of the area where I was to serve was strongly influenced by expectations that Jesus might come back anytime, and we would have to keep aware of "signs" of the end. They knew also that denominations requiring adult baptism by immersion had exercised such powerful influence for so long that I needed to have a good understanding of this question. My essays were satisfactory, and the oral questioning also passed.

The actual ceremony of ordination, including the specified questions and the actual laying on of hands, had to be done in a formal worship service of the presbytery. Beecher Wallace, an elder of Mattie Smith Memorial at Silver Point, invited the presbytery to come there for the service. Somebody raised the objection that that was nearly seventy miles east of Nashville. Beecher replied, "It ain't no farther for you all from Nashville to Silver Point than it is for us from Silver Point to Nashville!" The additional argument that this ordination service would be beneficial for the people at Mattie Smith Memorial, being a new congregation and unfamiliar with Presbyterian polity, swayed the decision to come to our place. Needless to say, the members from Buffalo Valley enthusiastically participated. My parents also came from Winston-Salem to be present, which I deeply appreciated.

The service included a sermon by me, my response to the questions for ordination, and formal charge to the local congregations. Next, an elderly minister, one who on occasion had formerly supplied the pulpit at Buffalo Valley, delivered the charge to me. Among his points, he charged me to be faithful in my study of scripture. He warned me to pay attention to it all and not to skip over the names of people in genealogies or of places in lists. Since then, in my long experience of studying and teaching the Bible, I have often recalled his charge. Those names are boring and difficult to pronounce, and therefore easy to skip. Yet one may fins details that call into question or perhaps even contradict a prominent Bible story line with which people tend to be more familiar. The ordination ended with my kneeling, and all those who were themselves ordained as elders, whether teaching or ruling, laid their hands on me during the moderator's prayer of ordination. I was honored and grateful that my father was one of those who laid hands on me at that time. My ordination occurred on August 19, 1945.

2. Culture Shock

I grew up in the mid-sized southern city of Winston-Salem, North Carolina, and Margaret in Louisville, Kentucky. We were both typical "city slickers." Though culture shock was not a familiar expression in the mid-1940s, that's what we experienced during the two years I served as a pastor in rural Tennessee. Our telephone service was a party line with two others, each with a different ring using the crank. To make a long distance call, we had to go through central and arrange a time for the connection. We didn't have a refrigerator or washing machine till our second year.

The manse was a five-room house with a full basement that included space to park our car. There was narrow access to space between the ceiling and the rafters. One entered the house directly into the living room, and on the left was a small side room that we used later as nursery after our son Bill was born. Behind the living room was the dining area with another room to the left, which we used as our bedroom. The kitchen and toilet were farther back.

Heating consisted of open fireplaces. There were two chimneys, each one serving fireplaces back to back, as it were in two rooms: on the right the living room with the dining room behind and on the left the two bedrooms. Ours was one of the few residences in town that had running water. Our supply came from a spring at the back of our lot that Mr. Wirt had had bricked up in such a way as to form a reservoir. From the reservoir, a pump drew water through a pipe to a tank inside the house.

We city softies were not up to doing without hot water. Though it was still wartime, I went to Nashville and managed to locate a used hot water system consisting of a small stove to heat the water and a storage tank. We used newspaper and corn cobs to start the coal fire when we wanted to take a bath.

It was summer when we moved in, but as fall came on, we found the fireplaces less than satisfactory for heating. Again, I went to Nashville and bought a coal stove, a round affair on legs standing less than four feet high, lined with firebrick and fed from the top. With proper technique, one could stoke the coal fire, close the draft below, and turn the damper down so as to keep the fire going all night, hence the name Warm Morning. We had to cut an opening in the chimney of the living room for the stovepipe, but the stove had to be located a bit too far away. After a while, soot built up along the level section of the pipe, so we would have to stop the whole operation and clean out the stovepipe.

In spring, I got a really bad cold and had to stay in bed for several days. Just at that very time, our water supply from the spring quit, and Margaret had to haul water in buckets. Later, we found out that during the rains, silt had accumulated in the reservoir enough to block the intake valve on the water pipe.

Indian Creek that ran behind our house and separated two distinct sections of the town flowed on to the Caney Fork River. That was a tributary of the Cumberland River, one of the principal waterways in Tennessee and Kentucky that flowed eventually into the Mississippi. During our time, several dams were under construction. They were not completed soon enough to protect against backwater in Buffalo Valley when heavy rains caused the rivers to rise. We weren't subject to headwaters, which might come suddenly and with disastrous force, but backwaters slowly rising from swollen rivers below inundated our valley. The year we were flooded, we had plenty of warning, and the members of the community teamed up to help all who were endangered. Our house was high enough for us to park our car under it, but the water actually reached about six inches into our first floor. The neighbors helped move everything out or tuck small things in the partial space above the ceiling, so we escaped serious damage.

Cleaning up afterward and restoring everything was a big job. My dad said that the expression "spring-cleaning" probably originated in communities that were subject to almost annual floods.

When we were able to return home, I discovered that we had overlooked my guitar, which was leaning behind an open door out of sight as we went back and forth carrying other things. It was ruined. Some of the smallest items we stashed above were so well concealed that we forgot about them until the time came for us to leave Buffalo Valley for good, and we rediscovered them finally in the course of clearing out everything.

3.   Rural Slums

The two years that Margaret and I lived in Buffalo Valley left a great impression on us, but we were such green city folks that we had hardly begun to get familiar with the ways of our country neighbors before we left to go to China. In an earlier generation, there had been extensive farming, principally corn. But the topsoil had washed off the hillsides, which were now overgrown with grass and grazed by cattle and sheep, with scrubby copses growing on the hilltops. The town consisted of an elementary school, a post office, two grocery stores, and a Presbyterian and a Campbellite Church (very conservative and related to the Church of Christ that call themselves Disciples). They had no pastor, but since their tradition included "the priesthood of all believers," the elders carried on weekly services including Sunday school. Once in a while, they invited an outside preacher to conduct a protracted meeting. They considered only the New Testament as canonical scripture, and since it didn't mention musical instruments, they always sang *a capella*.

I don't remember ever having heard what the official town population was, but I should say not much more than a thousand altogether. The lines were not drawn strictly, but the number of churchgoing people (i.e., excluding the infidels or nonchurch people) was fairly evenly divided between the Presbyterians and the Campbellites, with the former considered a bit superior in educational and economic status. In the general area, there may have been some people with Methodist, Baptist, or Holiness leanings, but there was no local church of those denominations. We weren't there long enough to become familiar with all the dynamics of personal and social relations, but we had the impression of generally cordial, civil conditions.

Indian Creek ran along the valley through the town in a general west-east direction. On a ridge stretching along the south bank of the creek huddled a jumble of huts and shacks, which could only be called a rural slum. Despite the differences that might exist among other townspeople, all were united in the conviction that "they" were not "us."

Above, I introduced Mr. Wirt and Miss Leona Jared, the most respected citizens of our village, and indeed, the surrounding area. Miss Leona was confined to a wheelchair and was greatly overweight because of her generally sedentary existence, but she was a renowned cook and seamstress. For her assistance, she employed a teenage girl called Avannah, who served as an extra pair of hands and feet. Avannah lived on the ridge across the creek, and Miss Leona was teaching her some manners and skills in addition to paying her a small stipend.

When I was at the Jareds' house one day, I overheard Miss Leona refer to the ridge where Avannah lived as the Philippines. That piqued my curiosity, and I immediately asked her about it. She burst out laughing. "Law, me," she said. "That goes way back to about 1900, the days of the Philippine insurrection. We used to get news about the fighting going on in the Islands all the time, and somebody said, 'Why it ain't no different from what goes on over yonder,' and somehow the name just stuck. Some folks call 'em the Islands, and some call 'em the Philippines."

During the two years we lived in Buffalo Valley, there were several residents of the Islands who achieved some notoriety. A young buck about seventeen years old had a reputation as being pretty much of a delinquent. He had got in some scrapes and was said to be living with an older woman whose name was Theoplis. I remember her name because of its similarity to a name in the Bible, but I can't recall his name. He was said to be having a quarrel with somebody on a farm several miles away, but I didn't know whether it concerned Theoplis or some other matter.

In due time, word went around that the young fellow had been gunned down. The story I heard was that he had been approaching the barn where his enemy was at work. He topped a rise behind the barn and was coming down the slope with the sun behind his back. From inside the barn, the other man saw him coming, grabbed a shotgun he had at hand, and let him have both barrels right in the stomach, cutting him practically in two. He was unarmed, but the killer claimed he thought he had a gun with him.

A girl who had come to our Sunday school a few times and lived up on a hill in sight of our house came to call on me. She said her dad wanted me to come talk to him about the killing. When I met him, he said the victim was his nephew, the son of his sister, but the parents had had nothing to do with him for quite some time. The uncle wanted to know if I would have the funeral for him. I said I would. I asked him if he had any preferences for hymns. He said, "Nope." Any particular Bible passages? "Nope." Will you have a history (that is, a biographical sketch)? "Nope." Silence. His eyes were downcast, and he sort of scuffed with his toe in the dirt. Finally, he looked up at me and said, "I tell you what, Preacher. If hit-a been me, I wouldn't-a took it."

The funeral was held in the Methodist church several miles away. It was bigger than our church but had not had a pastor or any services for a long time, and they expected there would be a pretty big crowd there. I had lived in the country long enough to know that funerals were always popular events, where lots of people gathered who never bothered to go to church any other time. This funeral was for a guy with a bad reputation who was a murder victim, so it was no wonder that lots of people showed up. The building was pretty well filled, and there were not a few, including some pretty rough-looking characters, standing outside looking through the windows and the door. I took the opportunity of preaching an evangelistic sermon urging repentance and faith in Jesus as Savior, but I don't know that I made any converts. I never was one to preach hellfire and damnation.

4. Baptisms at Buffalo Valley and Silver Point

While Margaret and I lived in Buffalo Valley, our first child was born in the hospital at Cookeville, the county seat. The facility was rather small and of less-than-class-A quality. It had been adapted from a one-time school building. Beginning on a Friday, Margaret was in labor for over two days, and I was there most of the time. As she had not yet brought forth by Saturday night, I had to go home and prepare to preach the next day, though the doctor told me she probably wouldn't be finished before I returned. After church on Sunday morning, I hurried back to learn that a boy had been born. The doctor had used forceps to take him, which left his head a bit misshapen. Fortunately, as his brain continued to develop, the cranium shaped up very nicely.

We named our son for his two grandfathers, William Archibald. For the baptism, we invited Margaret's father, the Reverend Dr. William H. Hopper, to bring Grandmother Ruth from Louisville and administer the sacrament. In Buffalo Valley, this was a special event. Nobody could recall an infant baptism within living memory. In the entire region from of old, the Baptists and the Church of Christ (popularly known as the Campbellites or, somewhat slightingly, as the "be dipped or be damned" folks) had monopolized debate and argument about baptism to such an extent that even Presbyterians and Methodists never considered baptizing babies. Some people in the area could still feel a subtle residue of holiness influence.

We deeply appreciated Grandfather Hopper's conducting the service. He also preached a memorable sermon on Psalm 1, comparing the well-founded life of a Christian with a "tree, planted by the rivers of water that bringeth forth its fruit in its season" (Psalm 1:3). The postmistress was one of a number of town folks who showed up for the baptism. On Monday morning when I went to pick up our mail, she expressed great appreciation for the entire event, concluding, "The twenty-third Psalm has always been one of my favorites."

Miss Minnie Denton was the widow of old Dr. Denton who had also been a prominent local citizen. She was a member of the Church of Christ, but once in a while, she came to hear me preach, and I included her in my rounds of pastoral visitation. Once, I asked her straight out, "Miss Minnie, suppose you all have a protracted meeting at your church and somebody gets under conviction and wants to be baptized. You're on the way to the creek, and he has a heart attack and dies right on the spot. Would you all consider that he was saved?" Without a moment's hesitation, she answered firmly, "No!"

Mr. Wirt Jared told me one of his elderly cousins became seriously ill and was not expected to live. He had never made a profession of faith, but he decided he had better get right with God before he died, so he asked the local Church of Christ elders to baptize him. This posed a problem as he was bedfast and near death, and therefore, it was beyond question to take him to the creek and immerse him there. But they could solve that problem. They would bring a rowboat with seats removed up onto the front porch, fill it with warm water, and put him in that. Not only so, but given his delicate health condition, they could even supply him a rubber suit that covered him completely, with only his face left exposed. They asked if he wanted to make use of that arrangement.

"Well," he opined, "the boat would be OK, but not the rubber suit. It don't seem like doing it thataway would really wash away my sins."

In the Mattie Smith Memorial Presbyterian in Silver Point, we had a weekly young people's meeting, which was attended by a number of youth not only in our congregation but also in the community at large. During summer vacation, we had a picnic outing for the group, and we were in a meadow along a little brook. I happened to notice a small snake in the edge of the water, which I recognized as harmless, so I picked it up behind the head and stretched it out by grabbing the tail with my other hand. As I displayed it among the youngsters, the girls naturally all squealed and acted properly frightened. Even the boys appeared doubtful. I approached one in particular, a hefty towheaded fellow who was by far the biggest of the whole bunch. "Here!" I said. "Don't you want to take this?" He threw up his hands in great alarm and stumbled backward a step or two, crying out, "I ain't no preacher! I ain't no preacher!" No snake handling for him!

Two sisters at Silver Point, nieces of elder Beecher Wallace, were active members of the youth group, and they indicated they wanted to make a profession of faith and join the church. We met together as a communicants' class for several weeks. When the question of baptism came up, they both insisted they wanted to be immersed. I was convinced they fully understood the symbolism of the water and that they did not believe immersion was a condition of their being saved. Since the Presbyterian Church recognizes the validity of all three modes, sprinkling, pouring, and immersing, I agreed to their preference. The problem was, where could we actually do the deed? Silver Point was located up on a dry ridge.

People had to drive six miles down to Buffalo Valley, park their cars, and walk perhaps as much as half a mile along the path down Indian Creek to find a pool deep enough to permit an adult to be fully immersed. But that's what we did. Members of the girls' family and of the church went along. By the time we arrived at the appropriate place and prepared to begin the ceremony, lo and behold, a group of idle onlookers had materialized as if out of thin air. Among them was Thurman Alcorn, the local justice of the peace, who lived across the road from the Presbyterian manse. Thurman's wife, Mabel, was a faithful member of our church, but Thurman was not. He was what some folks referred to as an infidel. This was my first experience of baptizing by immersion, and I admit it felt somewhat awkward. My unfamiliarity was not lost on Thurman. When it was all over, he said to me very matter-of-factly, "Looks like you ain't never done that before!" and I readily admitted that he was correct. I will say that I have difficulty picturing in my mind the apostles immersing three thousand people, all of whom responded at once to Peter's sermon on the day of Pentecost.

5. Learning Experiences

Two years was a rather brief time, but for us, it was a learning experience, and I hope it was for the local people. Those with whom we got acquainted both in and out of our churches were respectable and hardworking folks, but socially and theologically, they were considerably more conservative than we. There were two newspapers from Nashville, the *Nashville Banner* and the *Tennessean*. We asked which paper we should subscribe to, and they recommended the *Nashville Banner*. We did so, but being accustomed to the rather liberal Louisville, Kentucky, *Courier-Journal*, we decided after a while to try the other one. Both papers, though pursuing different editorial policies, used the same business staff and office. So once when I was in Nashville, I stopped by to ask to transfer to the *Tennesseean*. No problem! The clerk removed the metal plate with our address on it from the rack on one side and placed it in the rack on the other side. We liked the *Tennesseean* better.

As Thanksgiving approached, our first year there, I suggested we start planning for a Thanksgiving service. The prompt reply was that the local custom had always been that Thanksgiving Day was the time when everybody killed hogs and made sausage. I didn't make any effort to change that custom.

The gulf between the Presbyterian and the Campbellite churches was too deep to bridge effectively, but we conducted Vacation Bible School in Buffalo Valley on two summers. One of the teachers of the local primary school, a member of our church, helped with the VBS, and children from the whole community attended. We heard that in the Campbellite church after it was all over, they devoted several sessions to making certain their children had not been led astray. Once in a while, I overheard discussions of baptism, especially emphasizing going all the way under the water, illustrated by a proper hand motion. I avoided any sort of controversy and tried to keep cordial relations with all, being actually the only resident pastor in the whole area.

Mr. Wirt Jared told me he had been brought up in the Methodist Church, but he preferred the "Presbyterian Apology." He said he liked my sermons and would like to have some of them printed and distributed. I was very flattered at that, but I said I preached from an outline only and didn't have my sermons written out in full. I found that the two churches had no program of stewardship education to encourage members to pledge regularly to a church budget. I undertook to preach a series of sermons based on Paul's encouragement to the Corinthian believers to be generous in support of his collection to benefit the poor brothers and sisters in Judea. I don't know the effect it had on those who heard, but the discipline certainly strengthened my own understanding of the joys we have in sharing generously the rich blessings that God bestows on us.

Some years after we left, the federal highway I-40 running east and west through Tennessee was routed right through Buffalo Valley, destroying, among other things, Mr. Wirt and Miss Leona's house, the church, and the manse. Later, I heard that the local people were zealous enough to rebuild the church and carry on. I like to think that Margaret and I may have had just a little influence on that decision they made later on.

5

From Home to Foreign Missions

Margaret and I knew that our pastorate in Tennessee was a step in further preparation to go to China, and the people in Buffalo Valley and Silver Point had been fully informed from the start. During our time in Buffalo Valley, we went to Nashville to meet with the Executive Committee of Foreign Missions. From the earliest days, the Southern Presbyterians were strongly suspicious of centralized bureaucracy, and they dispersed their assembly-wide agencies, which they called Executive Committees, to different cities. The Executive Committee of Christian Education and Ministerial Relief where Father Hopper served was in Louisville, Home Missions in Atlanta, Religious Education and Publication in Richmond, and Foreign Missions in Nashville.

When we applied for appointment to China, Dr. H. Kerr Taylor, a member of the staff of the Executive Committee of Foreign Missions in Nashville who had formerly served in China, warmly welcomed us. Dr. Taylor had known Margaret in her active days with Presbyterian Youth. He had evaluated her as qualified to be president of the assembly-wide youth organization, but it was still too soon for a female to be elevated to that office. Dr. Taylor had earlier suggested she consider serving in China. Margaret mentioned this to me later and added, "He wasn't the right Taylor to steer me to China."

1.   Studying Chinese Language

The Mission Executive Committee had high language standards for career missionary appointees. For those going to lands where French, Spanish, or Portuguese was official, one year of full-time language study was prescribed. For those going to China, Korea, or Japan, it was two full years, if possible one in the U.S. and a second after arriving on the field. Our Committee sent candidates for Oriental assignment to the Yale University Institute of Far Eastern Languages. It had a distinguished history well known for its Yale in China program, but they had excellent courses in Korean and Japanese. So that was to be our location for a year beginning in the summer of 1946.

We still had our old Plymouth, and its second engine replacement was serving us well enough that we could visit family in Winston-Salem and Louisville before driving up to New Haven. We piled as many of our belongings as we could into the car, and on the front bumper, we attached the high chair that had originally been mine and that we now used for Bill.

We were one of three Presbyterian families, each with a small child. Our home was to be in Woodmont, Connecticut, several miles outside New Haven, right on Long Island Sound, in a summer home that had been "winterized." Two of our couples were studying Chinese and the other Korean. (More details of our living conditions are contained in my biographical sketch of Margaret.)

The Pacific War had ended, but in China, the civil war between the Red Army and Chiang Kai Shek's Nationalist forces persisted until Chiang's retreat to Taiwan. The fall of Beijing made it clear we could not go there for our second year of language study. These conditions made it questionable whether we could actually go to China. After debate in the Mission Executive Committee whether we should stay at Yale for our second year, they said we could go to China. A longshoremen's strike had shut down all the ports on the Pacific coast, so they told us to go to New York and book passage there. We got passage on a Norwegian freighter, the Ivaran, named for Ivar Anderson, the head of the shipping company. She had six cabins for passengers, who took their meals with the captain in the officers' mess.

2. On Our Way to China

Our course took us down the inland waterway along the Atlantic coast, stopping to pick up freight as we went. From our place on the upper deck, we could observe the sailors removing the hatch covers and the men on shore lowering the freight by power winches into the hold. Then it was through the Panama Canal, which was, of course, an interesting experience for us, watching as the little engines called donkeys on the side pulled us through the locks.

Once out on the Pacific Ocean and maintaining a steady speed, we became aware of the gentle rolling of the ship. It didn't bother Bill or me, but Margaret said it made her feel constantly uncomfortable, even though she never got really seasick. Besides, she said she had to chase Bill all the way across the Pacific.

Some distance beyond Panama in mid-ocean our engine broke down. The captain had told us his company ordinarily would have got rid of this ship long since, but during the war the Germans sank over half their vessels, and they had not yet been able to get enough new ones. The engineers worked steadily for about twelve hours while the ship, now idly drifting, rose and fell and rose and fell with the waves. That didn't sit well with Margaret, of course, but Bill and I went down where the deck hands were amusing themselves fishing. They actually hooked a small shark, which they hauled up on to the deck, where it lay gasping. We got a good look at its lethal teeth while it opened and closed its mouth as if wanting something to chew on. One of the sailors obliged by offering it a stick to bite. We were told that sharks' teeth developed as it were in ranks, one behind another. If a tooth were lost, another would rotate in from behind.

With the engine temporarily repaired, we limped along at a reduced rate of speed for several days till it conked again. Again, we were up and down with the swells, but no shark this time, while the engineers worked nonstop for another fourteen hours. In that fashion, we finally reached Manila, where we stayed for some days while the engine got a proper repair job and much of the ship's cargo was off-loaded.

Considerably lighter now, we headed southwest toward Hong Kong. Our course lay at about a forty-five-degree angle to the direction in which the waves were moving, so that our motion was a constant roll, portside down and starboard up, then the opposite, starboard down and portside up. By now, Margaret must have become somewhat inured to the waves' effect on the vessel, for she escaped real *mal de mer*, but it certainly was no fun for her.

In Hong Kong, we had a brief visit with Margaret's uncle Walter Hopper, who was the consul general. Bill, always curious, was eager to investigate everything, and we had to keep warning him to be careful while making distinctions between what belonged to Uncle Walter and what belonged to Uncle Sam.

By the time we left Hong Kong and headed due north for Shanghai, the old Ivaran had very little cargo left in her hold. This time, our course took us head-on into the waves, which now seemed to be a bit higher than before. As we rammed an oncoming wave, we would slide up till our bow must have been somewhat out of the water. When we got past the crest of the wave, we would flop down with a decided impact, up, flop, up, flop all the way to Shanghai, where we finally arrived sixty days after we got on board in New York.

The presidential election between Truman and Dewey took place while we were en route, and we depended on the wireless officer to keep us informed about the results, which we got from the captain at meal times. Like everybody else, we thought Dewey would win, but every notice had Truman ahead. We thought that represented metropolitan votes and that Dewey would overtake Truman. We said this to the captain each time when he reported, "You still got the same old president." His final report stated, "You still got the same old president, and you're gonna keep him!"

We arrived in Shanghai in November 1948 and found it swarming with refugees fleeing the Red Army's southward advance. In January 1949, we went to Taiwan as guests of the Canadian Presbyterian Mission. We taught English at the mission high schools in Tamsui, and I taught also at the seminary in Taipei. We stayed in Taiwan until February 1950.

When the Red Army had cleaned up on the mainland and threatened to attack Taiwan, President Truman and Admiral Leahy announced that the U.S. Seventh Fleet would not intervene. In view of the expected attack, the U.S. consul advised us to leave Taiwan. At the time, we had one son, Bill, and we were expecting our second child. We corresponded with missionaries in Japan, and they told us we would find a welcome at Shikoku Christian College, a men's school, which they planned to open in April 1950.

3.   We End Up in Japan

Margaret and I with our son Bill arrived in Kobe in early February 1950 and went from there to live in one of two mission residences in the city of Marugame in Kagawa-ken, one of four prefectures that comprised the island of Shikoku, smallest of the four main islands of Japan. Shikoku had been a locus of mission work of the Presbyterian Church (US)—Southern—for many years. Two mission families had lived in Marugame before the war, and the houses had been spared during wartime destruction. Jim Cogswell, who was also assigned to the college and had completed language study in Kobe, with his wife Peggy, daughter Peggy Ann, and baby son Jimmy lived in the other house. Our son Bill was almost four years old, and our second son, John, was born on May 5, 1950.

As it turned out, unforeseen by anybody, the outbreak of the Korean War in June of 1950 changed U.S. policy so as to protect Taiwan. But by then, Margaret and I had already settled in Marugame with our two children. Our third son, Samuel, was born less than two years later on September 15, 1951. In this way, our original sense of call to mission, contrary to our personal expectations and desires to go to China, landed us in Japan without any prior preparation. Little by little, I began to learn something of the history of Japan, the background of the Japan Mission, and the founding of Shikoku Christian College (SCC). Margaret and I had to pick up information gradually as time went on. In the next chapter, I provide some historical background.

4.   We Settle into our Life in Japan

In Marugame, we regularly attended Sunday worship at the local church, even though we didn't understand Japanese. English-speaking believers welcomed us warmly and helped us in many ways. We learned later that the church was affiliated with the Christ Reformed Church (popularly called Kaikakuha). It was one of a number of congregations that had had long relations with the missionaries of the Southern Presbyterian Church and that had withdrawn from the United Church of Christ in Japan (Kyodan) immediately after the war.

The college was in Zentsuji, a few miles distant from Marugame where we and the Cogswells lived. Lardner Moore, the president, and his wife, Grace, were already in their apartment on the college campus. He and Mr. Fukunaga, the dean, with a few other faculty members in residence were organizing the curriculum and observing the ongoing renovation of other buildings of the former Imperial Army cavalry regiment that was our campus. Classes began in April 1950. Some of the students had already begun their pre-ministerial studies the previous year at the Kobe Seminary, where Jim Cogswell had taught them Greek. We also had some newly entered first-year students, making a student body of perhaps as many as thirty altogether. I think we had about eight full-time Japanese faculty and missionaries. Jim and I commuted daily to classes in Zentsuji. I was limited to teaching English, but Jim taught some English in addition to Greek.

Besides Lardner Moore, the president of the college, the chairman of our board of trustees was Will McIlwaine of the Kaikakuha Seminary in Kobe. Jim McAlpine, who was treasurer of the Japan Mission and lived in Gifu Prefecture in Central Japan, was also a member of the board. Half a dozen or so of Japanese ministers were also trustees. All three of the missionaries had grown up in Japan and had served as missionaries of the Southern Presbyterian Church before the war. They had experienced and observed the government's increasing harassment of Christians and the imposition of state control over all churches, including the forced amalgamation of all protestant denominations to form the United Church of Christ in Japan (Kyodan). These men believed the true Christian faith had been almost fatally compromised, and they determined to start anew on a much firmer doctrinal and biblical basis. For the first several years of my relation with SCC when Lardner Moore was the president, I heard his side of the story, which included his criticisms of prewar conditions and his explanations of postwar policies of the Southern Presbyterian Mission. As time went on, I learned much more about the history of Japan and about the introduction and development of Christianity in that land that formed the general context in which the Southern Presbyterians had worked both prewar and postwar. All that was the general background of Shikoku Christian College. Therefore, at this point, I will insert a chapter to provide my understanding of that history.

PART THREE

Missionary Career in Japan

6

Background of Japan and Christianity There

1. History and Culture

Japan is a large archipelago consisting of four main and thousands of small islands in the West Pacific Ocean off the coast of Korea and China. If you imagine Japan lying off the Atlantic coast of North America, the northernmost point on the island of Hokkaido would be about the same geographical latitude as Montreal, Canada, and the southernmost tip of Kyushu Island would be about the same as Mobile, Alabama. Smaller islands farther south to Okinawa (the Ryukyus) would extend to about Key West, Florida. The total area of Japan is slightly smaller than California, but it is principally mountainous, and only approximately fifteen percent of the land area is arable. Japan is blessed with abundant water, but other than forests and some coal, it has very few other natural resources.

The people of Japan are from two general ethnic sources: northeastern Asiatics through Korea in the northern region and Pacific islanders in the south. An ancient principle in Japan recommends that families seeking a marriage partner for a child should strive for a couple consisting of one from the south and the other from the north. In this way, the two strains have been pretty thoroughly mixed over the centuries. Hokkaido in the far north is home to the minority Ainu, whose origin is still not fully explained. In contrast to the Japanese, Ainu men are very hairy, many sporting thick beards, and the women used to decorate their faces with tattoos. They used to inhabit the northern region of the main island Honshu also, but the Japanese called them northern barbarians and gradually pushed them farther north into Hokkaido. Ainu still suffer a certain level of discrimination.

Modern Japanese language has been standardized through universal education to conform to that of the general area of Tokyo, but many people in other areas may also speak local dialects in addition to the standard. Being separated by sea from the mainland, Japan was often late to receive certain cultural riches, including writing and advanced religion.

The indigenous religion of Japan is a kind of animism that acknowledges the existence of divine beings—eight hundred myriads of gods, *yao-yorozu no kami*—dwelling in any and all natural phenomena, especially those connected with agriculture and human and animal fertility. There is a patron deity (*uji kami* pronounced *ujigami*) who protects and prospers all the inhabitants of a recognized farming area. The *kami* lives unseen in the shrine the people provide for him. At festival times, the priest invites him to come into an elaborate palanquin so that young men can bear him throughout his domain to bless by his presence his people and to receive their homage in dance accompanied by drums and gongs.

By participating in seasonal celebrations such as planting and harvesting, all the local residents imbibe the spirit of solidarity that binds them to their neighbors. Most lasting traditions developed where climate and soil were conducive to wet rice culture. Constructing paddies and maintaining irrigation and fair distribution of water supply to the separate paddy fields necessitated a high degree of social organization and close cooperation. A colloquial saying derived from the Chinese, "drawing water to one's own paddy," is still used to criticize any kind of selfish actions. In some areas, the local *kami* may be the deification of the traditional person who was powerful enough to enforce the community discipline necessary for the agricultural well-being of all.

As metropolitan Tokyo has expanded very rapidly since the end of the Pacific War, residential areas have grown up where people never tried to farm and so never established communities. There is therefore no tradition of a local *ujigami* and no tradition of local festivals. Without their local god and community tradition, some of these communities have "borrowed" gods from other places and begun to devise their own festivals to promote community solidarity. In Japan, there is still much greater emphasis on this kind of social solidarity than there is on individual rights or the libertarian emphasis so strong in the United States. There is no evidence that people indulged in looting during the massive destruction and chaos resulting from the earthquake and tsunami of 2011.

The introduction of Buddhism from China began an extended period of Chinese cultural influence from about AD 550 to AD 780. The ruling power elite adopted Buddhism and writing to solidify control over the vast majority of the commoners and peasants. Using Chinese characters with Japanese pronunciation, they called the indigenous religion *Shinto*, usually translated "way of the gods" in English. Written Chinese is very inappropriate for Japanese, as the two languages are different in almost every linguistic characteristic. The fact that Margaret and I studied Chinese before we took up Japanese was not entirely useless, but as I say in comparison, if one wishes to learn English, studying Latin first will not be a total loss, but that's not the quickest way to learn English.

2. Japan Meets the West: The Gun and the Gospel

Japan's relative isolation prevented contact with Europeans for many centuries. Portuguese were the first the Japanese met when one of their ships was blown off course and sought shelter in the port of a small southern island in AD 1542. Trade with the Portuguese followed, and among other things, the Japanese obtained their first firearms. They copied and reproduced them, probably making some improvements, and guns began to spread rapidly in the land.

It was a time when the country was divided into warring states, each ruled by a feudal lord or *daimyo*—a big name. The court of the Japanese emperor was at Kyoto, but it had grown effete and weak over time, allowing the *daimyo* to compete against each other. The emperor's chief military commander, the *shogun*, assumed more and more authority, but competition for succession to that post exacerbated the general chaos. The gun was seen as an ideal addition to the swords, spears, and bows then available to the *daimyo* and *samurai*, the warrior class.

Following the opening made by trade, the Portuguese Jesuit priest Francis Xavier and a few companions including a Japanese refugee entered Japan to spread Christianity in 1549. In a relatively short time, perhaps enabled by the war-induced general spirit of unrest and insecurity (popular sects of Buddhism were spreading too), a surprising number of Japanese became attached to the Christian religion.

Priests of Portuguese and Spanish origin and different Catholic orders (some of whom had formerly been in the Philippines) followed Xavier's brief stay. They continued his policy of cultivating relationships with members of the ruling class, not only by their religious message, but also by facilitating trade. As a result of this top-down approach, thousands of Japanese masses followed their rulers' religious example. During the following half century, both the gun and the Gospel spread from far southwest Kyushu Island over halfway east and north on the main island of Honshu as far as Kyoto, the capital, and beyond.

The Shogun Oda Nobunaga consolidated his power by violent means. He destroyed temples of powerful Buddhist sects in and near Kyoto and slaughtered many of their believers because they were not sufficiently subservient. He favored the Jesuits through whom he gained advantages in trade, including acquisition of guns. It is thought that his relations with the missionaries had positive influence on the numerical spread of Christianity in the provinces.

The struggle to control the shogunate and finally impose unity on the warring *daimyo* and their feudal retainers, the *samurai*, was won in battle by Tokugawa Ieyasu in 1600, and he effected his total control by 1603.[10] Tokugawa considered the presence of the foreign Christians a threat to his power, for some believed they might form an opening wedge by which the European powers could gain control of Japan. There was already the example of the Spanish colonization of the Philippines. In addition, the authorities were outraged because the Catholics had tried to determine the proper Japanese word to express the Christians' *God* by appealing all the way to Rome to get the pope's decision.

Step by step, Tokugawa moved to counter this perceived threat, first by ordering the expulsion of the foreigners (not immediately effective) and later by persecuting believers. Twenty-four Christians including six missionaries were rounded up and forced to walk six hundred miles from central Honshu southwest to Nagasaki, exposed as objects of hatred and ridicule to crowds along the way. At the end, they were tied to crosses and tortured to death. They are still honored as the Twenty-Four Martyrs.

---

[10] Some years ago, the popular movie *Shogun* presented a fictionalized account of this development.

An unsuccessful revolt of severely oppressed peasants, many of whom were Christians, in one southwestern province resulted in the death of thousands. The Tokugawa shogunate erected notice boards everywhere calling Christianity an evil religion and forbidding the Japanese to practice it on pain of death. Using the fear of the evil of the foreigners and Christianity as prime motivation, Japan underwent a voluntary isolation from the rest of the world for over two hundred years.

During this time, the shogun collected and destroyed all guns, and all other weapons were forbidden to any but the warrior class. The *samurai* were subject to their local *daimyo* and forbidden to move elsewhere. Each *daimyo* had to maintain a family home in Edo, the shogun's hometown (which later became Tokyo, meaning "eastern capital"). The *daimyo* families lived there as virtual hostages. The *daimyo* themselves had to report in person at regular intervals to show loyalty to the shogun and receive his orders. The Japanese were forbidden to leave the homeland or even to move about freely within it. Japan built no ships capable of long voyages to other lands. Japan engaged in no aggression against another country. The only contact with the outside world was through a few Dutch merchants confined to Dejima, an artificial island in Nagasaki Harbor. What little the Japanese learned about the West was through what they called Dutch learning that seeped through this small crack.

Strict surveillance and control of the Christians was tightened. The shogunate used Buddhism as a tool. Every Japanese was required to register as a member of a local Buddhist temple, and they underwent an annual ceremony of pledging loyalty to Japan and rejection of Christianity by stepping on a Christian symbol, such as a crucifix or a representation of the Virgin and Child. Many believers who apostatized by this gesture maintained their faith in secret, especially in remote mountains or some of the very small islands. They used ostensible Buddhist objects such as miniature shrines with a feminized Buddha image inside, but with Christian symbols carefully worked into the decorations or hidden in the back or the bottom.

Western powers were eager to make contact with Japan to trade but were repulsed. Isolation continued for two centuries during which the Japanese people were, perforce, led to think of themselves as the "real" people, and mythology encouraged them to think of themselves as part of a divine family of whom the emperor was a direct descendant of the sun goddess. In 1853, Commodore Matthew Perry and his U.S. naval squadron of black ships with their heavy guns showed up and sent a message in diplomatic language with the unmistakable purport, saying, "Open up or we'll open you up!" Perry departed with the promise to return the following year, and in answer to the gun, Japan opened up. Thereafter, the U.S. stationed Townsend Harris as representative, who negotiated agreements on trade and permission for foreigners to live in designated port cities. Other Western powers also negotiated similar agreements called unequal treaties because they gave foreigners special privileges. The American Civil War intervened to forestall any possible U.S. imperialistic ambitions at that time.

3.   Christianity Renewed in Japan

Catholic priests came as chaplains with the French diplomatic team. When some of the hidden Christians became acquainted with them and observed their ritual practices, a few were bold enough to assert, "We are the same as you." The Japanese government began to round up these believers and transport them to exile within Japan. One ship carrying some of them stopped in the port city of Kochi on the Pacific coast on the southern side of Shikoku Island. Local Japanese were favorably impressed by the demeanor of the believers and felt sympathy toward them. They concluded that there must be something to be said for the faith they were accused of holding. In this way, ground was laid for the work of the Southern Presbyterian missionaries who reached Kochi several decades later and aided the growth of the church there.

Some protestant missionaries already in southern ports of China were quick to take advantage of the opening of Japan and came over. Among the earliest were the first Presbyterians, including the medical doctor James C. Hepburn and his wife in 1859. In addition to his medical work, Dr. Hepburn achieved fame for compiling the earliest dictionary of Japanese/English and devising a method of inscribing Japanese by means of the Roman alphabet. Others coming directly from the U.S. included three pioneers of the Reformed Church in America (RCA) who arrived in 1859 shortly after Dr. Hepburn. Samuel R. Brown was the RCA leader. He had family and other connections with Congregationalists and Presbyterians in both New England and South Carolina. Their group included Guido Verbek, an Americanized Dutchman, and he made an ideal liaison with Japanese interested in Dutch learning. Though Nagasaki had been and continued to be a locus of their work, the early missionaries tended to gravitate toward the new capital, Tokyo, and Yokohama, its port, settling in the nearby town of Kanagawa across the bay.

Spies infiltrated every group that the missionaries associated with and were among the numerous teachers and helpers necessary for the foreigners simply to exist. Two centuries of persistent antiforeign and anti-Christian propaganda prevented most Japanese from freely associating with missionaries, but some were eager to learn. The shogunate had grown weak over time and was unable to prevent serious rivalry between strict isolationists and those sympathetic toward an open policy. Radicals assassinated some foreigners, but both British and French warships retaliated by bombarding some port cities. The gun spoke again, and official Japan listened. Gradually, the policy of openness prevailed, aided by the fact that at the time, Japan was unable to defend itself if the Western powers should determine on a full-scale armed assault.

4. The Meiji Restoration

A coalition of leaders of provinces in the southwest forced the resignation of the Tokugawa shogun, brought the Emperor Mutsuhito (throne name Meiji) from Kyoto to Edo, now Tokyo, and proclaimed the new era of the Meiji Restoration in 1868. In practical terms, the emperor was only a figurehead who fronted the military junta that wielded growing power. To gain acceptance by the Western powers, they ceased persecuting Japanese Christians and removed the notice boards of prohibition without, however, announcing tolerance as an official government policy. They abolished the feudal domains and gave government bonds instead of the rice-based stipends to the *daimyo* and *samurai*. Aware of Western colonization that exploited China, Indochina, Africa, and Latin America, Japanese leaders lost no time in following the Westerners' example of an expansionist, colonial policy.

The government rushed to modernize by means of universal compulsory elementary education and by modernizing their armed forces. They accomplished the latter by making firearms the chief weapon and conscripting peasants into the army. These peasants were precisely those whom the *samurai* had always despised. When the government defaulted on the bonds held by the *samurai*, many of the former military class became impoverished. Justly feeling betrayed, the *samurai* rose up in rebellion in 1877, but the conscript peasant army with guns successfully defeated them.

[Note: This train of events stimulates me to engage in some speculation due to a tangential connection with my family history. Above, I wrote of my great-great-grandfather Major John Symington of the Watervliet Arsenal from 1851 to 1857. His successor, Major Alfred Mordecai, from 1857 to 1861 made further improvements, including devising a bullet press that produced uniform bullets at the rate of thirty-three thousand a day compared to less than ten thousand a day by the old press, which was constantly in need of repair. Only one other similar bullet press was made when the U.S. government requisitioned the first one for the State Department to include among a shipload of gifts for the government of Japan in 1860 as inducements for them to open their country to trade. I can't help wondering whether this efficient bullet press played a role in arming the peasant conscripts that defeated the *samurai* in 1877. Certainly, the Civil War in the U.S. also demonstrated the advantage of standardized firearms and the ultimate superiority of a citizen army compared to an elite class of professional soldiers.]

5.   The First Protestant Churches

Two years after the three Reformed Church pioneers came, James and Margaret Ballagh joined them. They lived closer to the larger community of foreigners near Yokohama and Edo/Tokyo. For years, Ballagh worked diligently conducting worship services for the expatriate community, which some interested Japanese also attended. He held services in Japanese for others as well, and young Japanese men regularly attended some of his other classes. In January 1872, a group of missionaries and other interested foreigners plus a few Japanese held fervent prayer meetings on behalf of Japan and the Japanese. A direct result of these meetings was the organization of the first Protestant Christian Church in Japan on March 10, 1872, in Yokohama, with eleven members. Nine of Ballagh's students were baptized that day, and two others were older men who had been baptized by other missionaries. Presbyterian David Thompson had baptized one named Ogawa, who was appointed an elder at that time, while the other was made a deacon. James Ballagh became the pastor, with the understanding it was temporary until a trained and ordained Japanese pastor could take the post. The missionaries, to emphasize that this was nonsectarian, named the church *Nihon Kirisuto Kyōkai*, Church of Christ in Japan. This was a bold move, for the notice boards prohibiting Christianity still stood, and government agents kept the church under constant surveillance, but without harassment.

In 1873, a second congregation was organized in Tokyo with cooperation from the Yokohama church and leadership by its elder Ogawa and Presbyterian missionary David Thompson who had baptized him. The second congregation adopted the same name and the same principles of doctrine and organization as the earlier church. A third such congregation was organized in Nagasaki in 1876.

Under Brown's leadership, the Reformed Church took the initiative to invite missionaries of other Protestant denominations to a conference in which they stressed the vision of a united Christian witness that did not reflect the denominational differences of the various foreign missionary organizations and the importance of a Japanese church with its own trained leadership. Unfortunately, in practical terms, this principle did not prevail, with the result that various other Japanese Protestant denominations gradually developed. However, the Presbyterian and Reformed churches faithfully adhered to the broadly nonsectarian principle, and the Church of Christ in Japan (with the nickname Nikki) became by far the largest Protestant Church. In comparison with the other denominations, the Nikki, in effect, represented the Japanese expression of the Reformed and Presbyterian tradition.

Following their early zeal to prepare the Japanese for leadership, both Presbyterian and Reformed missionaries taught courses that might be considered preparatory for a theological education, and a Reformed school that developed in Yokohama moved to Tokyo and joined with two Presbyterian schools in that area in 1883. The fruit of this move was the organization of Meiji Gakuin, of which Dr. Hepburn was the first president. Meiji Gakuin was a Christian school with the purpose of providing general education following the Japanese education structure, which included what we might think of as junior high, senior high, junior college, and senior college. For training ministers, there were preparatory and theological courses at Meiji Gakuin. The Presbyterian and Reformed missions that cooperated from the beginning stated clearly their purpose of preparing Japanese leadership to carry out evangelistic work, especially outside the port cities to which foreigners were restricted, and to train ordained ministers for the particular churches that were spreading. In time, the missions signed a covenant of cooperation by the missionaries, acknowledging and encouraging the autonomy of the Japanese church.

6.   The Presbyterian Church (US) Mission in Japan

James Ballagh sent a strong appeal to the Presbyterian Church (US, Southern) to come and join what seemed to be a time of great opportunity for Christian growth in Japan. The General Assembly approved, and later, the Executive Committee of Foreign Missions appointed two young men, R. B. Grinnan and R. E. McAlpine. They arrived in Yokohama in December 1885 and were welcomed by Ballagh. Later, McAlpine married Ballagh's younger daughter, Anna. Their son James McAlpine, educated in the Reformed Church, was later active in the Southern Presbyterian mission. When the first Southern Presbyterian missionaries arrived in Japan, they found the Church of Christ in Japan (Nikki) and the educational structure at Meiji Gakuin already in place, so they entered into cooperation without trying to begin on their own. Missionaries of the other Presbyterian and Reformed churches welcomed these newcomers, who accepted guidance from them as to the best location for them to extend the evangelistic and educational work that was already in progress.

The Southern Presbyterians began at once in Kochi City on the south of Shikoku Island, where they found a responsive people and established the church in Kochi that grew into one of the most influential congregations of the church. Miss Annie Dowd began educational work among girls that developed into Seiwa Girls High School. Over the years, their fellow missionaries spread their work farther north in Shikoku Island.

McAlpine went to Nagoya, the third largest city in Japan, which had earlier been suggested for the Southern Presbyterians and where other new arrivals joined the work. Mrs. Annie Randolph, who came from China, began educational work that grew into the Golden Castle (Kinjo) School for girls. Southern Presbyterians also settled in the port cities of Osaka and Kobe and across the Inland Sea in Kagawa Prefecture in the northern part of Shikoku Island, including the prefectural capital Takamatsu and the town of Marugame, where the Cogswells and the Taylors lived after the war.

The Southerners partnered with the Church of Christ in Japan, but Lardner Moore told me that they did not adhere to the same covenant as the others, choosing to do evangelistic work according to their own preferred pattern with more individual freedom and authority kept in the missionaries' hands. There was a sort of ongoing struggle on the part of leaders of the Japanese church to develop a greater degree of self-government and a resistance from some of the missionaries. The Southerners cooperated with Meiji Gakuin for a while, sending their ministerial candidates there for theological education. Over time, they began to feel that sending men from the provinces for education in Tokyo was not altogether suitable. Differences of opinion reached a climax when they objected to the choice of a systematic theology textbook. The Southern Presbyterian mission dissolved its relation with Meiji Gakuin and established the Central Theological Seminary in Kobe in 1907.

The world-famed Kagawa Toyohiko became a believer under the leadership of two Southern Presbyterian missionaries in Tokushima Prefecture, the eastern province of Shikoku Island. Kagawa's father was a nobleman, but his mother was a concubine, and the death of his parents led to his abandonment by the rest of the family. The missionaries Meyers and Logan befriended and lovingly cared for the young man, who early showed evidence of a brilliant intellect. During his crisis, he read and reread the New Testament and felt a call into ministry. He received assistance to attend Meiji Gakuin for several years, where he was said to have read practically all the books in the library, including works of Kant and Tolstoy.

Because of ill health, Kagawa dropped out of Meiji. But from there, he entered the Kobe Seminary. Kagawa's passion for the poor led him to leave the seminary dormitory to live in the slums among the urban poor. He was attracted to European socialist thought, which did not endear him to some of the missionaries and Japanese pastors. Eventually, he left the seminary altogether because of the lack of affirmation, indeed a certain feeling of opposition he sensed. There is no need to try to retell Kagawa's life story, but while I was still a boy in North Carolina, I had heard of Kagawa's great work and fame, and I bragged about missionaries of my own church having led him to Christ. In all my years of relationship with Southern Presbyterian missionaries in Japan, I never heard any of them speak favorably of Kagawa.

7. The Gun Wins Japan's Empire

Within a few decades, the *genro* or group of leaders who used Emperor Meiji as their figurehead, achieved rapid progress in emulating the expansionist policies of the Western powers. They supplemented their peasant army with a formidable navy, and in 1895, they seized control of the island of Formosa (Taiwan) from China. Moving into the peninsula of Korea and North China, the Japanese came into conflict with Russia, which eventuated in the Russo-Japanese War of 1904-1905. The war exhausted both sides, but the peace that U.S. President Theodore Roosevelt mediated gave Japan the victory and growing prestige in world affairs. Now with a free hand, Japan gained control of some northern islands from Russia and, in 1910, the entire Korean peninsula. They required teaching Japanese language in Korean schools and forced Koreans to give Japanese pronunciation to the Chinese characters of their personal names. Treating the Koreans as "fictive" Japanese, they required them to display loyalty to Japan by participating in State Shinto.

7a. State Shinto

Perhaps the most notable and surely the most effective means of controlling and mobilizing the Japanese people to give willing cooperation to Japan's imperial ambitions was the promulgation of State Shinto. As noted above, Shinto was the name given to the indigenous, basically animistic people's religion when Buddhism was first introduced around AD 550. Centuries of cultural and religious influence of Buddhism had pervaded Japanese culture and language, but Shinto persisted on every level and was practiced along with Buddhism without any sense of conflict.

The government built on this basic sense of solidarity cultivated by local Shinto practices and expanded it to embrace the entire nation. Each prefecture had a State Shinto shrine that ranked above the local ones, and the supreme national shrine was built at Ise. Exploiting details of ancient myths that were all but forgotten, State Shinto taught that the Japanese were a special race headed by their divine father, the emperor, who was directly descended from the sun goddess and himself was to be honored as divine—*Tenno*, king of heaven. Authorities classified religions as three: Buddhism, Shrine Shinto, and Christianity. State Shinto was not religious, they insisted, but only a public and patriotic expression of the ancient and eternal spirit peculiar to the whole people, who were themselves semidivine.

In 1889, in Emperor Meiji's name, the junta promulgated the first constitution providing for an elected diet, borrowing some features from western European examples but thoroughly Japanese nonetheless. Based upon ancient mythology predating written documents, it exalted the emperor as supreme, scion of the uninterrupted lineage of Emperor Jimmu, grandson of Amaterasu, the sun goddess who had sent him to earth to rule the divine land and people. Article 28 gave all subjects freedom of religious belief within limits not prejudicial to peace and order and not antagonistic to their duties as subjects.[11] The next year, 1890, the Imperial Rescript on Education was promulgated in the emperor's name. It briefly summarized the emperor's supreme authority and the duty of each subject to honor and obey him. Each school received a copy of this rescript, which they were expected to preserve as a sacred document together with a picture of the emperor to be posted in a prominent place where the students and teachers could hear the rescript read and bow in proper obeisance before the portrait. State Shinto shrines were built all over Korea, and teachers and students heard the reading of the Imperial Rescript on Education and did obeisance to the emperor in every school there as well as in Japan.

8.   The Origin of the United Church of Christ in Japan

Gradually, the central government extended and deepened its control over all religious bodies but with particular attention to the Christians. During those years, not only in the Nikki but also in most other denominations, the authority of the foreign missionaries was giving way to more local autonomy. The Religious Law of 1939 required that each religion must have official governmental recognition. A particular religion could receive this recognition only if it had a specified minimum number of adherents. The Catholics alone had enough members, but it needed all the Protestants together to meet the numerical requirement. Over the next eighteen months, a total of thirty-four denominations and

---

[11] Laman, op. cit. 277.

other Christian organizations, such as the YMCA and Salvation Army, negotiated a plan of union to form the United Church of Christ in Japan (nickname Kyodan). Despite government pressure, they refused to change the name to Japan Christian Church in order not to obscure entirely the worldwide scope of their faith.

The Church of Christ in Japan (Nikki) being the largest Protestant denomination had more prominent positions in the Kyodan and hence received greater notoriety in the Christians' public acquiescence to the policies of the military dictatorship. They became the principal targets of criticism and outright rejection from the most conservative missionaries, of whom some of the most vociferous were in the Southern Presbyterian Mission. The Christians' support of Japan's colonial policies in Korea was another cause of bitter condemnation. The government went to great lengths to spy on the Christians, to censor sermons, and to remove pastors from their congregations by conscripting them for military or other service. Moreover, the Christians, like all Japanese, knew only what the government told them. There is no question that many leaders as well as most Japanese church members lined up behind their native country and supported its war efforts.

9. Postwar Renewal of Mission Work

By the middle of 1945, Japan was near collapse. The U.S. Army Air Force using hundreds of planes and thousands of incendiary bombs had incinerated all but a few Japanese cities. U.S. military commanders MacArthur and Eisenhower predicted Japan could not hold out more than a few months. Japan was actually putting out feelers seeking terms of surrender. Despite all this, the U.S. applied "the gun" in its most extreme expression by dropping atom bombs on Hiroshima and Nagasaki.

When the Pacific War came to an end and freedom of religion was restored, many of the denominations that had been forced into the Kyodan withdrew and resumed their denominational identity. Most of the pastors, churches, and related mission organizations of the old Nikki (Presbyterian/Reformed), however, remained in the Kyodan, as did Methodists, Congregationalists, Disciples, and a few others. The foreign mission organizations that had formerly related to the member churches of the Kyodan, including the Presbyterian Church (USA, Northern), remained related to it and together organized the Interboard Committee for Christian Work in Japan to coordinate all the work with the Kyodan by the various foreign mission boards. Some of the Christian universities reopened their theological departments, but Meiji Gakuin did not reopen its theological department, for it had formed the nucleus of the Kyodan's seminary in Tokyo. As Tokyo Union Theological Seminary, it continued as the principal theological school of the Kyodan in the postwar reorganization. One should note that the postwar United Church of Christ in Japan became a full member of the World Alliance of Reformed Churches (WARC).

A group of Japanese pastors with close ties to Southern Presbyterian missionaries withdrew from the Kyodan to establish the Japan Christ Reformed Church (Kaikakuha), adopting the general theological position of the Westminster Confession of Faith and the Shorter Catechism. Early on, they reopened the Kobe Seminary to serve that church. Many of the former Nikki congregations in Shikoku (e.g., those in Marugame and other nearby towns) withdrew from the Kyodan and went with the Kaikakuha. Some Japanese pastors and congregations of the former Nikki also left the Kyodan but reestablished the former Nikki, calling it the Shin (or New) Nikki. As far as I know, the Shin Nikki still exists as a small Japanese denomination just as the Kaikakuha with original roots in Nikki, the first Protestant church in Japan.

The first Southern Presbyterian Missionaries to return to Japan after the war were Will McIlwaine, Lardner Moore, and James McAlpine. All three of them had grown up in Japan, were active during the ascendancy of the military in Japan, and had been interned at the outbreak of the war before being repatriated. They had also been closely related to the Japanese pastors who had established the Kaikakuha. These latter were among the first Japanese with whom they renewed relationships, and their interests were naturally with them and their newly organized church and seminary. McIlwaine readily affiliated with the seminary. Under the leadership of McIlwaine, Moore, and McAlpine, the Japan Mission of the Presbyterian Church (US) resumed its prewar policy of not relating officially to any national church. Individual missionaries were free to affiliate with either Kaikakuha or Kyodan. Several missionaries who had formerly worked at the Kinjo girl's school in Nagoya returned to their places there, and they and Kinjo affiliated with the Kyodan. Younger missionaries, who for the first time came to Japan, also had freedom of choice. Some went with the Kyodan, and some with the Kaikakuha.

Some of the younger missionaries began to refer to McIlwaine, Moore, and McAlpine as the Big Three.

These three also instituted an evangelism policy that differed from a basic practice of the prewar Nikki that they had strongly opposed. During a period when the Japanese leaders were exerting initiative, the Nikki decreed that only self-supporting congregations could be considered full members of the Nikki. Many smaller churches and their pastors that depended on subsidies distributed by missionaries were placed in a somewhat equivocal relationship to fellow Japanese Christians in the Church of Christ in Japan.[12] After the war, the Southern Presbyterian Mission subsidized the salaries of many of the pastors of the congregations in the Kaikakuha.

The establishment of Shikoku Christian College was already under way when Margaret and I inquired about Japan while we were still in Taiwan, and knowing only that it was to be a men's college and that there was a residence for us not far away, we had accepted the invitation to come and help in this new work. Lardner Moore was the president, Will McIlwaine was the chairman of the board of trustees, and Jim McAlpine, who was also treasurer of the Japan Mission, was a member of the board.

Several of the SCC students in 1950 had already attended the pre-ministerial classes that the Kobe Seminary had offered previously, and Jim Cogswell had instructed them in Greek, so they came to Zentsuji as second-year students. The Executive Committee of Foreign Missions of the Southern Church acknowledged the decision of the Japan Mission not to remain connected with the Kyodan and to give individual missionaries freedom to affiliate with the church of their choice. As for me, I was totally ignorant of the historical background at that time, and I was disinclined to relate formally to either church since I thought of myself as primarily an educational missionary at SCC, and at the time, I didn't know enough Japanese language to participate fully in any church. Owing to my detachment from the Kyodan and the relative geographical distance of Shikoku Island from the significant centers of public life in Japan at large, I remained untouched by serious struggles and problems in postwar Kyodan.

---

[12] Laman, op. cit., 462.

10. The Kyodan's Confession of Guilt

During the two decades following the war's end, people of conscience in the Kyodan began to consider the necessity of making a public confession of guilt for compromise and complicity with the military government and its wars of aggression. In 1966, the twentieth anniversary of the founding of the United Church of Christ in Japan, the Reverend Suzuki Masahisa was elected moderator of the Kyodan's General Assembly. In his office and over his name, he published a formal confession of guilt. Some welcomed it and treated it almost as though it were an official doctrinal statement, but others complained that it was not properly debated and voted. Hence, it had no official status. It receives scant attention in Gordon Laman's history.[13] Walter Baldwin, my colleague in the Southern Presbyterian Church who spent his entire missionary career in Japan faithfully engaged as partner in the work of the Kyodan, was intimately acquainted with Suzuki and placed a much higher value on his role. Baldwin collected and translated a number of Suzuki's writings and placed the confession in the total context of Suzuki's life and ministry. During the time Suzuki labored to advance his most important cause against some strong opposition, he was suffering from cancer, and he died not very long after it was made public.[14]

The 1960s and 1970s were turbulent times in the U.S., with the Vietnam War affecting every aspect of life. Japan also was deeply implicated by the extent of control exercised by the U.S. Indirectly, Japanese industry profited richly from American purchase of supplies, repair of military equipment, and rest and recreation for military personnel. Issues of war and peace, industrial prosperity, and materialism impacted heavily on the Japanese people and posed issues for sensitive Christians. Within the Kyodan, some felt they were once again being challenged to make difficult choices on issues that were not altogether clear, but which might have dire consequences.

---

[13] Laman, 607.

[14] Masahisa Suzuki, *The King's Way—A Personal Testament*. Translated by Walter P. Baldwin, (Privately published, Blurb.com, 2010

7

Shikoku Christian College (SCC)

Shikoku Christian College (SCC) was the realization of a desire of some in the Japan Mission to establish a school for boys as the earlier missionaries had founded the Kinjo or Golden Castle School for girls in Nagoya. After the war, the Japan Mission received considerable funds from the Presbyterian Program of Progress, a capital funds campaign of the Southern Presbyterian Church to restore mission work that had been interrupted or destroyed during the war. The Japan Mission thus could revitalize Kinjo, and they were able to purchase property in Zentsuji from the former Imperial Army as a campus for this men's school. Lardner Moore, the president of the school, told me that the Japanese Ministry of Education had considered using the extensive military property in Zentsuji to establish a national university catering particularly to students from the four prefectures of Shikoku island. When they abandoned that plan, the Japan Mission was able to buy a part of the property.

1. Early Years

Moore, McIlwaine, and McAlpine—the Big Three—remembered experiences at church-related liberal arts colleges in the U.S. in small towns or semi-rural locations in which all students lived in the dormitories. Conditions in Japan were quite different. Most mission schools were located in population centers where students could easily commute from home. Public transportation to Zentsuji was not ideal for commuting. We had one very desirable characteristic: in the center

124

of our property, there was a spacious area where the horses of the former cavalry unit could graze. Our buildings were all around the edges of this meadow, and we made a distinct contrast with other schools in cramped city spaces.

Without accreditation from the Japanese Ministry of Education as a school offering education beyond senior high school like Meiji Gakuin and Kinjo Gakuin, Shikoku Christian College started off with recognition simply as a "special school" (*Kakushu Gakkō*). The Japanese name Shikoku Kirisutokyo Gakuen might more accurately have been rendered Shikoku Christian Academy, but we all considered it a college like church-related colleges in the U.S. and referred to it as such, which accounts for the nickname SCC.

I began studying Japanese with a private tutor, but I didn't know enough to understand what went on in faculty meetings, though I attended regularly. None of the faculty had previous experience of teaching or administering a college-level educational institution, so the faculty spent a lot of time discussing every possible problem and question related to any phase of operations.

As mentioned above, some of our students had already made a start in pre-ministerial courses while in Kobe, where Jim Cogswell taught them. Several other pre-ministerial candidates were among those who entered as first-year students in 1950. The general atmosphere at SCC was family-like, with faculty and students and even some members of the board of trustees joining in softball games on "play day." Everybody had to attend chapel every day, and each faculty member in turn took responsibility for speaking in chapel for a week at a time. When it was my turn, either President Moore or English Professor Naitoh translated for me.

In order to qualify as a faculty member or a trustee, not only does one have to be a professing Christian, but he also has to subscribe to the Westminster Confession of Faith and the Shorter Catechism, which had become the doctrinal standards of the Kaikakuha, the Christ Reformed Church. Naturally, this requirement limited the pool of candidates from which to choose faculty members and trustees. To Lardner Moore, this did not present too great an obstacle, for the founders intended to keep the school small, averaging thirty students per year, for a total of 120 all living in the dormitory.

Under these circumstances, we passed the first year, with weekly faculty meetings often going on for long hours as we had to work out every detail not only of the curriculum but also of the administration. Discussions became heated at times, but we generally kept a good sense of mutual respect. For some reason that I never understood, President Moore had a serious disagreement with Dean Fukunaga, with the result that he dismissed the latter. Mr. Fukunaga and his family remained on campus for a year or so, living in the faculty residence to which he had been assigned until he found employment elsewhere. Japanese law gives great weight to the rights of the occupant of a residence, and the college could not evict the Fukunagas.

Because the new educational system in Japan required that all junior and senior high school students must take English, we, expatriate teachers at SCC, had many requests to serve as tutors. With relatively few students at SCC in those early days, we had extra time. Therefore, we organized what we called the English Night School, which met several times a week, offering various courses for English teachers of the public schools. It proved quite popular, and we became friends with many of the teachers in the area.

In the summer of 1951, early in the second year of SCC, Lardner and Grace Moore left Japan for their regular home assignment. By the action of the board of trustees and the Japan Mission, Jim Cogswell became acting president. During the home assignment of the Moores, Dr. George Landolt of Austin College in Texas came to the campus as adviser for a year. His wife, Doris, was a sister of Grace Moore. Dr. Landolt supervised the renovation of an old building to be our library. At his suggestion, we began to sponsor an English oratorical contest for high school students. He also encouraged us to seek accreditation with the Ministry of Education, and Jim Cogswell employed an elderly retired schoolteacher to investigate all the necessary conditions and to advise us on proper procedure.

Dr. Landolt chose the school's colors for us (the same as those of Austin College) and a Latin motto. He also drew up long-range plans for development, including blueprints for future buildings completely occupying our central green meadow. Dr. Landolt followed a rather brusque and independent manner of decision making and communication. He called the faculty together to inform us of his plans and ended his presentation by saying, "Anyone who doesn't wish to go along with these plans is welcome to leave." Publicity for student recruitment in 1952 included a poster that featured Shikoku Christian

College as an American school in Japan. We enrolled about fifty new students, the largest class up to that time.

When Lardner and Grace Moore returned from home assignment, he resumed his post as president and scrapped all of Dr. Landolt's proposals. He never made any use of the work that Jim Cogswell's assistant had done in the way of seeking accreditation. At the end of the school year, a mere handful of the first-year students remained.

In the summer of 1954, both the Cogswells and the Taylors returned to the U.S. for home assignment. Jim Cogswell began work on a doctorate at Union Seminary in Richmond, Virginia, researching and writing a history of the Japan Mission, *Until the Day Dawn*, a project that took him several years.

Margaret and I and our three boys went to Louisville. We were among the first missionaries to live in the Furlough Home, a facility that had been provided by the Women of the Church of which Margaret's mother had been national president. Enabled by my Patterson Fellowship, I earned a master's degree in biblical studies at the Louisville Presbyterian Theological Seminary during the year. I did my research and thesis on Jesus's quotations of the Old Testament. The result was a deep conviction on my part of the unity of the Bible and especially the importance of the Old Testament, which many Christians, especially in Japan, sadly neglect. Our opportunities to see Father and Mother Hopper were a great blessing to us all. It was especially so for Margaret, for it turned out to be the last opportunity she had for personal contact with her beloved father. He died before our next home assignment.

For two weeks in the summer of 1954, I attended a seminar at the University of Minnesota on the importance of general education courses in small liberal arts colleges. Dr. Cummings of the Executive Committee of Foreign Missions, being sympathetic toward me in my relation to SCC, recommended this study and made it possible for me to go. It was very stimulating for me to meet the faculty members of a number of small liberal arts church-related colleges and experience the cultural environment of the University of Minnesota. At lunch break one day, I topped a small rise, and below me I saw a number of students relaxing on the lawn. Almost the first that struck my eye was a couple consisting of a black male sitting next to a white female. When he leaned over and nuzzled her neck, I involuntarily felt an unexplainable rush of revulsion. I had never seen anything like that before, but it was symptomatic of the extent to which racist attitudes were so deeply embedded in my psyche in spite of all my attempts to overcome them.

I prepared a careful report of what I learned of the general education curriculum, and I presented it to Lardner when we returned to Japan. (Lardner never acknowledged receiving it or gave any indication that he even read it.) Instead of returning immediately to the college, however, we settled in Kobe for a year of full-time language study. Jack and Beverly Bridgman also came to Japan at that time and began two years of language study in Kobe. The Mission appointed Jack to teach biology at SCC.

We returned to SCC in the fall of 1955 after an absence of two full years. We lived in a house built for us on the college campus. Though I had had a year of language study and could understand a good deal more than previously, I still failed to get a lot of what was said. Still, I sensed immediately a completely different atmosphere on the campus and in the faculty meeting. Instead of the lengthy and lively discussions, everything seemed more or less cut and dried. We continued to attract a fairly good number of students to enter the first-year class, but only a few remained by year's end. I found out later that many of these students used SCC as a "prep" school and then took the entrance exams for accredited schools elsewhere.

Jack and Beverly Bridgman finished their second year of language study and came to Zentsuji. Jack had had experience teaching on a college level before coming to Japan, and he recognized too that not all was well. Meanwhile, Jim Cogswell completed his work on the history of the Japan Mission but did not return to SCC. He said he felt a call to evangelistic work with the church rather than to educational work. The Japan Mission assigned him to Ohgaki, near Nagoya, to work with the Kyodan. After a few years, Jim took up educational work at Kinjo.

During this period, I had several opportunities to learn more details of Lardner's attitude toward the former Church of Christ in Japan (Nikki) and the formation of the United Church of Christ, the Kyodan. Lardner was deeply critical of the extent to which the Japanese brothers had submitted to pressure from the military dictatorship and compromised the Christian faith during the Kyodan's formation and wartime existence. He predicted that eventually, the other churches also would leave, and it would become extinct (which never occurred). Lardner cited the example of some of the schools of our Presbyterian colleagues in Korea, which, he said, had been willing simply to shut down completely rather than compromise with Japanese colonial demands.

The Big Three more than other veteran missionaries felt very strongly about this issue, and there was a certain atmosphere of difference of opinion. Within the mission, it was planned to have a discussion of the issue of compromise and failure and whether and to what extent forgiveness and restoration could be granted. I don't recall just how it worked out, but Lardner and I were asked to be among those presenting different views. I of course had not personally experienced the very real and painful events of those days in Japan, but I could not take as uncompromising a line as Lardner did. To the extent that I was able, I reviewed church history on the background of the fourth century controversies that swirled around Christians facing a similar question of how to respond to failure under persecution among the Christians in North Africa. The Donatist party had taken a particularly rigid position on matters of purity and sanctity, and I couldn't help feeling that their position had been ultimately harmful rather than helpful. I knew it was impossible to draw strict parallels between the two situations, but gradually, I was drawing farther away from Lardner and his more conservative colleagues in the mission.

In due time, it became my turn to be moderator of our annual mission meeting. One important issue for our consideration was the question of whether our mission would advocate that the Southern Presbyterian Church support the proposed establishment of the Japan International Christian University (JICU). Not long after the end of the war, a prominent Presbyterian leader had publicly suggested that Christian people in the United States might conduct a joint campaign to raise funds to make possible a gift to show our love for our former enemies. The idea caught on, and within a year or so, an ecumenical committee had recommended as the objective of this gift to establish an outstanding educational institution that could provide well-trained leaders for the church and society in Japan. It was only natural that the General Assembly through the Executive Committee of Foreign Missions should inquire the official view of the Japan Mission. Predictably, the more conservative members opposed it, but there was also sentiment in favor. As moderator, I presided over the discussion without vacating the chair to offer an opinion. Voting was by secret ballot, and when the count was taken, it was a tie. As moderator, I had not voted, so it was left up to me to cast the deciding vote, which was in favor. I have never regretted that vote, and I am grateful that the Southern Presbyterians joined with others in this worthy endeavor. A year or so ago, a friend who had had a long relation of working for JICU informed me that a granddaughter of the current Emperor Akihito (throne name Heisei) was a student at the Japan International Christian University.

1a. Voices of Discontent

One afternoon, three of the Japanese faculty members made a formal visit to me at home. Mr. Naitoh did most of the talking as he was best in English, and he wanted to be sure I fully understood what they had to say. He began, "The Bible says that at the end of seven years, there should be a year of release. President Moore, who has been here seven years, is soon to go on home assignment, and we Japanese think the time has come for a basic change." The ground of their complaint was President Moore's total indifference toward getting accreditation. He had had very negative experiences under prewar Japanese government control of every aspect of education including worship of the emperor and all the other means of enforcing national conformity. Thus, he held the view that in order to satisfy the conditions for accreditation by the Japanese government's Ministry of Education, we would necessarily have to compromise our Christian principles and beliefs. He seemed quite content to remain a small, close-knit academy catering principally for pre-ministerial candidates in the Kaikakuha.

Although these Japanese colleagues all belonged to the Kaikakuha, they had more ambitious hopes for the school than that. They assured me that they represented the views of the other Japanese colleagues. "We must change the administration, broaden our base and our policy, and get accreditation so as to attract more students and become a true institution of higher learning," they insisted. They did not expect any change so long as the board of trustees under Will McIlwaine (himself so intimately involved at the seminary) continued to go along with whatever President Moore wanted. Mr. Naitoh likened the trustees to *narabi daimyo*, the feudal lords of old Japan who traveled to Edo on alternate years simply to sit in ordered ranks and give unquestioning assent to whatever the shogun decreed.

There was no question: I had to report this conversation to Lardner, which I did as soon as possible. He seemed incredulous. He said he would have to confirm for himself that all the Japanese agreed. Some days later, he reported that he had conferred with Mr. Kobayashi, a particularly intimate colleague, who supported him and told him that not all the Japanese felt the same way.

Meanwhile, in both the Japan Mission and the Executive Committee back in the United States, questions and criticisms about SCC had arisen and grown. Critics included people on both sides of the Pacific and on both sides of the Kyodan/Kaikakuha divide. They seriously questioned the comparatively large support for the college in terms of missionary personnel and financial cost when there were no signs of growth or success. We heard that within the Executive Committee, strong voices had called for the abandonment of this costly project.

While these deliberations were going on, a missionary colleague at Kinjo confided to me that upon reopening Kinjo after the war, Moore, McIlwaine, and McAlpine had begun making moves to take over control of that institution. Therefore, the missionaries at Kinjo had agreed to the proposal to start the boys' school to occupy the others and let Kinjo keep its independence. Nobody had anticipated the way things would develop subsequently.

The Executive Committee of Foreign Missions located in Nashville, Tennessee, had undergone some major changes since the postwar reopening of work and the establishment of SCC. Dr. C. Darby Fulton, general secretary of the Committee at the time, had been a second generation missionary in Japan himself. He was quite sympathetic with the Big Three and the pastors in the Kaikakuha, and he persuaded the other members of the Executive Committee to let the Japan Mission do pretty much as it wished without direction from the U.S. But during the last few years before Dr. Fulton retired, several members of the Committee had begun to call for a much more progressive and ecumenical policy. When Dr. Fulton did retire, the General Assembly chose one of those critics, Dr. T. Watson Street, as his successor.

1b. From Shikoku Christian Academy to Shikoku Junior College

Dr. Street was a well-known young theologian and church historian in the faculty of Austin Theological Seminary in Texas when he was elected a member of the Executive Committee. He resigned his faculty post at Austin Seminary to become general secretary for the Executive Committee for World Missions. Many of us welcomed his progressive policies, and we could understand why he would have doubts about Shikoku Christian College. Dr. Street had graduated from Davidson College and had been a Patterson scholar at Louisville Presbyterian Seminary ahead of me. Although I did not know him personally, I admired him greatly and shared many of his views, as did my wife Margaret. We corresponded with Dr. Street and other members of the Executive Committee, urging them to give the Japan Mission an opportunity to make some basic changes in hopes of preserving Shikoku Christian College, and many within the Japan Mission joined in the same effort.

The board of trustees of the college took up the question too. They had heard quite clearly that a very substantial majority of the faculty had lost confidence and wanted change. Now they heard the possibility of a cutoff of support from the Executive Committee in the U.S., so they had to make some very hard decisions.

As chairman of the board of trustees, Will McIlwaine had to bear the greatest responsibility for these decisions. His personal views coincided pretty much with Lardner Moore's, who insisted that relinquishing responsibility for planning and administering the college to the Japanese would result in making it just one more typical Japanese school. Will McIlwaine probably would have preferred for things to continue as they were, but he knew that was impossible. He knew that if the school were to survive at all, it would have to be in a different form. To his great credit, he did what he could to assure the continuation of Shikoku Christian College. He persuaded Lardner that no matter what happened, it would be best for him to resign as president. He told the board of trustees that over the past few decades, theology and mission policies of the Presbyterian Church (US) had changed from what they had formerly been when he himself came to the mission field, and therefore, he would not insist on trying to hold on to the old ways.

The board of trustees accepted the resignation of Lardner Moore and nominated Professor Tokunaga Shintaro as president. Will McIlwaine himself resigned as chairman of the board, and later, Dr. Kondoh Buichi, chancellor of Kinjo Gakuin (the Golden Castle Women's School) took his place. The trustees approved the other changes, and the details of which were worked out over the following months. The trustees instructed the new college administration to make an aggressive effort to gain accreditation as a junior college enrolling girls as well as boys. The curriculum would consist of two departments, English and Christian studies, with the latter one including courses in social work. The Executive Committee sent a committee of three experts, including one from India, one from an African American college in the U.S., and one from Davidson College, to see how things were going, and they gave their approval.

The trustees retained the English name Shikoku Christian College, but they changed the Japanese name from Shikoku Kirisutokyo Gakuen. The original Japanese name signified to an ordinary Japanese that the school's purpose was to specialize in teaching Christianity, but we had the much broader purpose of teaching liberal arts with a Christian foundation. The trustees chose Shikoku Gakuin Tanki Daigaku (in English, Shikoku Gakuin Junior College) as the new name. The term *gakuin* had been adopted by many Christian institutions of higher education when the Ministry of Education refused to grant them status as universities on the same level as the national universities at Tokyo and Kyoto. (Meiji Gakuin and Kinjo Gakuin are two examples.) Therefore, *gakuin* seemed appropriate for our purposes. Nevertheless, some in the Japan Mission and in the Executive Committee regretted the removal of "Christian" from the Japanese name of the college. A much-simplified statement of faith took the place of the Westminster Standards as requirements for faculty and trustees. The Japan Mission gave its approval to these and other changes and asked the Executive Committee of Foreign Missions to do the same. This they did and allowed us a year to work out the details of the transition to see whether we had a real possibility of succeeding.

Responding to our initial inquiries to the Japanese Ministry of Education, the authorities noted that all our buildings were renovated army facilities. They said we would need at least one new building designed specifically for academic purposes. With permission from the Japan Mission, the U.S. Executive Committee, and a grant of $10,000, we built an assembly hall that could accommodate the entire student body and that was adaptable to various other uses. Our daily chapel services were held there after it was completed.

We had a good deal of help from very able Japanese men in making the necessary changes. President Tokunaga had been on the faculty since the earliest days and provided trustworthy and dependable continuity and leadership. Dr. Yano, former president of Meiji Gakuin who had also served in the Ministry of Education and was a president of a secular university, gave us good advice and assistance in dealing with the Ministry of Education. Later, Dr. Yano became president of SCC and led us to accreditation as a four-year college. Professor Ito came to us from another small Christian college and contributed great faith, determination, and strength of character. In my personal view, Professor Tokunaga, Dr. Yano, and Professor Ito were in every sense of the word the "Big Three" who made a success of the transition from Shikoku Kirisutokyo Gakuen to Shikoku Gakuin Tanki Daigaku.

Mr. Ito took responsibility for the Christian studies department, and we invited Mr. Okada Totaro and Mr. Nishiwaki Tsutomu to join that department to develop the social work curriculum. They were both active members of the Kyodan. They attended the Kaikakuha congregation closely related to the college, but they were not warmly welcomed. Eventually, they were able to get a Kyodan congregation going in Zentsuji, which was in a sense the reorganization of the prewar congregation of the Nikki, whose church building had not been rebuilt after a fire. Under the new school organization, Margaret joined the faculty teaching social work, and I had the responsibility of teaching required Bible courses to all students as well as some advanced courses in the Christian studies department.

The administration submitted our formal application for accreditation to the Ministry of Education and waited for the response. Late one afternoon in winter, President Tokunaga came hurrying to our house wearing wooden clogs and the informal robe he wore at home. In his hand, he waved a telegram, which he had just received from Tokyo. The Ministry of Education had approved the accreditation of Shikoku Gakuin Tanki Daigaku. To my wife's surprise, as much as to President Tokunaga's, she threw her arms around him in a warm and joyful embrace. We had made it.

We had made the transition from a failed attempt at establishing "an American school in Japan" under the control of missionaries with a rather narrow theological point of view. We now set out on a new course to build an institution under Japanese administration more adapted to the needs and conditions of the time and place while maintaining the Christian faith and ideals that underlay our original founding.

Immediately, postwar, there was a rising demand for greater opportunities for education beyond high school. The Ministry of Education had not responded to this need, and private schools had sprung up all over the country. SCC was only one of many, with all sorts of purposes. All such schools depended on student tuition for operation, and compared to the elite national universities, tuition at private schools was very high. Eventually, the Ministry of Education recognized the inadequacy of this arrangement; and gradually, they began subsidizing private schools, though of course that enabled the ministry to exert greater powers of control. SCC did not experience intolerable demands and was glad to accept national financial help. This policy enabled SCC to get along without too heavy a burden on students, and we grew to about a thousand students, even though we were not considered anywhere near the top rank of private schools. We had dormitories for both men and women students, but the greater number of our students commuted from home.

2.   The Christian Character of SCC

From the early times, our faculty had some unusual members. Our first physical education teacher was a woman, and I believe we had a higher proportion of women faculty members than most Japanese institutions at that time. Without access to full data, I believe that Margaret's seminar on women's issues was the first in Japan at college level.

Mr. Matsuura, a very remarkable person, was one of a few blind college teachers in Japan. He was the son of a high military officer and himself a recruit in the Japanese Air Force near the end of the war. He was training for the *Kamikaze* suicide unit, with the aim of destroying an enemy navy ship by crashing his bomb-loaded plane into it. The war ended before he could carry out his flight, and he entered Kyushu Gakuin, a Christian institution. Through a mysterious cause, he began to lose his sight; and in a relatively short time, he became completely blind. He was in deep depression as he anticipated a useless life in contrast to the glory he would have won by sacrificing his life on behalf of his country. He was approached by one of the "new religions" that had formerly been repressed by the military government. Members of it urged him to come with them. They said his blindness was punishment for some wrongdoing, but they could help him. He happened into a Christian meeting where he heard the Bible story in chapter 9 of the Gospel of John. Jesus's disciples asked why a certain man had been born blind, was it his sin or sins of his parents? Jesus assured them the blindness was not caused by sin at all and healed the man.

Comforted by this idea, Matsuura also learned of a woman faculty member of the university, a Christian who was known to have cancer but who courageously continued to teach so long as she was physically able. Being welcomed by other Christians, Matsuura became a believer. He married a lovely Christian woman who became his faithful life partner. Later, Matsuura earned a master's degree at Boston University, where he made many American friends and admirers. After serving some years at SCC, he had an extended sabbatical and returned to Boston U for another degree, a doctorate, the *first* such accomplishment for a blind Japanese. He and his wife were a bright inspiration to all of us at SCC.

The college took first steps in overcoming many of the prejudices that were rampant in Japanese society and culture, where almost everybody assumed reincarnation or an individual's subsequent return to earth in another life after death. Any sort of mental or physical handicap was popularly believed to be punishment for some evil act in the previous existence. Hence, people with handicaps were routinely discriminated against, were deprived of employment or education opportunities, and often were simply hidden away by their own families. From the beginning at SCC, even though we were slow to provide accessibility, we decided that if handicapped persons who passed the entrance exam wanted to come, we would accept them. In time, we began to make progress toward accessibility, but never to the ideal extent.

Accreditation as a four-year college gave SCC an opportunity to have some noticeable impact, especially because there was no other school with a social work specialty anywhere nearby. In postwar Japan, the government's attempt to address the needs of disabled people ran into a lot of resistance because of popular superstitions as noted above. Members of our Social Work Department were able to assist the welfare office of Kagawa Prefecture in making a census of disabled persons, at the same time offering a Christian witness that might relieve people's anxieties to some extent. One member of that department took a special interest in autistic children. He formed a support group of parents of such children, and they organized an annual summer camp. He was a pioneer in that field, and his work spread further when it was only just becoming recognized as a disability that transcended national boundaries.

We also ignored the common practice of excluding Koreans, members of a large minority routinely discriminated against, though most of them had lived in Japan since birth. During Japan's imperial domination of Korea, they brought in many Koreans to do the most menial, dangerous, and underpaid labor, including women in the sex business. Postwar, it was simply impossible for them to return to Korea. They were foreigners, though forced to give Japanese pronunciation of the Chinese characters of their personal names. In popular Japanese opinion, Koreans were considered to be "a potential criminal element." They were registered, fingerprinted, and required to carry a foreigner's identification certificate at all times. The Canadian Presbyterian Church had an active ministry among Koreans, resulting in their own organized church. At SCC, we had Koreans in our student body sometimes. One of them became an assistant in our English language lab and later a faculty member. He married a lovely Japanese woman (one whom I had baptized at a small Kyodan church while she was a student). Already negative to their daughter becoming a Christian, her parents disowned her for marrying a Korean, but she found another family in the college and Christian fellowship.

In the same way, we ignored the ingrained prejudice against members of an even larger group with an ancient history dating from Japan's feudal period. Some people referred to them as the counterpart of India's *untouchables*. Originally, some may have been criminals, but most were captives of a defeated enemy or indigents reduced to abject poverty. Like Koreans, later, these unfortunates were given the most unclean, dangerous, and despised work, and they could never escape their condition. Some Japanese considered them to be subhumans. They were segregated in separate villages (called *buraku* in Japanese). These villages did not appear on any map, but their population was carefully counted and recorded. All Japanese have, besides their current address, an original "family address," that of their original ancestors. It was possible to identify *buraku-min* from their "family address," which they had to enter on any formal application for any purpose, such as for job, school, government assistance, etc. Officially, the postwar Japanese government decreed an end to discrimination against *buraku-min*, but it was still possible to consult illegal records to ascertain their address of origin. As in the case of Korean or handicapped applicants, we also accepted *buraku-min* who passed the entrance examination. Whether or not they "came out" was up to them. At SCC, besides our policy, we had courses that included teaching to oppose all sorts of discrimination.

One other contribution was in a sense peripheral to SCC, but I am glad to mention it. One of our trustees was the Reverend Nomachi, a Kyodan pastor of a church in Takamatsu, the prefectural capital some twenty miles from Zentsuji. Japan had suffered terribly from nuclear bombs on Hiroshima and Nagasaki, but immediately after the war, the annual public memorial for the victims and the protest against nuclear arms—with an anti-American emphasis—was monopolized by communists. Communist opponents of the emperor system and Japan's imperialism had been severely suppressed by the dictatorship, but afterward, many people acknowledged their courage and sympathized with the communists before the full implications of their policies became clear. Within the Japanese communist constituency, there was a split between those that followed Russian guidance and those that followed Chinese. So every August, there were two communist rival observances. As a result, many otherwise sympathetic people, including Christians, refrained entirely from those observances. Finally, Pastor Nomachi decided he could no longer leave everything up to the communists. So at first, with only a few companions, he went to Hiroshima to make a public Christian witness. In time, the true character of communism became clear; and with the additional pressure from the U.S., the Japan Liberal Democratic Party (which was neither liberal nor democratic) prevailed. Meanwhile, the Christian witness grew.

Another of our faculty members, Okamoto Mitsuo, had been a teenager during the occupation. An American serviceman had responded to his eagerness to learn English and taught him and helped him get an education in a very conservative Christian school, where he became a believer. Later, he studied in Germany and came to SCC as a teacher of German, though he had applied as a teacher of Christianity. When Mr. Okamoto first came to SCC, I was skeptical about his ultraconservative background, given my earlier experiences at SCC. But he was an open-minded and brilliant person, and on his own initiative, he became a student of peace studies, both in English and German. Mr. Okamoto opened the first course and seminar on peace in any Japanese university. He led the movement in Japan, writing and lecturing on the subject. Using funds and sabbatical time from SCC, he became known to such circles in the West.

Through Mr. Okamoto, I learned much about worldwide peace education and research. From him, I first heard that the small Central American state of Costa Rica had abolished its national army. President

Oscar Arias won the Nobel Peace Prize in 1987 for his efforts at peacemaking when President Reagan, Col. Oliver North, and others in the White House and Pentagon were funding the contra war against the Sandinistas in Nicaragua. The Presbyterian Church (USA) published information giving background and other facts focusing on U.S. imperialism. I shared this with Professor Okamoto, who was surprised and pleased to know that there were authentic Christians in the U.S. who did not support Reagan's policies.

When Mr. Okamoto had his sabbatical, Margaret and I urged him to take his wife, Tamayo, with him, which he did, and we lent them some funds to make it possible. In a later time, they repaid it all. Okamoto Tamayo was a brilliant person herself, and she later went in for a doctorate in Michigan State University, taking their three children with her during those years. During every break in the school year at SCC, her husband, Mitsuo, joined her and the children. Professor and Mrs. Okamoto were great assets to SCC and the entire community. Because of his national reputation, the University of Hiroshima called him away from SCC, giving him a much more prominent location for his peace and antinuclear activities. Tamayo also taught in another school in the Hiroshima region until they both retired. Professor Okamoto is the author of an essay in praise of Margaret that was published in a Japanese newspaper after her death. An English translation follows the biographical sketch of Margaret below.

3. My Term as President, 1978-1982

In early 1977, with the term of office of the current president of SCC coming to an end, several faculty members led by Mr. Okamoto came to me privately and asked me to let them nominate me as a candidate. I told them I did not consider it suitable for an American to serve as president of the college. Though I did not explain it to them, my chief reason for that opinion rested upon my early experience when almost total control by missionaries had met with opposition and had necessitated a thoroughgoing change. I gave them as other reasons the fact that I did not possess the necessary executive gifts needed to administer the college and my Japanese language ability was not up to it. Japanese decision making does not follow our American system of making a specific motion, getting a second, debating it, and voting yes or no. The

Japanese prefer to avoid the embarrassment of making a motion and losing it. Prior discussion can help determine whether an idea is good or not, and only if the feeling is right do they make a decision. Sometimes that feeling alone is sufficient, and they move on to the next item. To describe this process, they have an expression that is translated into English as "reading stomachs." I told my colleagues that not only was my colloquial Japanese inadequate, I was also very inept at reading stomachs. Sometimes I might note that suddenly, the discussion had moved to a different topic without my being fully aware of it, though the Japanese were satisfied. Privately, I said that I had a very low abdominal literacy quotient.

They went to Margaret to ask her to try to persuade me to accede to their request. She repeated the opinion that an American should not be president of this Japanese institution. To her, and later to me, they replied that the Japanese themselves should be the ones to decide on that particular point. After long and serious consideration and prayer, and with Margaret's consent, I agreed to let them nominate me. In any case, the result would be as they said: let the Japanese faculty and trustees make the decision. In the election, I received majority of the faculty votes, though not by a very wide margin, and the trustees concurred.

I faced several obstacles in beginning my term. First of all, I had to be absent from Japan for a while between the end of the school year and the beginning of the new one when I would take office. The Executive Committee of World Missions in the U.S. had made plans to hold a major consultation with missionary and national church delegates from all the major mission fields in which the Presbyterian Church (US) had significant involvement, and I was one of the delegates from our Japan mission. I had accepted the responsibility to attend that consultation long before the question of my being president of SCC arose. Thus, in my view, the transition from the previous administration to mine was not completely satisfactory.

A second major obstacle was my inability to choose the academic dean of the faculty. By custom and tradition, the faculty elected the dean, and the current dean still had two years to serve. I felt constantly thwarted because we disagreed on a number of questions, and his sympathies tended toward the man I had replaced.

Part of the reason I had been elected president was because Okamoto and several other faculty members wished to organize a new academic department and they sympathized with a large majority of the student activists who wanted to organize a student co-operative society to run a store to sell snacks, books, and student supplies. The previous administration had opposed both of those proposals. I myself had serious questions about them. I felt that from the early days after we achieved accreditation, the pace of development had gone forward too quickly, from junior college to senior college and then organizing new departments. Moreover, in the recent past, the whole country had gone through a period of extreme student unrest, somewhat tinged by communist influence according to some critics. Many people had a justifiable suspicion that a student co-op might become a serious problem.

Nevertheless, I refused to act on my immediate doubts to oppose these projects, but instead I facilitated feasibility studies of both of them. When our representatives went to Tokyo to inquire of the Ministry of Education about the possibilities of a new department, they found that we were delinquent in certain areas of our operation. For several years, we had admitted more students than our accreditation permitted, and we had been receiving more government subsidy than we actually qualified for. People in the Ministry of Education said they had warned us on this point previously, but our former president and dean had done nothing in response or even let the rest of us know. In working out the details of increasing the number of faculty to match the larger number of students, we found it practicable to organize the new department of social studies. Professor Ishimaru Shin, elected academic dean in the middle of my term, helped greatly to overcome our delinquencies and get the new department off to a good start.

In regard to the student co-op, besides the fear of student unrest, opponents insisted that our student body was too small to support a co-op adequately and that the college staff would have to take on unwanted responsibilities for management. A fairly large majority of faculty favored the co-op idea, but the staff was opposed. Upon investigation, we found that most co-ops were doing pretty well, the high tide of student unrest had ebbed, and even a relatively small operation had a good chance of success.

What I heard as a result of this preparation made me feel much better about the proposition. I became convinced that I should not try to hold the line against the students' desires. I felt that to do so would cause far more trouble than agreeing to give it a try. The board of trustees devoted a lot of time to discussion. They heard some rather strong negative attitudes fueled in part by some of the faculty members who opposed the co-op, plus the knowledge that many of the staff were against it, and perhaps some lingering anticommunist sentiments. Nevertheless, when the time came to make the final decision, I supported it strongly and actually threatened to resign if the trustees opposed it. I don't think anyone should make such a threat lightly. I had never done so before, but I was prepared to follow through on it if necessary. The trustees gave their approval.

Sugiyama Isao, who had become chief of the office staff during my term, supported me fully, even though he had his own personal doubts and had to suffer criticism from his colleagues on the staff and some of the faculty. Before I completed my term and Margaret and I left for the U.S. on home assignment in the summer of 1982, the co-op had started up. When I returned to Japan in early 1985, it was doing all right; and as far as I know, it has never caused any of the problems so many people had feared.

I had one other goal during my term of office, namely, to try to make a more equitable salary scale for the staff members in comparison to the faculty. In the earliest days of SCC, the general policy had been to try to pay compensation according to fairness and need, which in principle I thought was suitable for a Christian institution. I did not participate in policy making then, so I don't know the details, but there was no strict hierarchy of ranking among the faculty or among the staff with differentials in salary according to rank, though of course faculty salaries were greater than those of the staff. After the change from missionary domination, the college administration had adopted the accepted system of different ranks among the faculty and among the staff, with year-end bonuses and regular annual salary increases. Every year, we had to study, debate, and decide on the percentage of salary increase.

The representatives of the staff complained that they did not receive fair compensation. The faculty received many perquisites, such as funds for books, for travel, for attending conferences, and for sabbatical study. The staff said they did not receive pay commensurate with all the work they did, especially assisting the faculty. As I looked over the figures, it became obvious that the difference in salary between the faculty and the staff was set in such a way that the faculty rate of increase grew faster than that of the staff. Over the years, the gap between the faculty and the staff had been growing and would continue to do so unless we made some changes. At my insistence, the staff received a larger percentage increase than the faculty, though not so much as I had recommended. I hoped that by following this practice for a few years, we could eliminate the slower and unfair rate of increase for staff in comparison to faculty. I don't know how the administration has handled the pay scale question since that time, but I could not approve of the wide difference once it came to my attention.

Following the surrender of Japan, the U.S. government had established the Atomic Bomb Commission (ABC) in Hiroshima. American experts there did extensive examination of the victims and learned a great deal about radiation sickness. Yet they had not shared their knowledge with Japanese counterparts. Moreover, from the outset of the occupation, General MacArthur had strictly prohibited any publication of photographs, whether still or motion, of the bomb's effect on the people. All such pictures, whether taken by the Americans or by the Japanese, were rounded up and hidden away. During my presidency at SCC, it finally became possible to get access to this resource. But since the U.S. had possession of everything, the Japanese would have to raise money to buy even the pictures taken by national photographers. A public campaign to raise the necessary funds was launched, urging each individual to contribute enough money to purchase ten feet of the film— called the Ten Feet Campaign. I added my name and title to the list of sponsors of this campaign, and I made a generous contribution.

A growing communication between Japanese and Korean Christians related to the Southern Presbyterian Church resulted in establishing a formal relation between SCC and one of the several Korean colleges of Presbyterian background. With several others from SCC, I went to Korea to formalize the relationship, and we hosted a visit from a Korean delegation. Due to the circumstances, the details of which I don't know, our relationship was later changed from that school to another, but by that time, I was out of office and out of Japan.

My four years in the office of president took a heavy toll on my wife Margaret. We had already served on the field for four years of that five-year term at the time I was elected. We were eligible for a full year of home assignment, but the college faculty would not consider even a short-term leave of absence. During the ensuing years, Margaret, at her own expense, went annually to visit her mother, who was growing old and in very poor health. During the break in the school year early 1981, she visited her mother; and in the fall of that year when her mother died, she went back to the U.S. for the funeral. In January 1982, my mother died, and Margaret and I attended her memorial service in February. Thus, in less than a year, Margaret made three trips to the U.S. under stressful circumstances.

At last, we had our home assignment in 1982. We returned to Louisville, Kentucky, the first of September to serve as "missionaries in residence" at the Louisville Presbyterian Theological Seminary during the 1982-1983 academic year. I itinerated to publicize missions and taught a course in world missions in the spring semester. Margaret entered actively into the life of the seminary and took some courses for academic credit toward a master's degree in religious studies. In December, at the time of her physical examination, X-rays revealed that she had lung cancer.

During the surgery in early January 1983, faculty colleagues and students in Japan kept a vigil of prayer. A series of treatments with chemotherapy arrested the cancer, and Margaret completed the class work for her master's degree in May of 1984. That summer, however, tests revealed that the cancer had begun to spread, and she refused to let the doctors experiment on her with more chemotherapy. She died peacefully on November 26, 1984.

Margaret always gave her best for Shikoku Christian College, from the earliest days of small beginnings, in the dark days when its very existence was in doubt, through her years of teaching in the Social Welfare Department, and in her support of me during my term as president. Just a few months before she died, Professor Nakazono, at that time the academic dean, came all the way to Louisville to bring gifts and thanks. On behalf of the faculty and trustees, he gave fitting recognition to her contributions to the ongoing success of Shikoku Christian College. Part of Margaret's ashes rest in the Taylor family's cemetery plot in North Carolina. The other part rests in Japan, together with those of Christian sisters and brothers of the Kotohira Kyodan Church, where I used to preach sometimes and where Margaret played the organ for Sunday worship on occasion.

3a. My Subsequent Relations with SCC

I have noted above several of my accomplishments as president, for which I justly take credit. I also played a role in the decision about where to locate the college chapel. We held chapel services in the new hall we built to gain our first accreditation, but over time, we sensed that we should build a proper chapel. My immediate predecessor as president was an amateur architect, and he loved to draw plans. He had floated a plan to build a chapel in the *center* of our campus, landscaped to emphasize its majestic isolation. This might be considered a nice symbolic gesture, but it struck me as theologically inappropriate. Many Japanese Buddhist temples or Shinto shrines are located on mountaintops or remote places where people have to make a pilgrimage to reach them.

In the Bible, as I understood it, there was a serious debate whether God needed a temple at all, since the divine presence had always accompanied the Israelite people wherever they wandered. The prophet Nathan had thwarted King David's desire to build a house for his national God, YHWH, but his son Solomon had succeeded in building the temple in the capital city, Jerusalem. Even so, prophets such as Micah and Jeremiah had called attention to the temple's having become the focus of corruption and predicted its eventual destruction. Building the second temple later was also a debated issue, and its final destruction too had left the Jewish people to conduct their worship and study their scriptures in gathering places called *synagogues* found wherever communities of Jews lived dispersed all over the ancient Near East. Early Christianity had no central sanctuary, but like synagogues, their meeting places were scattered wherever people settled. It was only when Christianity became the official religion of the Roman Empire, to which it became subservient, that a central hierarchy centered on one supreme sanctuary became the official norm. I prepared a paper on biblical principles adapted to our local Japanese environment, and Professor Okamoto, one of my supporters, translated it into Japanese for distribution before we had a faculty retreat specifically to discuss the whole question. To my gratitude, the final decision was not to invade our green space but to locate the chapel in sight of the street that ran by our front gate and adjacent to our classroom buildings.

My predecessor was reelected president after me, and during my three-year absence, he designed and built the chapel in the location previously determined. To my disappointment, the building was not fully accessible, and it did not include rooms for various other student activities of a religious nature.

Besides these positive results of my tenure at SCC, I look back and discern two serious failures on my part.

First, I did not try to learn the details of the full implications of the lines of authority in Japanese institutions of higher education. Not counting the two highly prestigious national universities, there was a large number of private universities and colleges, including a number of Christian institutions founded by missionaries, some of them quite large. Kinjo Gakuin, our mission women's college, had classes from kindergarten to university-level graduate courses. Their chancellor, Mr. Kondoh, had been SCC's board chairman after the early reorganization, which was all very well. But eventually, he resigned, and we never had a satisfactory chairman for our board of trustees. In fact, for a brief time during one interim, I was the board chairman of record, though nobody instructed me exactly what I should do, and I didn't have sense enough to ask. In actual fact, according to Japanese rules, the chairman of the board of trustees can be a very powerful office, superior even to the president.

When my term as president expired, my predecessor was elected president again. I was absent from Japan for three years—home assignment prolonged by Margaret's illness. When I returned, I ranked only as a part-time professor, and I took advantage of the fact that I was not required to attend faculty meeting. Thus, I avoided the possibility of a clash with the president. Some years after I retired from Japan, I heard that he had succeeded in getting himself appointed chairman of the board of trustees, and thereafter, he solidified his authority over the subsequent presidents, deans, and faculty members. This is a cause of regret for me, though I have no idea whether my acting differently would have been effective in any way. Many years have passed, and I don't know what is the state of Shikoku Christian College.

A second regret concerns the relationship between Shikoku Christian College and the Mission Board of the Presbyterian Church (USA). I always took for granted a very intimate relationship between the Mission Board and the college, given the fact that despite the ups and downs that characterized our early years, the Executive Committee of Foreign Missions of the Southern Church had eventually given full support. As the college became self-supporting with national aid, it no longer received financial assistance through the Japan Mission. Still, the Executive Committee was willing to consider requests for qualified missionaries to serve full-time on the faculty, especially for teaching English. In addition, we had a number of young persons, including Jim Cogswell's son Jim Jr. who served for a year at a time teaching English, several of these being students from seminaries in the U.S.

While I was in authority as president, I should have taken the initiative to negotiate between the college, the Japan Mission, and the Executive Committee to draw up a formal covenant of mutual relationship. During my absence, the Northern and Southern churches had reunited. The Mission Board of the reunited Presbyterian Church (USA) maintained relations with both the Kyodan and the Kaikakuha, though the Northern Church had always related only to the Kyodan.

When I returned to Japan alone, I found that the head of our English department had applied to the British Council to send a young man to teach English. This Japanese English professor thought that "English English" was more authentic than "American English," so he had not bothered to apply to the Presbyterian Mission Board to send a missionary teacher of English. They would have been quite willing to do that, as they did it even for Kyodan-related schools that had been originally founded by other denominations. I met the young Englishman and his wife, who seemed very nice people and, I assume, effective teachers. But neither of them was an active Christian, and whether justly or not, I got an impression of at least a slight negative attitude toward the faith. That was the moment at which I became acutely aware of my failure to assure a clearly understood relationship between Shikoku Christian College and the Presbyterian Church. In the following years, my communication with people at SCC gradually dwindled away to practically nothing.

The last Presbyterian missionary member of the faculty, Dr. Harry Altman, professor of physics, was killed in a mountain-climbing accident shortly before he and his wife, Yukiko, were to leave for a yearlong home assignment. He was a remarkable person, highly talented in many ways, especially in music. During his college years, he had participated in a year abroad program in Japan and had married a Japanese woman, Yukiko, who was also very able. Harry had relations with a church in the U.S. that provided him with a set of handbells, which he introduced at SCC and formed a handbell choir. Our music professor had trained a choir to sing Handel's "Messiah" every year in which Harry participated enthusiastically. After I retired, at Harry's initiative, student singers from our Korean partner came to participate in the annual concert. Harry was the intermediary to ask me to find an American woman to be alto solo for the concert one year, which I succeeded in doing.

Harry became very sensitive to the injustice of the Japanese discrimination against Koreans in Japan by enforcing the alien registration law against them. Harry refused to be fingerprinted for a residence card when he returned from home assignment, which meant he could stay only a few months on a temporary visa. He then had to leave Japan for a while and then return for another temporary permit. In his absence, he and his family went to Korea, where they solidified their relations there.

Since Harry's death, his wife, Yukiko, stayed on a while at SCC but later moved to Tokyo, where she became a member of the staff of a Christian agency that ministered to women facing serious problems of abuse. Some of the women are Japanese, but the majority are from South Asian countries who had come to Japan to marry Japanese men but had later suffered rejection. Interracial children born of such unions also faced serious discrimination. In recent years, Yukiko Altman has retired; and as far as I am aware, there has been no Presbyterian Church (USA) missionary appointee at the college.

In 2000, when the time came to celebrate the fiftieth anniversary of the founding of the school in 1949-1950, the college administration made no special effort to ask the Mission Board to send a representative to the celebration. Dr. Insik Kim, the Far East area secretary at that time, would have been the appropriate person. But by the time he heard about it, he had already scheduled extensive travel to other East Asia countries, and it was too late for him to include SCC in his itinerary.

As for me, the invitation I received for that celebration specified that they would cover all my expenses for lodging and for my transportation from and to the airport at Takamatsu, about twenty miles distant from the college in Zentsuji. The invitation made no mention of my wife Wanda. By that time, I had too little interest in Shikoku Gakuin Daigaku in particular or in Japan as a whole to be willing to pay my own roundtrip travel expenses from the U.S. This decision may be counted against me as another failure. I still have ambivalent feelings.

PART FOUR

Margaret Hopper Taylor

8

A Biographical Sketch of Margaret Ruth Hopper Taylor

1. Family Background

Margaret Ruth Hopper was born January 15, 1922, in Louisville, Kentucky, the third daughter of the Reverend William Higgins Hopper and Ruth Eagleton Terry Hopper. According to her own account, before she was born, her name was William Jr. Nevertheless, her parents' desire for a son (William Jr. was born four years later) did not affect their attitude toward her as a daughter. She always expressed highest affection and admiration for her father, who, she said, never once gave her the slightest indication that as a girl she was in any way inferior to or less desirable than a boy.

Her father, William Hopper had grown up as the eldest son of a farm family in Stanford, Kentucky. The early death of his father placed heavy responsibility on him to see to the care and education of his younger siblings, which he discharged faithfully at the cost of delaying his own education for the Presbyterian ministry and his marriage. His mother spent her declining years in his home, and there, she died. He possessed a gentle, affectionate nature, but he had a very strict sense of moral values, constantly warning his children against even the appearance of evil. The Reverend William Hopper was a pastor of churches in Louisville and in Birmingham, Alabama, and later served as treasurer of the Executive Committee of Christian Education and Ministerial Relief of the Presbyterian Church (US) when it was located in Louisville. He was instrumental in the organization of the Board of Pensions, which was a great improvement over the old system of supporting retired or disabled ministers only by means of church-wide freewill offerings.

Ruth Terry Hopper provided a role model of an able, active woman of the day. She was one of a small minority of women who had college degrees in those times. As a student at the University of Louisville, Ruth Terry had joined the only sorority on campus. But since the sorority used the only meeting room available for the small number of women students, Ruth sensed the inequity of the situation and took the lead in dissolving the sorority—drawing down the wrath of the organization's national leadership. Before her marriage, she served a brief term as a dean of women at the university. As the wife of a Presbyterian pastor, she took active part in all phases of church work, from the local to the national. Later in life, she served as president of the women of the Presbyterian Church (US). She was one of its first women to be elected as a ruling elder, the first woman commissioner to the General Assembly to chair a standing committee. She was a delegate of her denomination to the Evansville, Illinois, Assembly of the World Council of Churches.

2. Margaret's Early Years and Education

In Margaret's early years, she showed the effects of her heredity and environment. She had a quick mind and a sharp intelligence. She said her most vivid memory of her years in public school was being constantly bored in class. She was an enthusiastic participant in all sorts of activities—sports, journalism, drama, and music. The high schools of Louisville were sexually as well as racially segregated. Though this policy had some distinct drawbacks, it worked to her advantage in giving her opportunities to develop leadership abilities without facing the culturally sanctioned unfair advantage over girls that male students frequently enjoyed.

Margaret attended Shawnee High School in Louisville's West End, which was considered inferior economically, socially, and culturally compared to the East End. Thus, her environment shielded her from temptation to snobbishness and strengthened her sense of solidarity with less affluent people. She also did not suffer academically, for she won highest scholastic honors. She was editor of the school newspaper and cherished an early ambition to edit the *New York Times*. She took first prize as solo cellist in a statewide music competition, and she won a scholarship to summer school in Chautauqua, New York, where she did college level study of speech and international politics accredited by New York University.

3.   College and Graduate Study

When Margaret graduated from high school in 1938, her second sister, Martha, was a rising senior at Centre College, and the Hopper family budget could not cover the expenses for two daughters at that Presbyterian school. Therefore, Margaret lived at home and attended the University of Louisville. According to her own estimate, this was one of the most formative of her educational experiences. Some of her most influential teachers were refugee scholars who had fled Hitler's Germany. While some students made fun of their queer English, Margaret was able to appreciate their depth of scholarship and their social and political concerns, which she carried with her when she transferred to Centre College in her second year.

Attractive and popular, Margaret enthusiastically entered into the students' social life on campus. This did not, however, dampen her interest in social concerns of a different kind. Majoring in sociology and political science, Margaret continued the study of subjects that had attracted her attention since high school. Indicative of her involvement in trying to improve the lot of sharecroppers, she posted in her dormitory room a copy of Millet's painting *The Man with the Hoe* and the poem of the same name. She joined the protest against the U.S. sale of scrap metal to Japan to be made into weapons turned against China. Few of her schoolmates at Centre understood or sympathized with these interests. Yet they elected her to the Student Honor Council, which administered the honor system in effect on the women's campus at Centre (the men's campus did not have the honor system). Again, she took highest scholastic honors, being elected a member of Mortar Board. (Centre did not have a chapter of Phi Beta Kappa.)

During her youth, Margaret had been active in the churches where her father was pastor, teaching and accompanying hymns in the Sunday school. She was active in the Presbyterian youth program locally, regionally, and nationally. She became a member of the General Assembly Youth Council, which enabled her to participate in decision making at the highest denominational level and attend nationwide ecumenical youth meetings. One of the adult advisers of the denomination's youth program asserted that Margaret Hopper was best qualified to be president of the council, but times were not yet ripe for a woman to receive that recognition. She strongly criticized the Montreat Conference Center management for segregating the black young people and wanted to make a formal protest. However, she couldn't rally sufficient support for such a move.

Had the Presbyterian Church at that time admitted women to the ordained ministry, Margaret would probably have gone to seminary after graduating from college. But since the ministry was not an option, in order to respond to her sense of call, she enrolled in Kent School of Social Work of the University of Louisville to prepare for a career in that field. She wrote her thesis on a documented history of the National Youth Administration in Kentucky, one of the Roosevelt New Deal programs initiated in response to the great depression.

In addition to studying, Margaret worked part-time as a caseworker in Louisville General Hospital. This brought her into intimate contact with the effects of poverty, unemployment, and alcoholism. She was also sensitized to the effect of callousness and indifference on the part of many of the people who had responsibility for dealing with recipients of assistance. She was particularly incensed by hospital interns and residents who, she thought, were sometimes deliberately cruel to people on the charity wards, as though punishing them for some wrongdoing. As a Christian, Margaret had a keen sense of one's responsibility for personal sin and wrongdoing. But her study, experience, and direct observation convinced her that there were systemic weaknesses in society contributing to poverty and crime which needed to be addressed by political action. She accepted the logic of the necessity for public welfare and assistance programs, yet she knew that within such programs, there was a need for social workers with a deep sense of call and commitment and an understanding and sympathy for the unfortunate people to whom they were responsible.

4. Marriage

Margaret was in her first year of graduate study and I in my first year at Louisville Presbyterian Theological Seminary when we met at the home of Dr. and Mrs. Louis J. Sherrill. Dr. Sherrill, professor of Christian education at the seminary, invited me and several other students to his home for after-dinner dessert one evening. Mrs. Sherrill (another role model for Margaret), whose grown children had left home, had also enrolled in the social work master's degree program, and she invited Margaret and another young woman from her class. After that first meeting, Margaret and I dated fairly frequently; and several months later, I told her I loved her and wanted to marry her. Only then did I learn that she had a number of other admirers, and it took her a while to make her choice.

During the courtship, I introduced my father to Margaret when he came to Louisville on business. He was a typical Southern male chauvinist and a vocal critic of Roosevelt and the New Deal. In no time at all, he and Margaret engaged in a spirited debate, and I finally had to ask them to find some other topic of conversation. After we became engaged, Margaret went with me to my home in Winston-Salem, North Carolina, during Thanksgiving holiday in 1943 to meet the rest of my family. I think she got a mild impression of provincialism when one cousin, knowing she was from Louisville, asked, "How are things out in the West?"

We married on September 5, 1944, after she had completed her master's degree and at the beginning of my senior year in the seminary. I had a full scholarship and received some income as student pastor of the Presbyterian Church in Charlestown, Indiana. We lived in Charlestown, as did several other student pastors of churches in the area, and I commuted four days a week to school. Margaret had a part-time job with the Presbyterian Board of National Missions as a visitor calling on people who moved into the area to work in the local DuPont powder plant. We needed a car, and Margaret used her small savings to buy one. During wartime, all we could get was an antiquated Plymouth sedan that constantly needed some sort of repair. During the four years we used it, it required major engine overhaul twice.

Before I finished seminary, I had a deep sense of call as a missionary to China. The immediate impulse came through a talk at the seminary by a veteran China missionary of the Presbyterian Church (US), but it stirred childhood memories of a visit to my home of another China missionary. For some years after that early visit, I had talked of going to China as a missionary someday, and the latest experience seemed to confirm and reinforce my early inclination. Margaret concurred in this decision without hesitation. She and her family had always had deep interest in the overseas work of our church. Her father had wanted to be a missionary, but the delay in his education made him too old for appointment. He had helped and encouraged a brother and a sister to go as missionaries to Korea. Margaret's own interests and studies had given her an outlook transcending narrow provincialism.

5.   Minister's Wife in Tennessee

The war was still in progress when I finished seminary in May 1945, so we had no possibility of going to China. To gain experience in the pastorate in the U.S., we went to the village of Buffalo Valley, Tennessee, where I was the first resident pastor of the old Presbyterian Church there and a newly organized one six miles away at Silver Point. Margaret and I, both city bred, took considerable adjustment to rural life. She pluckily put up with all the inconveniences, including a house without hot water, heated by open fireplaces. I installed a water heater and a coal-burning stove by myself. We got our water pumped into the house from a spring, but during the winter when I was sick, the spring silted up, so the pump wouldn't work, and Margaret had to haul water as well as coal. During a flood the next spring, we had to move everything to the second floor and vacate the manse because of the backwater, which rose six inches into the first floor.

There were many hovels in the rural slum section of Buffalo Valley, and thus, we became acquainted with poverty in the U.S. outside the urban areas. There was a clear economic differential between Presbyterians and others in the town. I did not limit my pastoral visitation to the Presbyterians, and I conducted several funerals in the area during our two years in Tennessee though no members of either of our churches died. Margaret participated in the women's study groups taught by the local home demonstration agent, but these hardly touched the lives of the poor. We lacked the resources, knowledge, and time needed to address their problems.

Our first child, Bill, was born in Cookeville, the county seat. Margaret was in labor for over fifty hours, and I stayed with her as long as possible. I had to preach on Sunday, however; and by the time I returned to the hospital, the doctor had taken Bill by forceps. Our neighbors were shocked that Margaret planned to sleep the baby not in the same bed with us, not even in the same room with us, but in a totally separate room. They expressed further puzzlement by asking, "You ain't going to take that little bitty baby to Chiny, are you?" But we were, and we eventually did. When we left Buffalo Valley in 1947 to study Chinese language at Yale University, we couldn't help wondering just what had been the total effect of our ministry there. For us, however, it was part of our learning process. We came to have a deep admiration for many of these rural people, who outwardly seemed uncouth and who lacked the educated polish that most urban Presbyterians value so highly. Their patience in adversity, their hard work to make do with relatively little, their basic human qualities, and their Christian faith endeared them to us.

6. Preparation for Missionary Service

Full-time language study at Yale tested our patience and endurance. Three families, missionary appointees, each with one small child, lived in a "winterized" summerhouse (that is, one equipped with a furnace) facing Long Island Sound in Woodmont, eight miles out of New Haven, Connecticut. Wives and husbands had to fulfill the same language requirements, so we shared all housekeeping duties on a unisex basis. On Saturdays, we did shopping, laundry, and housecleaning. Five days a week, we had to finish breakfast and get the children to the nursery school before our classes started at 8:00 a.m., pick the children up after we finished at noon, and go home to get lunch. We were supposed to spend afternoons and evenings in study and drill, and most of us followed the regimen conscientiously. Margaret and I were in the most advanced section of our Chinese language class.

By the end of our year's study, summer 1948, the Pacific War had ended, but civil war wracked Mainland China. The Mission Board equivocated whether to send us to Beijing for our second year's required language study according to policy. It was off again, on again. After summer vacation, Margaret and I were told to go back to Yale to continue our study there, and I went ahead to find an apartment. Hardly had we begun to settle in when the Executive Committee of Foreign Missions decided we could go to China after all. We got our things together, bade farewell to our family, and, in mid-September, boarded a superannuated Norwegian freighter in New York bound for Shanghai. The voyage took sixty days. Our son Bill was not quite two and a half but was very energetic. Margaret used to say she chased Bill all the way across the Pacific.

Disembarking in Shanghai, we found the place swarming with refugees, for Beijing had fallen and the Red Army was southward bound, sweeping all before it. We "celebrated" Thanksgiving and Christmas at the Winling-Lu missionary guesthouse with our colleagues, and in early January 1949, we went with three veteran Presbyterian missionaries to Taiwan, where the Canadian Presbyterians welcomed us as guest workers. The Taiwanese speak different Chinese dialects from what we had studied, so we found communication difficult. We taught English in the mission schools and continued language study.

From missionaries and from acquaintance with Christians, we learned to love and respect the Taiwanese. We sympathized with them because of their suffering under Japanese colonial rule followed by the unjust treatment of Chiang Kai-shek's Nationalist forces (Kuomintang). When the Nationalists fled from Mainland China before the Red Army, the Taiwanese had welcomed them, but they promptly massacred over a thousand of the most able Taiwanese leaders. The Nationalists reduced Taiwan itself to the status of simply one of the fourteen provinces of all China, of which Chiang's Kuomintang claimed to be the legitimate government. Misled by the China lobby, many people in the U.S. never understood this historical fact. Hailing the Nationalists for anticommunism during the cold war, the U.S. accepted their fictional claim to be the real China and systematically supported this small minority in their repressive policies against majority of the Taiwanese.

Some years after we left Taiwan, we entertained in our home in Japan a professor of law from the Massachusetts Institute of Technology who had just come from Taiwan where he had been a guest of the government. He gave extravagant praise to the officials he had met. "They are really quite open and democratic," he said. "They told me, 'Just point out whatever in our laws needs to be changed, and we'll change them.'" When Margaret asked him, "Did you talk to any Taiwanese nationals?" He had to admit he had not. It turned out that he was totally unfamiliar with the true nature of these "open and democratic" people who had given him such hospitable treatment and the status of the Taiwanese people from whom he had been insulated.

We were in Taiwan less than a year before the communist forces had consolidated their victory on the mainland. Everyone assumed that they would attack Taiwan soon, and President Truman announced that in such case, the U.S. Seventh Fleet would not intervene. In view of the possibility of invasion and the fact that we were expecting our second child, we accepted the advice of the U.S. consul to leave. We learned that our Presbyterian Mission in Japan was about to open Shikoku Christian College and that we would be welcomed there. There was an old mission residence for us in Marugame City, about five miles distant from Zentsuji, where the school was located.

7. Missionary in Japan

When we landed in Japan in February 1950, the country was still deep in economic distress following total defeat. Because of shortage of supplies, foreigners could not buy food on the local market. We had special ration stamps to order imported goods from Kobe or Yokohama. Cooking had to be done on charcoal stoves and bread baked in a small electric oven. The occupation authorities gave missionaries the privileges of Army Post Office (APO) service and accommodations in special cars on the railroads. Both of us felt uncomfortable about these marks of privilege.

Three months after our arrival, our second son, John, was born in the U.S. army hospital in Osaka. Margaret and Bill had gone to the Mission guesthouse in Kobe during the final wait, but I remained on duty at the college in Shikoku. By the time I reached the hospital, John had already arrived. He was the largest of Margaret's babies, but she had not had such a lengthy labor as with Bill. On her second morning in the hospital, a nurse brought her a pile of diapers and turned over to her full responsibility for caring for John.

Returning from Osaka to Marugame, we rode a ship on the Inland Sea. Ordinarily, it's a nice overnight trip with bunks to sleep in, arriving at home port about breakfast time. This time, however, a heavy fog blanketed western Japan, and we didn't reach home till nearly night. Margaret could nurse John, but Bill got very hungry, with no meal service aboard. Kind Japanese passengers shared fruits and crackers with him.

Sixteen months subsequently, our third son, Samuel, was born. Margaret enjoyed a more leisurely stay in a Japanese hospital in Kobe and the assistance of a nice Japanese nurse.

The sheer mechanics of daily living, compounded by lack of knowledge of the Japanese language, put a great strain on us all, but especially on Margaret. What seemed to weigh heavily on her mind was the necessity of employing Japanese helpers. She had faced the same situation in Taiwan. Intellectually, she knew that the economic situation in both countries made it desirable for as many as possible to find some kind of employment, and she knew that under the circumstances, we alone were incapable of taking care of ourselves and doing any sort of mission work besides. Still, having dedicated herself to a career of service, first as a social worker and then as a missionary, she felt it ironical that one of the first acts she had to do when arriving in Taiwan and later Japan was to hire people to serve her and her family.

With her limited vocabulary and a very expressive range of body language, she managed fairly well, and she did her best to relate as much as possible on a human level without emphasizing rank. She greatly appreciated the response of our Taiwanese cook to her egalitarian manner. When a second family came to live in the other side of the house where we stayed, we had to relocate our kitchen to an outhouse. "How will I ever let you know when we need something at the table?" she asked our cook. "You could write me a letter," he suggested with a grin.

As time went on, Japan became more affluent. There were many more desirable jobs than housework, and housekeeping itself became easier. Margaret welcomed these changes, though she regretted that she had let our boys be waited on so much by the helpers without learning to take more responsibility for themselves.

We stayed in Japan nearly three and a half years to complete our first term of service before returning for home assignment. Margaret taught two nights a week at the college, where we offered special English classes for public school English teachers. She took main responsibility for managing the household and caring for the two smaller boys, whom she was unwilling simply to turn over to an amah or nursemaid. Using materials from the Calvert School of Baltimore, she began first-grade lessons for our eldest son. As our younger sons came along, she taught them too. In all, she taught a cumulative total of twenty pupil years to our three children in addition to classes she taught at the college. As the children left home one by one to go to high school at Canadian Academy in Kobe, she took on a heavier course load at the college.

We spent our first home assignment in the year 1953-1954 in Louisville, where I got a master of theology degree at the Presbyterian Seminary. We especially enjoyed nearness to Margaret's parents, and this year, in retrospect, became more precious to her, for it was the last time she could be with her beloved father, who died before we had our second home assignment. Margaret always believed that of all the members of her family, her father gave her the most unquestioning and unswerving appreciation and support. His death was a heavy blow to her.

Instead of returning to Shikoku Christian College, we spent the next eight months in language study in Kobe. Though neither of us knew any Japanese when we first went there, I had studied a few hours a week with a private tutor while teaching at the college. With the two babies coming so close together and her other responsibilities, Margaret's opportunity for language study had been severely limited. So even though it meant living in yet a different residence for most of a year, we recognized the necessity for the effectiveness of our work. Even so, this language study time compared poorly with what we should have had, namely, two full years of formal class work.

We had expected to concentrate on language study that year in Kobe while our boys attended Canadian Academy, but in Margaret's case, a special assignment from the Japan Mission encroached upon her study time. She was appointed to head the publicity committee to help raise money through the Presbyterian Women Birthday Offering (US) in order to build the Yodogawa Christian Hospital in Osaka. With her usual wholehearted enthusiasm, verve, and ability, she led the campaign that resulted in the largest Birthday Offering in the history of the church up to that time. Besides planning the campaign, Margaret wrote much of the publicity material, including a biographical sketch of Dr. Frank Brown, the missionary doctor who had taken the lead in the medical work. She also served as a missionary member of the board of directors of the hospital in the early years and for some time thereafter. Her criticism that the Mission did not move fast enough in the direction of giving administrative responsibility to the Japanese was one reason for her later resignation from the hospital board.

All too aware that our language preparation was still inadequate, we returned to Shikoku Christian College. A house for us was under construction on the campus, but we had to stay with friends for about six weeks till it was finished. When we moved into our new home, this became our seventh residence since we married, besides the various hotels, guesthouses, and ships we had stayed in for anywhere from ten days to three months along the way. By this time, Bill was doing fifth-grade Calvert study at home, John was attending Japanese kindergarten and doing first-grade work at home, and Sam was soon to start kindergarten. In the spring of the next year, John entered first grade in the Zentsuji public school, and Sam followed in due course, but both continued their English studies with their mother using the Calvert School materials.

Our weekday schedule was as follows: Early in the morning, John and Sam came and got in bed with Margaret, who guided their Calvert studies, while I prepared breakfast. My routine was to alternate eggs and toast one day and hot cereal the next, with liberal portions of fruit and milk. Then the two younger boys set off for the local elementary school. At our evening meal when we were all together, Margaret used that opportunity to ask what they had learned at Japanese school or to share with Dad what they had learned in Calvert. If one of them had a cold that kept them home from school, Marg used that opportunity to get in at least a double session of Calvert.

Margaret conscientiously fulfilled her multiple roles as wife, mother, teacher, and household manager. She was always careful about nutrition—a staunch advocate of green leafy vegetables—and made every effort to plan a balanced diet for all of us. Japan in the early postwar years was faced with many deficiencies, including food supply, especially during the winter months. Carrots and cabbage were almost the only fresh vegetables available, and Margaret warned me to be prepared for them to appear frequently on our table. I was to eat them without complaint and set an example for the boys. From their earliest years, our sons learned to eat everything. When they lived in the dormitory during their high school days, they made no complaints about the food in the dining hall, while other students were quick to complain. My son Bill reported to me that the Taylor boys told the others, "Just eat all you want and leave the rest to us."

After Bill had already left for MIT in the U.S., John and Sam came home for winter holiday. At lunch one day, there was a platter containing carrots and celery among other raw veggies. I looked at it and said, "I always did think rabbits were stupid animals." The two boys' ears pricked up almost noticeably, and they said, "What? What did you say, Dad?" "Nothing, nothing. Forget it." Margaret intervened, "It's OK. Go ahead and tell them." So I told how their mother had instructed me to eat carrots and cabbage all those years and at least pretend to like them. They both agreed that they never had any idea that I thought otherwise.

During our second term on the field, Margaret devoted much of her time to the children, but she did teach some classes at the college, and she also served on various committees of the Presbyterian Japan Mission organization. The Mission again called on her ability at writing and editing to prepare the annual report to the Executive Committee of Foreign Missions and the church at large. She did her usual excellent job, highlighting that we Presbyterians devoted ourselves to the same types of ministry as Jesus, preaching, teaching, and healing. She regularly wrote informative letters, which were mimeographed and mailed out through the Missionary Correspondence Department of the Executive Committee (the letters were familiarly called MCDs). Favorably impressed by the Japanese school system, she wrote an article for the *Saturday Evening Post* entitled (by the editor) "My Japanese Educated Children" and appropriately illustrated.

We had sent along some snapshots that might accompany the article, but the editor engaged a professional photographer, John Launois, to come and stay as a guest in our home for a few days. John spoke fluent English as well as his native French, but not Japanese. His Japanese wife accompanied him. She spoke Japanese and French, but no English. We Taylors spoke Japanese and English. (Though I had studied French in high school and college, I was not up to colloquial conversation.) Our mutual communications were interesting, to say the least.

By this time, we felt that after a great deal of moving about for nearly ten years, our missionary career and our family life were at last becoming settled. Margaret herself had matured as a person, as a woman, and as a missionary, and people were paying her some attention.

8.   Teacher

Margaret was a born teacher. She never forgot how bored she had been in school. She thought our son Bill was probably typical of most children. "He loves to learn but hates to be taught," she said, and she did her best to make learning interesting both for our boys and for her college students. The money she received for her article in the *Saturday Evening Post* she used to help finance a family trip through Europe on our way to the U.S. for home assignment in 1960. Margaret took the initiative in planning the whole thing, including the purchase of a Volkswagen camper bus that was home for us as we made our way about in ten European countries. All through the year preceding the trip, she prepared the boys for it; and after we returned to Japan and she resumed the homeschooling, she found opportunities to recall some of their experiences.

Always conscious of the inadequacies of her Japanese language ability, Margaret worked hard to find illustrations and activities to liven the classroom atmosphere. She did her best to challenge the students and broaden their minds. Her seminar on women's problems was probably the first to be offered in a Japanese university. It gave her real satisfaction to help raise the consciousness not only of women students but also of some of the men. On the faculty of the Social Work Department of the college, she taught developmental psychology, cultural anthropology, and psychology of the handicapped (our college had an accredited course to train teachers of handicapped children). She made the students spend a day blindfolded, in a wheel chair, or with one limb disabled in order to help them understand the plight of the handicapped. She had a senior seminar in which she guided a number of students in research and writing their graduation theses.

Shikoku Christian College had a majority of women students, but the faculty was preponderantly male. Margaret did all she could to encourage the search for more women faculty members, and her efforts met with some success. She encouraged the other women to be more assertive, but they never attained her level of courage in speaking out. As Japanese women in Japanese society, they were subject to more pressures and dangers than was Margaret, a foreigner. The college administration, in its desire to increase the proportion of men students, tended to give preference to men in borderline cases, but this always stirred Margaret's strong opposition, and sometimes she was able to get admission decisions made on a more equitable basis.

Making full use of the college's allowance for study and travel connected with teaching, Margaret joined the organizations of both professional social workers and teachers of social work. She attended the international venues of these associations in Tokyo, and she joined the Japanese delegation to attend the meeting of the Asia section, which met in Teheran, Iran, with a side trip to Egypt before returning home. An avid reader, she was always ready to recommend books to people, and many, including the Executive Committee of Foreign Missions personnel, expressed their appreciation for her helpful suggestions. As in the case of the MIT law professor, Margaret was always quick to try to give people she met new insights or added information from her growing store of study, observation, and experience.

In our later years at the college, Margaret's views and opinions were appreciated and sought in the wider society. For a year, she wrote a column translated into Japanese for a bimonthly publication for Japanese social workers. She received appointment as a member of a committee of Kagawa Prefecture (roughly equivalent in level to state government in the U.S.) in charge to make a survey and recommendations concerning the establishment of a new senior high school. She responded to invitations to speak to women's groups, to senior citizens, and once to an entire high school student body. She spoke to the high school students on the subject of human rights. The teacher who had been instrumental in inviting Margaret had her class write their reactions, many of which she shared with us. One student had written, "Her Japanese was sort of odd, but she certainly said some important things."

Margaret's MCD letters always elicited response, mostly positive. She tried to cover a broad range of subjects related to life and work in Japan, including social, political, and economic matters, as well as a more narrowly defined "missionary work." One church executive in the U.S., whose official position was such that he automatically received all the MCD letters sent out from the Executive Committee, said he routinely placed the interesting and informative letters in one pile and the predictably typical missionary letters in another. When he finished his term, he checked out the two piles; and in the interesting and informative stack, he found only those from Margaret.

9. Controversialist

Not all responses were positive, however. As a social worker, Margaret knew the importance of birth control and family planning. She believed that the "Japanese miracle" of rebuilding industry and economy after the war had been greatly facilitated by the fact that Japanese women could limit the number of children to those they really wanted and could afford to bring up. As a positive consequence, measurable improvements took place in the quality of education and family life, the status of women, and the number of teen age mothers and abused children. In the early postwar years, the Japanese used antiseptic, inexpensive, and safe abortion as a major means of birth control. Margaret did not condone the irresponsible or casual use of abortion and worked toward the successful promotion of other means of birth control. But she always insisted that safe abortion should be an option and that women should have a high degree of freedom of personal choice. Not only in MCD letters but also in the media in the U.S., she expressed these views. As a result, she received her share of negative criticism, some of it of a scurrilous nature.

"My Japanese Educated Children" in the *Saturday Evening Post* got some positive reaction. One reader, however, wanted to know why the author went as a missionary to Japan if they had such a good school system. Margaret never attempted to justify the missionary calling by denigrating everything about the people among whom she lived and worked. It distressed her to see some missionaries' almost totally negative attitudes toward the Japanese. Perhaps those examples encouraged her more positive attitude, but I think too that her basic sense of fairness and justice motivated her. Her conflict with the Mission and the hospital over the question of Japanese leadership should also be seen in this light.

Certainly, the Japanese themselves appreciated her. When she was fighting cancer, a group of students folded one thousand paper cranes and sent them to her as an expression of love and prayers on her behalf. Some of them had prayed all night in Japan the day Margaret underwent surgery in the U.S. She received another thousand cranes from a group of women whom she had met through participation in the local UNESCO Club. When news of her death was reported in Japan, one of our Japanese colleagues at Shikoku Christian College wrote a memorial that was printed in the regional newspaper. It was entitled "An American Woman Who Loved Japan," and it took special note of Margaret's characteristic practice of always looking to find the best in everyone.

The *Saturday Evening Post* paid Margaret a generous check for her article, but when the treasurer of the Executive Committee learned of it, he demanded that she hand it over. This was his interpretation of the rule requiring all missionaries to turn in any money "over and above" the salary they were paid for doing work outside their regular missionary duties. The question was hotly debated both in the Japan Mission and in the Executive Committee, but the final decision went in Margaret's favor. Such creativity was not to be equated with, for example, getting paid for teaching English in a public school or a private class.

As time went on, Margaret found herself more and more in conflict with the Executive Committee over questions of missionary pay and the status of women. A missionary couple counted as two missionaries, whether the wife devoted herself chiefly to household tasks or worked full-time as, for example, a hospital nurse or a schoolteacher. The

Executive Committee calculated a couple's pay according to the median salary of pastors in the U.S. with adjustments made according to overseas conditions. If missionaries earned any money "over and above" the salary, they had to give it to the Executive Committee. After our boys grew up, Margaret became a fully tenured professor at the college, taking on all the responsibilities the status entailed. The school administration did not recognize both husband and wife as full-time faculty, but they offered to pay her on the scale as a part-timer. She declined the offer because the rule about extra pay would simply mean that she turn the money over to the Executive Committee.

At the same time, she protested that the rule discriminated against missionaries. The median salary for pastors in the U.S. did not include any money their spouses might make, and in the case of home staff on the Executive Committee, their spouses too could hold their own jobs. Yet during a recent reorganization of the staff, the Committee had declared that all employees were "staff" of the one Executive Committee, some serving at home and some serving overseas. Margaret wrote to the director of World Mission, stating her objections and pointing out the great discrepancy in salaries, not only between home staff and overseas staff, but also among different ranks of home staff. She sent copies of the letter to members of the Committee, to the home staff, and to a number of missionaries in various fields. Missionary salaries did not change as a result, but home staff salaries became a bit more equitable, as one of the beneficiaries told us.

It came to be known later, however, that in special cases, the Committee had allowed some missionary wives to keep the money they earned. This was never publicly announced, but it was said that permission might be granted in response to the request. Learning of this, Margaret told the college she would be glad to accept the pay they had previously offered, and she informed the Committee authorities of her intention. Since the Committee made no response, she kept the money. Most of it she placed in savings accounts in the U.S., but she used some of it to buy Japanese art and crafts for which she had developed an appreciation. Some time later, the Committee revised the missionary handbook, reinstating the old rule requiring the return of "over and above" earnings and interpreting it strictly. Still, Margaret refused to comply.

As his term was coming to an end, the moderator of the General Assembly Executive Committee of Foreign Missions (whom we had known for some years) wrote an appeal to Margaret to abandon her obstinate position and follow the rules. In reply, she wrote, "One of the heroines of recent history is Rosa Parks, who refused to move to the back of the bus when she was ordered to do so. What you are saying to me is 'Margaret, move to the back of the bus.' I won't do it."

Margaret had always taken every opportunity to learn more and upgrade her own knowledge and skills. For example, during our 1960 home assignment in Richmond, she had, at her own expense, taken some courses at Richmond Polytechnic Institute (now Virginia Commonwealth University). On our home assignment in 1968, the board granted us one-half of the tuition expenses for both of us to study at Harvard Graduate School, which was among the most stimulating experiences either of us ever had. At the height of protests against the Vietnam War, Margaret participated in some student rallies. She and other women students, angered because they had to go to a separate classroom building to find toilet facilities for women, threatened a "sit in" protest.

Margaret always urged other missionary wives to study on furlough. It always pleased her when they took her advice and saddened her when they didn't. At least two had said, "Why spend the time and money? It won't make any difference in our salary . . ." To Margaret, this response gave clear evidence that the system itself not only discriminated against women but also encouraged them to internalize the inferiority the culture imposed on them.

10. Householder

As the daughter of a Presbyterian pastor, Margaret early experienced the problems faced by ministers required to live in houses not their own but provided by the church they served. Missionaries faced similar problems. Mission housing had to conform to certain standards so as to accommodate different families over the years. Plans for the house that the Mission built for us on the college campus could embody a few, but by no means all of our personal preferences.

Lardner and Grace Moore, an older missionary couple at the college who had lived all their lives in mission housing approached retirement and return to the U.S. with no home in prospect and with no equity in a home. That situation roused a lingering concern in Margaret's mind. Later on, after our children were grown and gone, a younger family was appointed to the college and came to Kobe for a year in language school. The question arose of providing housing for them when they came to the college. There was no room left on the campus for a house there, so people had to consider finding land and building outside.

The new folks correctly pointed out that the house we occupied would be more suited to them with their growing family, so why shouldn't we Taylors be the ones to take on the matter of a new residence? With this incentive, Margaret got the idea of avoiding the hassle of trying to plan another house within the constraints of mission rules. "Why don't we," she suggested, "buy land and build our own house?" asking the Mission to pay us a housing allowance as more and more churches in the U.S. had begun to do for their pastors. Besides, the Mission was already renting housing for some missionaries. She had some savings, and we had not drawn on the income from a trust fund set up for me by my father. He had done the same for each of us four Taylor siblings, and we all found the fund helpful in getting our own homes.

Nobody in the Japan Mission or the Executive Committee in the U.S. had ever thought of such a thing before, so it took a while for the authorities to agree, but finally, we got their approval. While waiting for the process to take its course, we had been looking around, and we found a place in the town of Tadotsu on the Inland Sea, about four miles from Zentsuji. Japanese friends of ours at the college, Professor and Mrs. Nishiwaki, whose children were also grown, were interested in moving out of college housing, so the four of us cooperated in negotiating for the purchase of enough land for us both to build. The property lay within a semirural neighborhood in a small Japanese town, and without the joint negotiations involving our Japanese colleagues, the owners of the land would probably not have gotten agreement from their neighbors to sell to us Americans.

We concluded the whole transaction just before leaving for home assignment at Harvard in the fall of 1968, and the Nishiwakis tied up the loose ends and built their house during our absence. By the time we returned, Margaret and I had a pretty good idea of what we wanted. She succeeded in making it a tasteful combination of Western and Japanese features. We built the house to suit ourselves, but I had no difficulty in selling it to a Japanese when I left Japan in 1986. The years Margaret and I spent together there in our own home were among our most enjoyable, even though we underwent a certain level of stress during my term as president of the college, our long period without home assignment, and the death of both our mothers.

11. Feminist

I believe that Margaret's innate sense of justice enabled her instinctively to recognize and resent unfair treatment wherever it existed. Living in Japan where discrimination against women was more flagrant than in the U.S. sharpened her natural sensitivity to women's problems. Having lived in Taiwan and Japan, she had a personal acquaintance with Asiatic people, which spurred her very early opposition to the U.S. war against the people of Vietnam. She gave wholehearted support to the struggle for racial equality in the U.S. Yet she observed that within the movement, women were most often shunted out of positions of real leadership and consigned to menial and secondary duties. She predicted that the rights of women would be the next important goal of the struggle for justice, and she was determined to play a part in it. She knew from experience that those in control of power don't voluntarily surrender it. Women would begin to get equal treatment only when they themselves began to take initiative.

All this was in her mind as she defied the Executive Committee. She felt compelled to speak out on her own behalf. Naturally, there were those who accused Margaret of being crassly mercenary. She did not deny the desirability of the money, but with her, the issue was broader than that: this was a battle for the recognition of the dignity and worth of women. In a society that commonly measures worth in monetary terms, women fully deserve such recognition. For a woman to remain silent when mistreated is to share complicity in her own degradation, and therefore, Margaret determined never to let people get by with behavior or attitudes that degraded women.

I became one of the earliest targets of her counterattack. From my Southern upbringing and the example of my father, I had learned habits and attitudes that Margaret resented; and in time, she reached the point at which she would not put up with them any longer. Never in public, but always in private, she would take me to task for insulting or denigrating behavior. She was smart enough to recognize that not all of my unpleasantness was directed against her personally. She could identify many of them as products of cultural formation, which I could change if she responded in reasonable terms and spoke in the context of respect and love. She helped me have a significant attitude adjustment.

In 1971, we had an emergency furlough of six months because of the illness of Samuel. We spent that time in Louisville, and in keeping with her practice, Margaret took some courses at the University of Louisville. We lived in the Furlough Home on the campus of the Presbyterian Seminary, and she became a supporter and confidante of several women students who were struggling for better treatment and recognition in that male-oriented institution.

Meanwhile, I spent much time in the library researching the Bible teaching about women. At Margaret's suggestion, I read Kate Millett's *Sexual Politics* in which the author accurately described the widespread denigration of women in real life and in literature. While I agreed that she accurately described the way men have mistreated women, I thought that Millett was wrong to place so much of the blame on the Bible and Christianity. With my consciousness already raised by Margaret's efforts, I studied scripture with a new perspective. I learned to read the Bible in a historical and cultural context. I saw that aspects of male dominance and female subordination and acceptance of slavery and polygamy, which one could easily find in the Bible, differed hardly at all from the near-universal characteristics of the ancient world. I found the same bias against women in Egyptian, Mesopotamian, Chinese, and Japanese cultures. Absolutizing the patriarchal texts in the Bible as church "fathers" like Tertullian and Augustine had done made biblical religion no different from the pagans in that respect. I began to understand and appreciate Kate Millett's resentment and reflect on the culture in which I had grown up.

Yet within the Bible itself, I found other texts to call in question the cultural dominance of patriarchy. The Bible's unique feature lay in God's taking the initiative to deliver the Hebrew slaves out of Egypt. The deity stood, not with the oppressing power structure, but with the oppressed. This good news acted as subversive yeast in Israelite society to challenge all aspects of injustice and oppression and to cause some improvement in the status of women. In Jesus, I found the climax of a process leading toward the true equality of women and men. Growing out of my biblical research, I wrote the essay "MALE-FEMALE-NATURE-SCRIPTURE," which later appeared in the Shikoku Christian College journal *Treatises*, and "Liberation for Women, A Biblical View" in the *Japan Christian*

Quarterly. Without being aware of the emerging liberation theology, I was already part of its flow.

As Margaret's instinct for justice had stimulated me, my biblical studies gave her even greater confidence as she carried on the struggle within the church. That summer of 1971, at the Furloughed Missionary Consultation and the World Mission Conference at Montreat, she had the opportunity to test her mettle. When we had come home for our year at Harvard in 1968, I had come directly to the U.S. in time to attend these conferences at Montreat. Margaret, however, took her own time and money and came home via Siberia and Russia, giving herself another opportunity to observe firsthand a different part of the world and a different group of fellow human beings. She flatly refused to attend those Montreat conferences. She complained that male chauvinists dominated them and that they did her more harm than good. The board authorities practically ordered Margaret to attend the conferences the summer before we returned to Japan, and in response to her complaints, the planners gave her an opportunity to make a presentation on women's concerns. That was to take place on the last day of the World Mission Conference when all those in attendance divided into five groups to go in turn to each of five programs on different subjects, including Margaret's. She went well prepared.

As soon as Margaret arrived, she placed posters in prominent places, drawing attention to discrimination against women in society and in the church, but somebody tore them down. She put up new ones, and she announced publicly what had happened to her material. This only spurred greater interest. At both the Furloughed Missionary Consultation and the World Mission Conference, she participated actively in the discussion following each lecture (all of which were given by men). Margaret would stand up and announce, "The women's liberation movement gives you a grade of so-and-so for that talk for such and such reasons . . . ," and then she would specify her criticisms. By the last day of the conference, the place was abuzz. One youth delegate, who later held a prominent position in the reunited church organization, testified that she had never before seen a woman operate with the courage and skill that Margaret displayed. Some of the men who received low grades from her were resentful or mystified, but others had the good sense to seek her out and try to learn what she was talking about.

After we returned to Japan, Margaret did a similar work of consciousness-raising at Lake Nojiri, where a number of missionaries had formed an association at a modest summer vacation place. One year, she and I and several sympathetic colleagues planned the weekly theological discussion, a standard feature of every summer program. We had Bible lectures and presentations of various facets of the women's movement. Again, teenage girls saw in Margaret for the first time a new kind of role model. Not only so, but a number of missionary wives who felt frustrated in their family life or mission organization or both began to seek out Margaret for advice. She experienced special satisfaction and joy when, at her urging, several wives went in for graduate study, one of whom achieved a doctorate.

The organization of the Nojiri Lake Association was patriarchal. Husbands were house owners of record and members of the association. In case a husband could not attend the annual meeting, his wife had to have special permission to act as his proxy. We had bought a small cabin and registered ownership in Margaret's name, not mine. She became active in the politics of the association and succeeded in having the constitution changed so that both husband and wife were recognized as voting members.

Sunday worship at the Lake had always featured a man preacher, but gradually, the climate changed enough so that the worship planning committee asked Margaret to be the first woman to occupy the pulpit on Sunday. When we returned to our cabin after the service that day, we found on the porch an anonymous note ordering her to read certain Bible passages, those which fundamentalists customarily cite when opposing the ordination of women.

Margaret never shrank from debate or controversy, and as I pointed out previously, she refused to remain silent when people denigrated women. Leaving church in Richmond, Virginia, one Sunday morning, she held the preacher's hand, looked him straight in the eye, and said, "Do you realize you used three illustrations in your sermon this morning and every one was a put-down of women?" He was momentarily stunned, but then in typical blame-the-victim response, he cried, "Dear lady, we preachers have such a hard time finding illustrations! Surely, you're not going to take these away from us." But she was adamant in insisting that he become sensitive to this matter. While being confrontational, she seldom or ever was threatening, and I was always impressed by her attitude, which tended to disarm rather than alarm her interlocutor. In this way, I think she got much more positive response than some overly aggressive militant feminists. She was not a man-hater but a true lover of humankind, all made in God's image. She firmly believed that the liberation of women, the true equality of men and women, would actually mean the liberation of men from sexist stereotypes that limited them in so many ways. I acknowledge her help to me in achieving progress toward liberation from cultural limitations to freedom, which God offers to all through Christ as revealed in the Bible.

12. Fall of 1982 in Louisville

For eight years, Margaret and I did not have a real furlough from our responsibilities in Japan. We had qualified for home assignment in 1978, but in the fall of 1977, the faculty of Shikoku Christian College elected me president for a four-year term beginning April 1978. The dean of the faculty was not willing for me to take even a three-month leave of absence during that time, so we stayed on. Margaret's mother was in declining health in a nursing home in Louisville, so she visited her each year. The 1981 visit took place in the summer, and Mother Hopper died in the fall, so Margaret returned to the U.S. for the funeral. Early in 1982, my mother also died, and Margaret went with me to that memorial service. Thus, she made three rather stressful trips to the U.S. within nine months. I can't help thinking that this may have contributed to the onset or the growth of the cancer that finally took her life.

Following her annual physical examination in the fall of 1981 in Japan, the doctor had said he would need to pay attention to her right lung the next time she came for an exam. However, my term as president of the college ended March 31, 1982, and we left that summer for home assignment as missionaries in residence at Louisville Presbyterian Seminary, expecting to get our exams in the U.S. On the way home, we spent about ten days in London, enjoying leisurely visits to museums and attending several plays. Margaret tired rather easily, so several times, I went out by myself walking along canals and picturesque neighborhoods or attending a concert at St. Martin-in-the-Fields.

We had brief visits with our son Bill and Roberta, our grandsons Ken and Ron, and John and Samuel. We arrived in Louisville the first of September. Mark Ruppert, a senior at the seminary, met us at the airport. Enthusiastic about world missions, Mark urged us to take responsibility to teach a course on that subject in the spring term. Classes at the seminary had already begun when we arrived. We met with Dean Louis

Weeks and Professor Harold Nebelsick, who seconded Mark's request that we team teach a missions course in the spring. From the start, Margaret agreed enthusiastically, and I went along too, even though I knew it would be quite a task. Neither of us had specialized in missiology as an academic subject, and simply having been missionaries hardly qualified us academically.

At the meeting with the dean, we also learned of a new one-year degree course offered by the seminary, master of arts in religious studies, designed for missionaries and others from overseas who had only a year to study but who might be able to earn a degree during that time. Dean Weeks wanted someone to try out the new course, and Margaret decided to make the attempt. In anticipating our retirement after our final term of service in Japan, she had expressed a desire to find some kind of employment in the U.S., and she thought an additional degree would qualify her for a more useful kind of service.

She signed up immediately for four full-time classes—systematic theology, philosophical theology, sociology of religion, and American church history. She found it rather hard going, for it involved subjects somewhat removed from her own field of social work and she was a bit late getting started, but she threw herself into the study, taking it seriously and doing rather well. For my part, I audited several classes, started preliminary preparations for the forthcoming missions course, and traveled some to speak about world missions.

We began regular attendance at Second Presbyterian Church, one of our eleven supporting churches, where Margaret had her membership. The pastor, Glenn Dorris, recommended that she stand for election as an elder, and she was subsequently elected at a congregational meeting.

Soon after our arrival in Louisville, we registered to vote in the Democratic Primary prior to the congressional election coming in November, and we wanted to exercise our citizen's voting right. Margaret did not lose any time in writing to the Louisville *Courier-Journal* on the question of militarism and population control. She got some positive response, but also some scurrilous remarks from a Ku Klux Klan member.

We had already decided to retire in Louisville, so we began looking at houses. We made the acquaintance of a very able and helpful real estate agent, Patti Thomas; and through her, we bought a house on Alta Vista Road, in walking distance of both the Presbyterian and Baptist seminaries. Margaret was the one who took the initiative in all this, and she entered enthusiastically into the bargaining process that resulted in our getting the house for a very reasonable price. Patti Thomas managed the property for us as a rental.

Because of all these activities, we both put off getting our physical examinations, ignoring the rule of the Executive Committee that missionaries on home assignment should do that before engaging in any kind of work or itineration.

I had my physical examination with Dr. Robert Shaw III, recommended to us by an old friend of the Hopper family. Then I left for New York to attend a meeting of the Society of Biblical Literature and stay with my son Samuel. Margaret went for her examination after the exams when classes ended for the holidays. When she had her chest X-ray, the technician told her there was a suspicious spot on her right lung and took more shots. That afternoon, she went to see Dr. Shaw for the first time, and he seemed to have difficulty knowing how to report on the findings, as he had never met Margaret before and didn't know anything about her. She sensed his difficulty and said, "It's all right, Dr. Shaw. You can tell me quite frankly. I'm a Presbyterian." By that, of course, she meant that she had strong faith in God's predestinating providence and was prepared for any kind of news however bad it might be. She often quoted her father as saying, "Presbyterians ought not to worry about things." As she recounted to me her remark to Dr. Shaw, she added, "He must have thought he had a mental case on his hands."

She convinced Dr. Shaw that she wanted him to tell her exactly what he thought, and he said the spot on her lung was something serious. It could be TB, some sort of fungus (a remote possibility), or cancer. He gave her a skin test for TB, which within a short time proved negative. Margaret telephoned me and Samuel in New York to tell us what was going on and as much as she knew up to that time. She said Dr. Shaw had strongly recommended that she enter the hospital for a bronchoscopy to get a sample of the tissue to determine whether or not it was cancer. But it was nearly Christmas, and we were expecting Bill and Roberta, Ken and Ron, and Samuel to be with us in Louisville. Therefore, she had decided to wait till early January to have the biopsy.

Christmas was a happy occasion with all the family with us, except John. But naturally, it was somewhat clouded by the prospect of the forthcoming tests. We had decorated a tree, and there were lots of presents for everyone. Samuel brought along the computer printout of the book he was writing, *Shadows of the Rising Sun*. The whole family participated in reading and commenting on it. Samuel accepted a lot of our suggestions, but not that by Margaret that he should use more inclusive language instead of some of the sexist expressions found here and there. We all thought it was well done and were very proud of Samuel.

On the last Sunday of December, we all attended Second Presbyterian Church in Louisville, where Margaret was ordained and installed an elder. I had the distinct privilege of sharing in the laying on of hands at my wife's ordination. Only the family and Mac Brewer, a distant cousin of Margaret's who was a medical doctor and a member of Second Church, knew about her questionable medical situation at that time. She had called Mac as soon as she had the news from Dr. Shaw and had Mac's approval of Dr. Nightingale, the surgeon recommended by Dr. Shaw to do the bronchoscopy.

Performed early in January, the biopsy revealed adenocarcinoma of the lung, with possible involvement of some of the ribs. The question was whether to operate or to attempt some other form of treatment, such as radiation or chemotherapy. Dr. Nightingale would do the surgery, and the cancer team of the University of Louisville School of Medicine would direct the latter. Margaret was very positive in wanting the surgery, even though it might not be effective and in any case would be rather radical—possibly involving removal of the entire right lung and parts of the ribs nearby. The oncology people spoke of chemotherapy as a means of "prolonging survival," words that caused my stomach to turn over when I heard them. Nobody spoke about a cure.

Up to this time, every new bit of information we got had been "bad news." But Margaret was not downcast. She had a sturdy faith. We read the Bible and prayed together often during these days, and she took special courage from the great promises in Romans 8, "I consider that the sufferings of this present time are not worth comparing with the glory that is to be revealed to us . . . We know that in everything God works for good with those who love him, who are called according to his purpose . . . For I am sure that neither death, nor life, nor angels, nor principalities, nor things present, nor things to come, nor powers, nor height, nor depth, nor anything else in all creation, will be able to separate us from the love of God in Christ Jesus our Lord." People at the seminary and Second Church were especially solicitous. Margaret appreciated their concern very much, but she really preferred not to have visitors.

13. Battling Cancer, 1983

After careful consultations involving all the medical people connected with the case, it was decided to do the surgery. We had kept the family informed, and people at Shikoku Christian College had called, and they knew the plans. They arranged a chain of prayer continually throughout the hours before, during, and after the surgery, even though that meant that it was nighttime in Japan. Friends in the various churches also joined in the prayers.

I went to the hospital on the day and sat in the waiting room a long time. Other people were being called out from time to time, but no one came to inform me. After several hours, I went out and made inquiries and found that there was another waiting room where I should have sat. The surgeon, having finished the operation and unable to find me, had gone. I found Margaret in the recovery room. I spoke to two residents who had assisted at the operation, and they told me that the cancer had spread too far for surgery to have any effect, so they sewed her back up. This information also caused my stomach to turn over. The residents urged me not to tell Margaret her true condition, but I knew I could never deceive her. When she woke enough for me to talk to her, she naturally wanted to know the exact result, so I told her. This was another heavy blow, but she took it bravely, although her first reaction was one of anger.

Later, we got a fuller explanation from Dr. Nightingale. The cancer had spread over a rather wide area between the lining of the chest wall and the lung. This had not been of sufficient opacity to show up on the X-ray and could not have been verified except by surgery. To remove part or all of the lung under these circumstances would have aggravated the condition and caused an even wider and more rapid spread, he told us.

As time went on, we learned a few things about cancer in general and lung cancer in particular. It seems that there are perhaps hundreds of different kinds of cancer. Some grow rapidly, others slowly. Some may be removed surgically, others not. For some, very effective treatments have been devised, for others not. Among the five or more different types of lung cancer, Margaret's was not the kind commonly associated with smoking. Lung cancer grows slowly, and by the time an X-ray can detect it, it has already reached a rather advanced stage. In light of what they learned through the tests in Louisville, the doctors could reexamine the X-rays taken of Margaret's lungs in Japan in September 1981, and they realized that there was a very faint irregularity in the right lung at the place where the cancer later showed up. How long it had been growing inside her or what had caused it, no one could say. For some years, Margaret had complained of being easily tired and not having much energy nor being able to sleep well. Whether these were symptoms that the cancer was already at work in her or whether they were general conditions of physical weakness that made her susceptible to cancer, I don't know.

We hear from time to time of people who complain bitterly when they learn they have cancer. "Why me?" they ask. Some of our friends told Margaret they would fully understand if she too railed against God. One who had experienced both serious heart disease and cancer said that cancer frightened and discouraged him most and made him cry out, "My God, my God, why hast thou forsaken me?" Margaret never took this attitude. She said, "If I ask why me for this cancer, I also have to ask why me for all the many wonderful and rich experiences of blessing I have received throughout my life." For her, life had been good. She was not afraid of death, only of the possibility that dying might be painfully prolonged. At the same time, she had a strong will to survive, and she was ready to undergo the next treatments as soon as she recovered sufficiently from the surgery.

Dr. Thomas Woodcock directed the chemotherapy treatments using two drugs, cisplatinum and velban, in a protocol he had devised and which had helped some patients to have a prolonged survival and better quality of life for a while. Even so, the treatment was classed experimental, and we had to sign a release. The drugs, especially the cisplatinum, are highly poisonous and attack all the cells in the body, but they are more destructive of the rapidly growing cancer cells than others. They do cause loss of hair and severe nausea and may damage the kidneys and hearing.

Margaret had to spend four to five days in the hospital in order to monitor all her physical functions after receiving the drugs. She was terribly nauseated and uncomfortable for some time and quite debilitated after she came home. Tests indicated that the drugs had had an unexpectedly severe effect on the electrolytes, minute trace elements in the blood that control the action of the heart. When these had been brought into balance, she was much better and could get up and around at home. A few weeks later, she went as an outpatient to receive a dose of velban, the less drastic of the two drugs.

After several more weeks, she went back to the hospital for the second round of velban and cisplatinum. This time, they knew better what to expect, and she did not have such a severe reaction, though she was very nauseated as before and she began to lose her hair. Eventually, it all came out. She wore a turban all the time and put on a wig when she wanted to dress up, but I admired the symmetry and beauty of the shape of her head.

During the spring of 1983, I taught the World Mission course by myself at Louisville Seminary. When Margaret was in the hospital, I had a cot in her room and stayed with her. The Furlough Home Board employed a seminary student once a week to do the laundry and run the vacuum for us, which helped greatly, as I did all the shopping and other housework. The Executive Mission Committee was generous and accommodating in every possible way. They paid all our medical expenses. They told me my top priority was to take care of Margaret. Harry Phillips and Insik Kim of the Division of International Mission made special visits, and Cliff Kirkpatrick, general secretary of the Division of International Missions, and Lew Lancaster, a former colleague in Japan with the Atlanta Board, called on us when they came to Louisville for a meeting.

While Margaret was in the hospital for one of the treatments, we had a visit from our eldest son, Bill. He and an associate had developed a seminar on artificial intelligence, which they presented here and there. He stopped by Louisville after one presentation in Chicago. Margaret's brother Bill Hopper also visited her when in Louisville to interview a senior student prospect for employment at the church where he served on the ministerial staff.

At the seminary commencement in May, Margaret made a special effort to dress and put on her wig, and we got to the chapel just before the service began and sat on the very back row. Had all gone as expected, she would have received her degree at this time, and she very much wanted to congratulate her classmates on their graduation. After all the degrees and other awards had been given out, the president, Dr. John Mulder, announced a special award and called Margaret to come forward. This was totally unexpected. As she walked down the aisle, all her classmates gave her a standing ovation. The president then read a citation commending Margaret's courage and her inspiring example.

Concord Presbytery in North Carolina of which I had been a member since we left the U.S. for mission service in 1947 elected me a commissioner to the General Assembly to be held in Atlanta, Georgia. The Presbyterian Church (US) to which we belonged and the United Presbyterian Church (US) had negotiated for many years with a view of reuniting and healing the breach that had occurred during the Civil War. Everyone anticipated that the general assemblies of both denominations, meeting in separate halls under one roof, would approve reunion. I considered myself honored and privileged that my presbytery had chosen me a commissioner.

We conferred with Margaret's doctors, and they arranged the treatment schedule so that she could go with me to Atlanta. In the cycle of the treatment, she felt at her best at that time. She took great pleasure in attending this historic meeting. She met many dear friends and made new acquaintances. She even joined in the parade when the two assemblies, having voted to unite, left the convention hall and marched into downtown Atlanta, where Mayor Andrew Young greeted us. Margaret's going at all was made possible by our son Samuel, who came from New York to travel with us to Atlanta and back to stay with us in our hotel room and to be with his mother while I attended sessions of the Assembly. As a freelance writer, he could arrange his time to accommodate us, and he had previously come from New York several times after Margaret's treatments began.

During the spring and early summer of 1983, Margaret had four of the complete cisplatinum/velban treatments. By that time, the drugs had begun to affect her kidneys. X-rays did not reveal any shrinkage of the tumor, but it had not grown. Margaret was disappointed that the cancer had not shrunk, especially in view of all the pain and discomfort she had endured. She really did not believe that the chemotherapy had helped her. The doctors insisted, however, and I am inclined to believe them that the drugs, being systemic, had prevented any spread of the cancer to other parts of the body, which often happens in cases of lung cancer.

For radiation treatment, Margaret next came under the care of Dr. Babi Jose, a very able and compassionate doctor from India. She went for treatment five days a week for two weeks, had a week off, and then repeated the daily schedule for another two weeks. The radiation was much less drastic than the chemo. She felt no side effects and could eat and get about pretty well. At the end of the course, X-rays showed the tumor had shrunk by about half, and she got negative results from tests for metastasis. This was very encouraging, but Dr. Woodcock would go no further than to say that her cancer was "in partial remission."

That summer, we had another visit from Bill, Roberta, Ken, Ron, and Samuel. This was a pleasure for Margaret, though she did not have the energy she would have liked to play with her grandsons and do other fun things with the family. We exercised as much as Margaret was able, taking walks after sundown and swimming in the pool at the Baptist Seminary.

14. In Remission, Academic Year of 1983-1984

When the seminary school year began again in September 1983, Margaret resumed her interrupted studies. The Division of International Mission appropriated $500 to help with the tuition costs of her study, a great psychological help as a vote of confidence as well as a financial contribution. She again took a full course load and entered enthusiastically into study and discussion.

Samuel's book came on the market in the early fall, and friends said Margaret greeted its appearance as if it were a long-awaited grandchild. She took pleasure in giving copies of it to close friends. We were deeply touched that Samuel had dedicated the book to us.

In mid-October, we both attended a seminar for missionaries on home assignment held at Columbia Seminary in Decatur, Georgia. We saw many old friends among our colleagues and met others for the first time. Dr. Johannes Verkuyl, a world authority on missiology from the Free University of Amsterdam, gave the principle lectures. We also attended two lectures by Dr. Jurgen Moltmann, guest professor at Emory University Candler School of Theology. Margaret had profited from the Moltmann books she had read for her theology course, and she enjoyed hearing the author in person. One sad experience was meeting with Todd Reagan, one of our colleagues from Japan who was in the last stages of cancer. She died just at Thanksgiving.

At the seminary, Margaret attended regularly the meetings of the Women Caucus. Out of her own experience and struggle for equality both here and in Japan, she could help many of the younger women. She impressed them by her courage and persistence in working for women's rights in the Presbyterian Church in the early days when there were so few involved and the barriers were so strong. Margaret always generously gave me credit for responding positively to her activism in providing biblical and theological foundations for liberation and equality and for supporting her in her quarrels and debates with some of the church bureaucrats.

Some husbands of Women Caucus members and some of the men students showed enough interest in the movement to wish to attend the meetings too, and sometimes they received invitations. Margaret supported a proposal to open the Caucus meetings to the entire seminary community. She believed in equality and nondiscrimination for all, and she saw excluding men as a reverse kind of discrimination. She also argued that women should welcome any men who wanted to come, as it would help their understanding of the problems and in the long run benefit everybody. Many of the others shared these views.

However, some of the women had evidently had rather traumatic experiences of oppression or discrimination and had very negative attitudes toward men in general. They seemed to feel that the Caucus was almost the only place they could have full support and acceptance. They strongly insisted that the Caucus should remain restricted to women only. Some became very emotional about the issue. In the end, the group decided to respect the special needs of these women and did not put the question to a showdown vote, but Margaret was disappointed.

Meanwhile, the session of the Second Presbyterian Church began a process of setting goals for the next decade. A special committee proposed fourteen objectives for the Session to discuss and revise before asking the congregation to adopt them. When Margaret saw the report, she noted three neglected areas, and she spent a good deal of time in wording proposals and marshaling supporting information. At the Session meeting, she suggested adding these goals: doubling the number of missionaries supported by the church, actively promoting programs to strengthen marriage and family life, and making peace a high priority for the entire congregation. The Session adopted all three of these proposals (even though there was some heated opposition to the third one), and the congregation adopted the entire expanded list of objectives. Before Margaret died, the church achieved her first proposal, doubling the number of missionaries.

Margaret took a course in pastoral counseling. The class separated into groups of three for practice. A counseled B, B counseled C, and C counseled A. Margaret's "counselee" was a special student, a young man from a broken home who had a very difficult relationship with his mother, resulting in extremely low self-esteem and almost-total lack of confidence in relating to women his own age. Margaret knew his problems were beyond her own competence, and fortunately, he was receiving professional counseling also, but she did her best to help him understand his own abilities and good points and have more self-confidence through her evident and genuine appreciation of him and friendship with him.

Margaret's "counselor" admired her courage in facing the reality of a terminal illness. He saw no need to emphasize this point, so he tried to suggest ways in which her life could become more enjoyable. He asked, "If money were no object, what would you like most for Arch to give you?" She said, "I would like him to give me a diamond to replace the one I lost fifteen years ago out of my engagement ring."

When Samuel came to be with us at Christmas, I reported this to him; and with his encouragement and monetary contribution, plus the same from Bill, Samuel and I picked out a diamond ring and gave it to Margaret on Christmas day as a gift from the three of us. She was completely surprised and deeply touched. I had given Margaret the original engagement ring on her birthday on January 15, just slightly more than forty years before. For her part, she wanted to give me a good guitar, and she had Samuel go with me to pick out the one I wanted. So Christmas that year was a very happy one, even though Bill and his family were unable to join us as originally planned because of a bad back condition that made travel impossible for Roberta.

Although the younger Taylors were unable to be with us, Bill had sent along a copy of the printout based on the seminar on artificial intelligence. This was to be published privately for sale to corporations interested in the subject. Though it was somewhat out of Margaret's field of experience and knowledge, she conscientiously went through it all, made suggestions about style, and indicated places which needed clearer explanation for the benefit of nonexperts like her. As always, her cogent comments helped improve the final version. The book was published in time for her to see it. She and I both read it again and noted typographical errors that were later corrected.

Professor Okamoto Mitsuo and his family visited us during the Christmas holidays. Professor Okamoto was a colleague of ours at Shikoku Christian College, and his wife, Tamayo, had brought her three children with her to the U.S. in order to study for a doctorate at Michigan State University. More than any others, the Okamotos had responded positively to Margaret's urging of the faculty wives to keep up their intellectual abilities and not allow themselves to get completely bogged down in housework. This meant, of course, that she also encouraged the husbands to cooperate in making this possible. So while

Mrs. Okamoto worked on her own studies, her husband continued to teach at SCC and served one year as a guest lecturer at Selley Oak Colleges in England. Every extended holiday, he came to the U.S. to be with his family, and they shared many activities together. So it was a great satisfaction to Margaret and me to have this visit from them and to hear firsthand about their various experiences.

During the J-Term (January), Margaret worked over several chapters of her book on raising the status of women in Japan. She had originally started writing the book at the request of the Lutheran Church's publishing house in Japan—it was to be translated into Japanese. However, by the time she finished the first draft, the publisher had changed his mind. Dean Weeks accepted her revised and updated chapters and gave her credit for independent study toward her degree. Margaret appreciated this, of course, but it was a great disappointment to her that she could not get the whole book published.

In the spring term, Margaret again took a full course load, and I taught the class in World Mission for the second time. Regular checkups at the cancer center showed no signs of metastasis, and although Margaret's energy level did not seem to increase, it appeared as though her condition had stabilized. We began to think about going back to Japan in the fall. She would not teach at all, but I would resume my regular responsibilities. We corresponded with the board and with the college, and I sent in descriptions of the courses I planned to teach. She had her passport renewed. Since the end of the treatments, Margaret's hair had begun to grow again, fuzzily at first, but with a good color, no gray at all, and it grew long enough to take a permanent wave.

As always, Margaret took a great interest in politics, and she followed the democratic presidential primary campaigns very closely. Both of us were deeply impressed by Jesse Jackson, and as the campaign went on, we became convinced supporters of his. As registered Democrats in Louisville, we attended the caucus meeting in our precinct. There were very few blacks in our precinct, but people from both the Presbyterian and the Baptist seminaries had worked hard for Jackson, so he got some delegates out of our precinct to the state convention.

One of Margaret's seminary courses was a study of the psalms, and under the direction of Professor Johanna Bos, the students worked up a "festival of psalms" which they presented at the seminary. It represented an ancient processional into the Jerusalem temple, with priests bearing the ark and worshippers following. Then the students offered the psalms they had written, some recited and some sang. Margaret had composed "A Lament" based on her experience of illness, honestly describing the deep distress of her soul, yet expressing thanks for God's blessings in the past and ending on a chord of praise. She read this as part of the psalm festival program, and it greatly impressed the hearers.

"A Lament" was later published in the *Presbyterian Survey*, in the *Seminary Times*, in an MCD letter from the board, in various congregational newsletters, and even in Morse Saito's column "Battling Windmills" in the *Mainichi Daily News* in Japan. There has been widespread response to it from overseas as well as from the U.S. It seemed to touch a sensitive chord and meet a need felt by many people.

A Lament

O Ruler of the universe,

There drops before me a dark curtain
Shutting out the light of years ahead I had hoped to spend on
   your beautiful earth.

The physicians say my body houses a killer disease.
They have no cures.
Earth's healers cannot heal.
Their treatment is painful and debilitates.
This frame that has carried me where I wished to go for sixty
   years now totters and weakens.

Physical pain and lethargy I can bear, but am I never to see
   the ethereal glory of the cherry trees across the sea unwrap
   their heavenly beauty again?
Will the emerald isles of the Inland Sea not rise once more
   before my eyes?
Is the handclasp of friends soon to be no more?
How can I say goodbye to the sons of my womb and their
   children?
Heaviest of all is the thought of the final closing of my eyes on
   the loved face of my life's partner, who cares for me in my
   illness as gently as a father does his little child.

Is this your will, O God?

All my life you have blessed me beyond remembrance with
    gentle parents and loving friends.
So many doors of travel and learning have you opened for me.
Years of good health and joy of living have you poured out for me.
You have spared me through hurricanes at sea, earthquakes on
    land, and on miles of travel.

None of these great blessings have I earned.
I can only repeat my song of thanks for all your saving wonders,
    for your marvelous creation of nature and human kind.
Keep me close to you, O mighty God. I trust in you through
    every valley.

Praise your holy name! Praise be to God!

As commencement time approached, Professor Nancy Ramsey told
me that staff members of Women's Concerns at the General Assembly
Mission Board had prepared a citation to be presented to Margaret at
that occasion, recognizing her contributions to peace and justice causes,
especially on behalf of women. She had not known about this, and she
received it with a standing ovation when she was granted her diploma.
Another surprise came to Margaret from the Women of Strathmoor
Presbyterian Church, the second of our two supporting churches in
Louisville. They invited her to come and lead the installation service of
the new officers for the coming year, and on that occasion, they gave her
a gold pin and a certificate of honorary life membership in the Women of
the Church.

The successful completion of the master's degree and the various
awards were made the subject of a write-up that appeared in the
Presbyterian Outlook to which Margaret had been a frequent contributor.
Besides these evidences of appreciation, she received innumerable cards
and letters during the long months of her illness. Because her cancer was
so serious and so protracted, many people felt moved to write to her, and
a number of them sent beautiful expressions of appreciation for Margaret's
work and example in the cause of liberation. Had her illness been short
and her death quick, she might have been spared a great deal of pain
and discomfort, but she would not have received these expressions of

appreciation which did so much to encourage her and to make her realize that the seeds she had sown produced a great deal of fruit than she ever imagined. She used to get discouraged sometimes because of the seeming lack of response to her teaching and earnest efforts, but the last year of her life especially brought forth many powerful affirmations for her.

The commencement at Louisville Seminary on May 27 was a very joyful occasion. Samuel came from New York, and a host of friends and well-wishers at the service and the reception afterward gave her special greetings and expressed congratulations and appreciation. I think this was one of the great high points in her whole life.

15. The Last Months

Although Margaret successfully completed the degree studies, as summer drew on, she became noticeably weaker. She suffered shortness of breath with even minor exercise. The June checkup at the Cancer Center showed that fluid collecting in both her lungs, including the hitherto unaffected left one, caused the breathing problem. Further, the bone scan showed up some "hot spots" in the spine and ribs. The cancer had metastasized. The doctors said they could offer another type of chemotherapy, but when we asked more specifically about it, they said it was highly experimental, there were as yet few dependable statistics on its effectiveness, and it had rather severe side effects. Samuel was still with us at the time, and the doctor left the three of us to discuss what to do. Margaret soon made it clear that she preferred not to undergo such radical treatment with so little prospect of improvement. Tearfully, Samuel and I agreed with her.

In July, Margaret and I flew up to Boston. Bill met us and showed us the lab where he worked on the artificial intelligence project. Then he drove us to their home in New Hampton, New Hampshire, an old house, which he had only recently bought and which was in process of extensive renovations. Margaret and I had a room to ourselves downstairs, and she could withdraw there alone when she needed rest, but she enjoyed playing with Ken and Ron, and she was very interested in the house and all the plans and possibilities for its repair and decorating.

During our stay in New Hampshire, the Democrats held their national convention in San Francisco, and Margaret avidly followed it on TV. She was much impressed by Cuomo's and Jackson's speeches, and she especially rejoiced at the nomination of Geraldine Ferraro for vice president. The weather was fine, and she played outdoors with the boys as much as possible, encouraging them to climb trees and do other things they had not hitherto been able to try out. We were there about two weeks, and Samuel came briefly, so it was a happy time for all, though we knew it was the last time Margaret would ever visit the younger Taylors and it was probably the last time for them to see her.

Knowing that her remaining days were very limited, but uncertain as to how long she would live, Margaret signed a "living will." She stated her desire not to have heroic measures applied in order to prolong her life, for to her, that would only mean prolonging the process of dying and making it more difficult both for her and for her loved ones. She sent copies of the "living will" to our lawyer, Drs. Woodcock and Shaw, and our pastor, Glenn Dorris.

Margaret and I both hoped she would live to see our fortieth wedding anniversary on September 5. I asked whether she wanted me to invite a few friends on the occasion of the anniversary, but she was not sure she would be physically able to attend a party. While she was thinking this over, we had a call from Jean Morrison, wife of Seminary Professor Clinton Morrison, who offered to have a party for the celebration at their home. Margaret and I made up a list of about ten couples to invite. We wished it had been possible to have a big celebration with a long guest list, but that was not practicable. As it was, it took special effort for Margaret to go, but she found it a very gratifying experience. Jean gave a lovely party. Our friends present represented a total of several hundreds of years of married life, and Glenn Dorris offered a beautiful and appropriate prayer.

A little later in September, we had a visit from Professor Nakazono Yasuo, a colleague of Margaret's in the Social Welfare Department of Shikoku Christian College. He came all the way from Japan as the official representative of the entire college community to bring gifts and greetings—farewells also implied. When we left Japan, we had full expectations of returning, and our Japanese friends could not rest content never to see Margaret alive again, so Professor Nakazono did the honors for all of them. This gesture of love and concern impressed the seminary community and was written up in the Louisville *Courier-Journal*, as well as in several of the church papers and magazines.

Professor Nakazono spent two nights in Louisville, one each at the home of the seminary president and the dean. He was honored at a reception at the seminary, where he expressed great appreciation for the assistance of the Presbyterian Church to the development of Shikoku Christian College and told something about the school's distinctive contribution to Christian witness and service in Japan.

In preparation for Professor Nakazono's coming, Margaret rested and stored up strength as much as possible beforehand. She was her usual cordial, charming self and made a great impression on the newspaper reporter and our visitor. However, it was a heavy drain on her both physically and spiritually. She was deeply honored by what the college was doing in recognition of her, but she also knew that there was an inescapable finality implied by it. About that time, we had a call from Professor Doi, another SCC colleague, who had recently arrived in Nashville to study for a year at Vanderbilt. He wanted to bring his family to visit us, but Margaret was not able to face up to it.

She did have one last objective to accomplish before she died: to vote in the presidential election. As soon as possible, she applied for an absentee ballot. In due time, it arrived, and she insisted on filling it out and having me mail it immediately, as she did not wish to take any chance that death might prevent her from voting for Mondale/Ferraro and registering her disapproval of the Reagan administration.

We had gotten in touch with the local hospice organization which sent a nurse, Libby Call, to take charge of Margaret's care whenever needed. Another visit from Bill Hopper all the way from California was much appreciated. Margaret now spent most of the time in bed and began to have increasing difficulties in breathing. Libby consulted with the doctors, and Margaret went to the hospital to have some fluid removed from her left lung. She declined to have a lengthy procedure done which might have prevented further accumulation in the good lung but opted instead for a short procedure which drew off about a liter from the left side.

In order to facilitate breathing, we had an oxygen machine put in the room at home, and Margaret used this from time to time. She had a lot of phlegm in her bronchial tubes and often had coughing spells, but she could not get rid of much sputum. Within two weeks, the breathing situation worsened, and Libby Call could tell that fluid had collected in both lungs. Margaret was on oxygen, and she went to the hospital by ambulance. Dr. Nightingale removed a liter of fluid from each lung and inserted a tube in the left side to allow for continual draining.

Margaret had finally agreed to have the longer procedure done. That involved putting a caustic drug into the space between the lung and the lining of the chest. This would cause irritation and scarring of the tissue on both surfaces, which would then grow together, thus making it impossible for fluid to accumulate any more. Margaret went under general anesthetic for this operation but still suffered extreme pain, much more than the doctors had anticipated. The doctors took this as a good sign: the drug must have spread over a large area, and therefore there would be very little space left for fluid to collect. Dr. Woodcock prescribed some medication which he expected would counteract the mental depression he thought he saw in Margaret, and this, together with stoppage of the collection of fluid, should enable her to have a fairly good quality of life for some months. On this optimistic note, we left the hospital and went home again.

Margaret had hesitated to take the mind-elevating drug, for she had always opposed chemical alteration of mental states. She also knew that the drug she was taking could have serious side effects. So after a few days, she stopped taking it. It soon became obvious that the lung drainage operation had not resulted in the expected physical improvement. The degree of pain increased, requiring stronger medication; and before many days, fluid again accumulated in the chest cavity.

Margaret desired at this time to stay at home under the care of Libby Call of hospice until the end came. However, as more and more fluid accumulated in the lungs, she had increasing difficulty breathing, and frequent coughing spells racked her whole body. In consultation with Libby, who also talked to the doctors, Margaret finally concluded that she would have to go back to the hospital where she could get sufficient relief from pain and from the panic of inability to breathe so as to be able to end her life peacefully.

In her mind, Margaret was prepared to die, but her vital signs continued fairly strong. Despite the fact that EKG tests showed that she had suffered a slight heart attack some time between January and June 1984, her pulse was steady. Though she ate practically nothing, she did not look emaciated, for her body retained a good deal of fluid. It would have been entirely possible to feed her through a nose tube, put another tube in her chest to keep the fluid draining, and hook her up to a respirator to regulate her breathing. In this way, she might have been sustained for an indefinite period of time.

Such a procedure, however, was not at all what she desired. For some time, even before she became ill, she had made a study of the medical and ethical problems associated with the beginning and end of life. In her classes at Shikoku Christian College, she and her students had read and discussed euthanasia and related questions. As mentioned earlier, she had signed a "living will," which the doctors had assured her they would respect. Therefore, it was with full certainty that she would not leave the hospital alive and that she entered it for the last time.

Soon after being admitted to the hospital, she had me go to the Lions Eye Bank nearby and give formal notice that she wished to donate her eyes. The doctors and nurses attending her were informed of this.

The pain had increased to the level that she could no longer retain medication administered by mouth—her system rejected it. She received stronger sedation intravenously, and little by little, she ceased to speak or even respond when spoken to, though the nurses said she could still hear and understand. So they and I continued to speak to her. I read the Bible and prayed aloud, and from time to time, I sang hymns.

Near midnight on November 25, I woke up when the nurses came in to check on her and renew the medication. I dozed off again during their ministrations, but one of them woke me to say that Margaret was noticeably weaker and that she probably would not survive much longer. I got up and sat by her bed. Besides talking to her to express my love and devotion to her, I read the Bible, prayed, and sang,

> Sun of my soul, thou Savior dear,
> It is not night if thou be near;
> Oh! May no earth-born cloud arise
> To hide thee from thy servant's eyes.
>
> Be near to bless us when we wake,
> Ere through the world our way we take,
> Till in the ocean of thy love,
> We lose ourselves in heaven above.

Shortly after midnight, early on November 26, the end came. She seemed to gag, her breathing stopped, her head dropped a bit to the right, and some spittle dripped from her open mouth. I closed her eyes, wiped the dribble from inside and around her mouth, and washed her sweaty face, which seemed to turn yellowish when she died. I combed her hair and tried to tie a handkerchief in such a way as to keep her jaw from sagging open, but without success. At that point, the nurses came in, and we lowered the bed so her mouth didn't hang open.

The resident was called to confirm Margaret's death, and within half an hour, the eye specialist came to take her eyes. I asked whether they were in good enough condition to use for cornea transplants. He said that the lab would have to test to make certain, but that they seemed all right to him. They had two patients waiting for transplants. He had already received another donation a few hours earlier, so it was altogether likely that at seven o'clock that very morning, two people would receive the gift of a new opportunity to see again. I only hope that the person who received Margaret's eyes is able to see what she saw.

With her usual foresight, Margaret had long since had me make all the arrangements with Pearson's Funeral Home to see to having her body cremated and the usual obituaries sent to the newspapers. Margaret also said she wanted to be buried with me, and I had promised to see to that. I had corresponded with various family members and found out that there was space in the Taylor cemetery plot in Winston-Salem. We had gotten permission for both of us to be buried in the same space, right next to my father's grave, using one stone for both of us. All this we had accomplished before she died, so she had no anxiety with regard to any of these details.

So the morning she died, Pearson's came to take Margaret's body to their funeral parlor, and I went to identify it as next of kin. I expressed a desire to go to the crematorium and stay the entire time and received permission, even though that is not customary in the U.S. I remembered having been present when our missionary colleague Merle Kelly's body was cremated in Japan, and I thought it much more civilized and respectful than just turning the "remains" over to the funeral home and later on receiving in return a box of "cremains" (what they call the ashes).

The crematorium consisted of a big furnace set at the rear of a concrete block building like a garage. The operator brought me a folding chair to sit on, for it took several hours for the body to be completely consumed. The operator of the crematorium was very kind and understanding. It was after six in the evening by the time the cremation was finished. I suppose that ordinarily he would have just waited till next morning and then delivered the ashes to the funeral parlor, but for my sake, he stayed on. When it was over, I selected some of the fragments of bone and divided them into two portions, one to be buried in Winston-Salem and one to take with me to Japan. Margaret had requested this, and our Japanese colleagues and friends seemed very pleased at this decision. A memorial service was held at the seminary in Louisville and another one later in Winston-Salem where she was buried.

16. Afterward

When Margaret and I bought the house in Louisville, Patti Thomas assured us that we had gotten an excellent bargain because the owners were so eager to sell and their agent had not helped them as he should. She said if we wished, she could help us sell it later at a much better price. Our renters had moved out to a home of their own, and it became clear that Margaret and I would never occupy the house together. We told Patti to put it on the market. I gave the title of the house to the Louisville Presbyterian Seminary with the proviso that the money realized from the sale would be a challenge gift to start a fund to endow a faculty chair of missions at the seminary.

Before I returned to Japan, I bought another smaller house, which Patti Thomas rented out to a young couple during my absence. I arrived in Japan in 1985 in time to begin the spring semester at Shikoku Christian College as a "guest professor" paid by the school. Though the Mission Board paid my travel and covered my medical expenses, I was no longer officially a missionary of the Presbyterian Church (USA). With me, I carried back to Japan a portion of Margaret's ashes, which were placed in the cemetery plot owned by the Church of Christ (Kyodan) in the town of Kotohira. Over the years, from time to time, Margaret and I had attended that small church. If their young pastor was not yet ordained, I would go monthly to preach and conduct communion and, from time to time, baptize new members. Whenever we went, the congregation was pleased to have Margaret accompany the hymns on the pump organ. She was a skilled and sensitive accompanist who greatly helped congregational singing. The church's plot stands near an entry to the large city cemetery in Kotohira, where the vast majority of graves display Buddhist symbols. On the church's plot, a large stone bears the words from Philippians 3:20, "Our citizenship is in heaven." A slab of granite in front of the stone covers a hole in the ground, giving access to shelves below where small packets of remains of other believers and their families are kept. Margaret's ashes are there, and her name is inscribed with the others on the base of the stone above.

Many Japanese people have what seems to us Westerners a morbid fixation on death and the necessity of commemorating the dead and performing ceremonies of various kinds to assure their peace in the afterlife. I have been told that the practice originated during the years of Catholic practice following Xavier's ministry. The Japanese Protestant Christians I knew have no such compulsion of obligation toward the dead, but they do have healthy customs of formal remembrance and appreciation of their departed loved ones. Besides our attendance at the Kotohira church, Margaret and I most often attended the Kyodan church in the college town of Zentsuji, which did not have a cemetery plot. On the Sunday nearest the first anniversary of Margaret's death, the pastor of the Zentsuji church conducted a special memorial service after the regular morning worship, and we all adjourned to the fellowship hall to enjoy a light meal together. As we sat around the table, one after another shared with us their memories of Margaret and what she had meant to them. Having come back alone to Japan and living in the house she had planned and built, I experienced some deep loneliness from time to time. But this communion of saints, including also the spiritual presence of Margaret herself, brought great solace to me. As I listened to their testimony concerning Margaret's influence on their lives, I had a renewed sense of what she means to me.

I grew up in the 100 percent segregated white supremacist South. My family and the surrounding culture were strongly patriarchal. The Southern Presbyterian Church into which I was baptized and brought up reinforced this culture using biblical arguments opposing racial and gender equality. My mother was always in the shadow of my father, and I never saw her express anger against my father, despite the fact that he often belittled her and sometimes let his quick temper carry him away.

Margaret helped me to a different way of understanding the Christian faith I professed and evaluating the culture, which too easily seduced the leaders and the members of the church. In the course of history, the Christian church in the U.S. came to support the elimination of polygamy and slavery from our culture, even though the Bible itself never demanded their abolition. In the twenty-first century U.S., many women, of whom Margaret was closest to me, demonstrated the ability and dignity of women, which called into question the continued recourse to biblical texts to maintain their subordination. To remain true both to these brave women and to the fundamental principles of justice and liberation that worked their transforming way through the Bible, the rest of us finally had to take a stand for the right and the truth.

Margaret's patience with me and the grace God gave me to respond positively to her criticisms preserved our marriage, even as we saw the marriages of some of our contemporaries founder and break over their inability to adjust to the rising expectations of women and a more enlightened understanding of the Bible.

My quest for the biblical teaching on women led me farther and farther into the paths of activism for peace and justice. What Margaret felt and responded to instinctively, I achieved by serious biblical study and observation of the world about me, encouraged also by her. Out of my own deeply held convictions, I have committed myself to work for the equality of women and men, for women's reproductive rights, to overcome racial prejudice and discrimination, for equal rights for persons of all sexual orientations, for the abolition of death penalty, and not only for the reduction of armaments, but for the abolition of war. As I have involved myself in these causes during the years since Margaret died, I do so with the very real sense that I am carrying on the quest of her goals for humanity under God and that she continues to be not only an example and a teacher but also an inspiration and a presence.

All Saints Eve, October 31, 2000/revised June 10, 2013

An American Woman Who Loved Japan

In Memoriam, Professor M. H. Taylor

Okamoto Mitsuo

Margaret H. Taylor, professor in the Social Work Dept. of Shikoku Christian University, is dead. The cause of death was lung cancer. She was sixty-three years old, hardly the age to die. In the summer of 1982 in good health she returned to the United States with her husband A. B. Taylor, former president of the University. Home assignment was to have been for only a year, yet she never set foot on the soil of Sanuki[15] again. How regrettable that she could not return to Japan where she had lived over thirty years, since 1950.

Having traveled through Europe on the way home, Margaret, feeling herself in her usual good health, had a routine physical examination which showed some abnormality in the right lung, and following the physician's advice, she had a more precise test. In January 1983 it was diagnosed as lung cancer. In response to the doctor's proposal to remove the cancer by surgery she underwent an operation. However, it was

---

[15] The ancient name of Kagawa Prefecture, still used as a familiar term.

already too late for surgery to be effective. Recovering from the operation, she underwent treatment by chemotherapy.

The Patient's Right to Know

All during her treatment Margaret knew that she had lung cancer. Because patients in Europe and America possess the "right to know," doctors are obligated to inform them of their true condition. Also, the attitude toward cancer over there is quite different from that in Japan, I believe. They don't make a taboo of cancer as we do in Japan. Prof. H. E. Teht, who came in October from Heidelberg University to lecture at Shikoku Christian University, knew that he was a cancer patient. In Europe and America, even if cancer cannot be cured, it can often be controlled. The period of remission may be a year, five years, even ten years.

The first time I made a visit to Margaret was in March 1983. Suppressing a painful feeling of tragedy in my heart, I landed at the airport in Louisville, Kentucky. However, as her husband Arch, who had come to meet me, talked with me in the car, I began to realize that my exaggerated emotions were the product of the special Japanese sensitivity concerning cancer. Arch was quite matter-of—fact and betrayed no special sense of tragedy. "Margaret is preparing supper, so I came alone to meet you."

What? A cancer patient cooking supper?! I could hardly believe my ears, yet it was so. Margaret entertained me, the guest from afar, with her own home cooked dinner. We talked about family and friends. It was a bright, happy atmosphere, altogether like that in the Taylors' home in Tadotsu. "I'm getting tired. Please excuse me, but I have to go to bed early." So saying she went off to her bedroom, but until that moment I had completely forgotten that I was in the home of a sick person.

A Deep Social Concern

I believe it was in 1968-9 that Margaret and her husband were studying at Harvard University. They attended class taught by Edwin O. Reischauer, former American Ambassador to Japan. This was an important experience for her. Her depth and breadth of understanding of Japan were much influenced by Dr. Reischauer, one of the rare persons who thoroughly know and admire Japan.

After she returned to Japan from Harvard, she entered even more enthusiastically than before into the struggle to achieve social justice. She believed that both Japan and the U.S. were shamefully backward in social services and thus failed to achieve peace in the true sense of the term. She engaged in a fierce battle against the customary discrimination against women. Even the Presbyterian Church US was not spared her criticisms on this point, and she often wrote letters to the President of the United States.

In tracing her career, one must understand that its motivation was the ethical requirements of Christian faith characterized by abstinence from tobacco and alcohol, sexual morality, conjugal love, child rearing, and family values. But it also extended to broader concerns like welfare, social justice, and political and economic issues. It was reported that this fall she declared, "I refuse to die before the elections on November 6." Her opposition to Reagan administration policies was unmistakable.

Thus, she was critical of U.S. policy toward Latin America. She could not countenance the U.S. invasion of Grenada and intervention in the domestic affairs of Nicaragua, El Salvador, and Honduras. "The U.S. is always supporting oppressive regimes, and that is a mistake," she often said to me while she still lived. She was a person who, for an American, showed an unusual social concern.

Recognition of Japanese People's Strong Points

Early on, Margaret discerned the strong points of the Japanese. I believe it was because she loved Japan that she could see the goodness of Japan. This was long before Japan had become an economic superpower and foreigners' evaluation of Japan had undergone a radical change.

For example, she gave high marks to the Japanese policy of birth control. This is a minority view among Americans. In the recent election it was a controversial issue, and Geraldine Ferraro, the vice presidential candidate who advocated birth control, ended as the representative of the minority. Margaret understood that because of birth control, "every Japanese child is a desired child." Children are a treasure in Japan, and therefore "total strangers on buses and trains will give up their seats to children," she observed in an article, "What Other Countries Can Learn from Japan."

In short, she was a person who paid close attention to others' virtues and good characteristics. For her, this way of discovering other people was the starting point of social intercourse and education. Her three sons all attended Zentsuji Central Elementary School, and she brought up her children with distinction. The third son Samuel most recently published a critically acclaimed book about Japanese studies with a large publishing house (professional name, Jared Taylor, *Shadows of the Rising Sun*, translated by Mitsunobu Yamamoto, Kobun Sha publisher). Her appreciation for Japan is thus passed on to the next generation.

The Consummation of her Warm Affection

The last time I visited her was in December 1983. My wife is doing graduate study in Michigan while caring for our three children. All of our family together drove the more than 700 km to Louisville, as we sadly realized it might be the last time we could see Margaret. Yet she appeared to be in good health. We all went to a steak house downtown for dinner, and I remember that she ate a steak with gusto. It was after the completion of the radiation treatments that had followed the chemotherapy, and the spread of the cancer had been halted. "If her condition continues like this, we may see her back in Japan next spring or fall," I wrote to my colleagues.

I realize more and more that we can never fully understand our human fate. Never imagining that it would come to this, I can never again see that Margaret who said goodbye to us, saying, "Come back again!" We have lost this American woman who loved Zentsuji, who loved Sanuki, who loved the Inland Sea, who loved Japan, to which she had dedicated her life. According to her last wishes, half of her ashes are to be brought back to Kagawa-ken. Surely, her warm affection for Japan achieves its consummation by this act.

A memorial service for her is to be held at Shikoku Gakuin University on December 9, at 3 p.m.

Okamoto Mitsuo, Professor, Shikoku Gakuin University. English translation from the *Shikoku Shimbun*, Japanese newspaper, 12.7.84

PART FIVE

Retirement and Second Marriage

9

I Retire from Japan

While I was back in Japan after Margaret's death, President Reagan was supporting the contra war against the Sandinistas in Nicaragua. I developed a strong antipathy to that war, which I shared with my colleague Okamoto Mitsuo. He was pleased to learn from me the policy statements of the Presbyterian Church (USA) General Assembly office that clearly did not conform to a general support for the war. Much popular Christianity in America tolerated Reagan's policy on the grounds of opposing anti-God communism. In the back of my mind, I had a desire to go to Central America personally to observe the conflict if possible. My employment status was rather vague—Shikoku Christian College paid me though neither at the same rate nor with the same responsibilities as Japanese faculty members. The Mission Board of the now-reunited Presbyterian Church (USA) paid my travel to and from Japan and covered my medical expenses, yet I was not a "mission coworker" according to official terminology in those days. I was nearly sixty-seven years old, so I decided it was about time to retire. I planned to finish at SCC at the end of September 1986.

1.   Unanticipated Economic Advantages

Due to circumstances I did not fully understand, my economic situation had changed considerably in my favor. For years, like all other expatriate Americans in Japan, I had had to pay income tax both to Japan and to the U.S. As living expenses in Japan grew along with the economy there, this requirement fell heavily on the Americans. The salaries of employees of U.S. companies were taxed at what they considered an exorbitant rate, which made people reluctant to take a post in Japan. Therefore, Japanese law was changed to increase the minimum amount of the Americans' income subject to tax. As a result, the income I received was not high enough to be taxed at all. The financial officer on the staff at SCC kept me informed on all the various details and enabled me to take advantage of every legal possibility. When I finally ended my relationship with the college, they paid me a bonus, something I had never anticipated. It was by no means what a Japanese faculty member would have received after a career like mine devoted to SCC, but for me, it was a generous plus, which escaped tax and which I invested in the Presbyterian Foundation in the U.S. I receive income from it, but at my death, the remainder will be returned to Shikoku Christian College.

Meantime, I had found a purchaser for the house Margaret had planned and where we lived so happily, though for such a short time. The lady who operated one of the best restaurants in Zentsuji said her daughter was finishing college and would be coming back to help run the restaurant. She would be married soon, and her mother wanted to secure the house for her. I congratulated her mother and said I hoped the daughter and her new husband would be very happy. "We haven't picked out the husband yet," she replied. "We just want to make certain about the house."

A little later, the mother got back in touch. She said she wanted to complete the purchase since during the few months before I left Japan, some emergency might arise. I might have to go back to the U.S. for some unforeseen reason. She said she would feel more at ease if she paid the price and got the legal deed, though I could still stay on rent-free till I left. That suited me fine, and we agreed on a date to close the deal. We would meet at a place that was near the college campus and the center of town. On the appointed day, we met. A lawyer accompanied the purchaser, who also brought along a big stack of cash. The largest denomination of Japanese currency was a ten thousand yen note, so it required quite a pile of them. Fortunately, the bank where I had my account was not far away, so we were able to carry the money there and get it properly deposited while the purchaser got the deed.

2.   A Long Way Home

My youngest son, Samuel, was unmarried and was a freelance writer in New York City, so he was able to come help me pack up my things. He said his most enjoyable experience was a reunion with some of his elementary school classmates. They could yak yak yak freely in the local dialect and enjoy eating local delicacies while reminiscing old times. After the movers had taken my freight, Samuel and I set out on the western route back home, beginning with China. Our first stop was Hong Kong, where we encountered the first of the many problems facing foreigners trying to get into China proper. Avoiding guided tours, we did what we could, not what we especially wanted. At that time, foreigners had to use a special currency some folks called funny money for all purchases, and we were supposed to stay only in designated hotels at a higher price.

2a.   China

We managed to get railroad tickets as far as Zhengzhou on the Yangtze River, north about halfway to Beijing, where we had wanted to go. Westward, we went to Luoyang, which was famous for hundreds of Buddhist sculptures carved into the face of a high rock cliff. During the Cultural Revolution, Chairman Mao Tse Dong had incited hordes of young people—called the Red Guards—to try to eradicate traces of Buddhist religion, including the most prominent of those religious works. To us, it was still an impressive sight.

Farther west, we went to Xi'an, site of the tomb of China's first emperor, Qin Shi Hwang Ti, who was principally responsible for building the Great Wall. His tomb in Xi'an contained the buried army of hundreds of life-sized terracotta soldiers, horses, chariots, and other accoutrements to serve him in the next life. I couldn't help wondering about the daily life of the multitudes of peasants the emperor had pressed into forced labor to build his tomb as well as the wall. It was a conspicuous example of the gap between the rich and powerful few and the poverty stricken exploited masses, something like building the pyramids of Egypt, I thought.

Our trip was made less problematic because I remembered some of the Chinese language I had studied at Yale in preparation to go to China, slightly strengthened by recent review. Samuel also was able to help. In

Japanese school, he had become familiar with Chinese characters, which form the basis of written Japanese. We bought a local map of Xi'an's public transportation routes, and we could plot our way by means of the names of places. We could identify a place by the characters of its name (true pictographs), even though we couldn't actually pronounce it correctly. We were able to change some of our dollars for the standard Chinese money, but we had to do it unofficially on the street.

From the railroad station in Xi'an, we started out on foot, and we noticed a sign over a door with characters that we recognized. In Japanese, it was pronounced *ryokan*, but I recalled *lyugwan* in Chinese— it was an inn. We stepped inside, and I engaged in sort of a conversation with the clerk, asking whether we could get a room. He responded no. I asked whether he was full up, and he said no. Then I asked if it was because we were foreigners. He seemed to hesitate, and I persisted, so at last, he relented, accepted our payment, and showed us to a room. We had beds consisting of mats a couple of inches thick laid on a platform of thin boards that sagged a bit under our weight. We shared the washroom and toilet with other patrons. Samuel and I had already purchased our own towels, wash pans, and drinking cups, which were standard necessities for Chinese travelers.

I knew that the town of Zentsuji, where SCC was located, was said to be the birthplace of a Buddhist monk named Kō Bō Dai Shi, who had spent years at a famous Buddhist temple outside Xi'an before returning to Japan to establish another sect of Buddhism. We rented bicycles and toured the countryside on the way to that temple. It was harvest time for the Chinese variety of maize, and we saw great loads of it. We stopped to observe a brick-making operation. From a hopper containing the proper mix of clay and water, a man extruded an amount of material into a form the proper size and shape for a brick, which was then cut off and set out to dry sufficiently in the sun to be fired in a kiln later. Through many centuries, all the buildings in and around Xi'an and the vast city wall itself were made of brick, and the forests for miles around had been cut down to provide fuel for brick making. When we arrived at the temple, we saw busts of the chief abbots for generations past, but we were not able to get any enlightenment about Kō Bō Dai Shi's stay.

Farther west from Xi'an, we learned of a distant mountain valley that was a site of another series of Buddhist shrines that the young Red Guards of the Cultural Revolution had not discovered. It was well worth our effort to reach it, for it was very colorful and well preserved, although it was of smaller scale than Luoyang. We found our way there by public transportation, but we had no prior plans to return to our base. We were fortunate to see a bus with Elder Hostel markings on it, so we caught a ride back with that group.

From Chongqing, the wartime capital of Nationalist China, we rode a ship down the Yangtze River to Shanghai. On the vertical cliffs to our left, we could see where the narrow footpath had been carved for the gangs of men who used to pull the Chinese junks upstream, whence they could go back downstream with the river current. Most river traffic is now motorized, and we saw only one small junk being pulled by humans. Since our visit, China has dammed the river, and the gorges of the Yangtze have been flooded to produce electricity, so the towpaths are now under water. I understand thousands of people were deprived of their land and relocated elsewhere because of the lake that formed behind the dam.

Motor ships have long since made the onerous towing obsolete, but we could still see ample evidence of exploitation of mere manpower, a work done by people whom foreigners had learned to call coolies many years ago. We observed several men wielding sledgehammers, demolishing a rather large brick building. We saw men pulling heavily loaded two-wheeled carts. On the banks of the river at Chongqing, we saw men with wooden yokes over their shoulders and heavy loads hanging on either end of the yoke, trudging up and down the steep steps to load or unload boats in port. Two men might carry an especially heavy burden slung beneath a stout pole between them. On the way to the Buddhist carvings in the mountain, I caught a glimpse of one man in mud above his knees, guiding a water buffalo to plow a field. A phrase I had learned while studying Chinese occurred to me over and over: *chr ku*—eat bitterness.

During my years in Japan teaching the Bible, I became more and more deeply convinced from the creation story in the first chapter of Genesis: there is only one God, Creator of everything and everyone, who transcends all the gods of all the world religions. The God revealed in Genesis created humanity in the divine image, male and female together, and gave us dominion over the rest of creation as partners of God. After years of teaching the Bible from this starting point, I had become convinced that if it is true that God is one and humans are all images of God, this one must be God for all people, and all people must be, in a real sense, children of this one God and hence brothers and sisters to each other. My increasing understanding of evolution assisted my conviction of the basic oneness of humanity within the whole created world. I reflected on the comfort and security of my life in comparison with the multitudes of Chinese among whom I was now moving—why do so many of them eat bitterness while my life, by comparison, is so sweet? I had a deep impression of our common humanity, which has continued with me ever since and influences my understanding and interpretation of the Bible and human life.

Samuel and I made our way back to Shanghai on a riverboat we boarded at Chongqing, and thence, we went back to Hong Kong. We made a brief side trip to Macau, which was still under the colonial authority of Portugal, but we saw no lure in the gambling houses that give Macau worldwide fame and attract thousands of tourists every year. There was at least one architecturally famous Buddhist temple, which we saw, but of which I have only a vague recollection. At this point in my life, I regret that I did not keep a proper journal of our adventures.

2b. Pakistan

Our next stop was Pakistan, where my wife Margaret's brother Bill Hopper and his wife, Mollie, were representatives of the Presbyterian Church (USA) Mission Board. We landed first in Karachi in the far south, where we changed to fly on to Lahore. The local city was in an uproar from what we could learn from the English language newspapers. A day or so before, a small plane had been shot down and crashed, and everybody wondered why. It turned out that the pilot had happened to fly over an outdoor wedding party for seven couples. Guests on the ground were celebrating by firing their guns in the air, which apparently caused the crash. There was a semiofficial suspicion that some shooters may have deliberately aimed at the plane as it happened to pass over, and the seven bridegrooms had been arrested by the time of our visit. We were long gone before the final result of the inquiry became known.

As we went about Pakistan, we couldn't help noticing the large number of shops where firearms, mostly handguns, were displayed for public sale. We heard that people were permitted to make their own weapons. Apparently, there is as little effort to curb gun violence in Pakistan as there is in the U.S.

In my view, there was a striking difference between China and Pakistan. In the latter, there seemed to be hordes of children everywhere, each followed by a swarm of flies, and garbage was strewn everywhere. China had enforced the one-child-per-family policy, so there were fewer children in view, and they were much better cared for. The streets and sidewalks were kept much more neat and clean than those in Pakistan.

The Hoppers lived in Lahore, near the border, with India in east central Pakistan, which had been an administrative center of Presbyterian mission work for nearly a century before the division of Pakistan from India. As we understood it, most of the Christians in this part of Pakistan were descendants of Hindu untouchables, who had responded most positively to the Christian message early on. Still very poor, they had been unable to leave when the division occurred. They were a distinct poverty-stricken minority in the proudly Muslim state of Pakistan. The Presbyterians had built schools and hospitals over the years, and a good deal of property remained on the Pakistan side, though because of many economic and political factors, not all of it could be fully utilized. The government had taken over all the former mission schools, including Foreman Christian College in Lahore.

Bill said that squatters had occupied some vacant mission property. A group affiliated with the Bible Presbyterian Church, a fundamentalist splinter group led by Carl McIntyre, had taken possession of a building on the campus of the Gujranwala Theological Seminary. This information reminded me of another "brotherly" gesture of the McIntyre faction: when commissioners of the former Southern and Northern Presbyterians filed out from the hall after voting for reunion at the 1983 General Assembly meeting in Atlanta, members of the McIntyre group greeted us, holding signs accusing us of heresy and blasphemy.

The Mission Board had sent Bill Hopper to try to straighten out some of the property problems. In Pakistan, he also applied his earlier experience in Iran to give added support to the office preparing and publishing materials for literacy, education, and evangelism. Bill and Mollie took us on a visit to the Memorial Christian Hospital at Sialkot well known for developing an effective eye operation that restored sight to thousands of patients every year. This was in addition to its full service as a general hospital staffed principally by Pakistani doctors and nurses, with the aid of a few American coworkers.

We were to be in Pakistan over a week, and Bill asked if I would preach at the English worship on the coming Sunday evening in the

Foreman Christian College chapel. The service was for expatriates—missionaries and others—and some English-speaking Pakistanis. My brief experience and observation in this land had greatly reinforced in my mind the sense of privilege and blessing that had come to me totally beyond my deserving in comparison with the masses of poor and indigent Pakistanis. The conviction that one God must be God for all was strengthened, and I preached my very first formal sermon on God's plan of salvation that included all of the human family based on Genesis 1:27-28 and Romans 5:12-21 and 11:32.

In the years since then, Pakistan finally returned control of the educational institutions to the Presbyterian and other missions and the Christian Church of Pakistan. There had been a noticeable decline of standards during that period, but I understand quality has been gradually restored.

Incidentally, we encountered firsthand a serious personal problem. An American woman who had married a Pakistani had come to try to recover her son whom her husband had taken with him when he abandoned her and returned to Pakistan. She had joined the small American community in Lahore, and Bill and his Pakistani associates were doing their best to help her. This was only one of several similar examples. Her prospects of success were slim, we understood, given the superior status and authority of a Pakistani man in a contest with a woman, especially if she were a foreigner and at issue was a boy child.

Either in China or in Pakistan, I had picked up a "bug" of some sort that caused diarrhea. Even though Samuel had been much more daring about eating and drinking stuff available from carts on the public street, he never seemed to suffer any bad consequences. Mollie shared such medications as she had available, but nothing seemed effective. Only a few weeks later, back in the U.S., I learned that I had amoebic dysentery, not the common sort most of us are liable to catch once in a while here. Fortunately, I didn't suffer any lasting physical damage.

10

Activism Back at Home

In Louisville at the end of 1986, I settled in the house I had bought before I returned to Japan and which was now available since the young couple who had rented it had left. At this time throughout the U.S., thousands of solidarity groups were meeting regularly to monitor and oppose Reagan's contra war against Nicaragua. Most of those activists strongly believed that public demonstrations by millions of people all over the country the previous year had stymied what they thought was a serious desire by Reagan to invade Nicaragua as he had previously done on a smaller scale to Grenada.

I promptly joined a neighborhood group led by George and Jean Edwards. George was a professor of New Testament at the Louisville Presbyterian Theological Seminary, and he and his wife were the organizers and effective leaders of the Louisville chapter of the Fellowship of Reconciliation (FOR), the oldest international interfaith organization devoted to world peace and reconciliation. I had heard a lot about George, who had been a conscientious objector against Word War II and had done alternate service at an institution for the violent mentally ill before going to the seminary. This was my first opportunity to get to know him and Jean personally, and for me, it proved to be a most rewarding and enriching friendship. They lived in walking distance of my home on Strathmoor Boulevard, and we participated in many actions through the years.

I learned that an organization called Witness for Peace had been sending delegations to Nicaragua for several years—George Edwards had already participated in one of them—so I began to consider joining one myself. Father Jim Flynn, a local Catholic priest who had led such delegations, made a presentation at the Presbyterian Seminary early in 1987, and I was able to sign up for a delegation being planned for November that year.

1.   The Hiroshima Day Observance

Meanwhile, I also attended the monthly meetings of the FOR. I was not particularly active, but I did contribute the name for the monthly newsletter *FORsooth*, and I took an active part in the local committee to plan the annual Hiroshima Day Observance. This activity had already been going on for well over a decade and was still attracting a fairly good audience. Jean Edwards was its most effective leader. We sponsored an outstanding speaker, and we floated candlelit lanterns on a pond in a local park in memory of the dead as is done in Japan. There it's done in a flowing stream that will carry the lanterns down to the sea. Louisville's FOR organized the participation of a number of churches, plus the local congregation of the Soka Gakkai. That is the local group affiliated with a popular Buddhist organization in Japan that has many congregations in North America. Most of the Louisville members are Americans, but there are several Japanese, including a few who are *hibakusha*—survivors of the Hiroshima or Nagasaki bombs. They are naturally reluctant to speak out, but the local FOR and other sympathetic folks are able to inspire their confidence so that they can bear their personal testimony.

One year, we sponsored a display of photographs taken by Joe O'Donnell, who as a young photographer in the Marine Corps had actually visited both Hiroshima and Nagasaki not long after the bombs fell. The Nagasaki bombing had failed to target the principal military installations in the city because incoming clouds threatened to obscure everything, so the crew just dumped the bomb more or less at random. The part of the city that suffered the most damage was the district where the Catholic cathedral was located and was home to the largest concentration of Christians in all Japan.

For Joe O'Donnell, the experience of seeing and photographing the damage had affected him so deeply that after the war, he locked his negatives in a trunk in his attic and tried to forget the whole thing, but it continued to prey on his mind. He had been brought up Catholic, and he had been persuaded to attend a spiritual retreat. One of its features was a life-sized papier-mâché sculpture of Christ on the cross, with flames rising up on either side. It was the work of a Catholic sister. The paper she used to form Christ's body consisted of pictures and printed narratives describing the nuclear bombings. The retreat experience persuaded Joe that he should use his pictures to demonstrate the horrors of war, particularly of nuclear bombs. Evidently, the radiation he absorbed at ground zero in both cities had affected him. By the time he came to our observance event, he was seriously ill with cancer, and we weren't certain till the last moment that he would be able to come at all. To top it all, a member of our committee succeeded in locating the statue of Christ. It had been stored away, and insects had chewed up a lot of the flames, but the Christ figure on the cross was still whole.

Naturally, this was one of our most effective Hiroshima Observance events. In a discussion afterward, Joe told of an opportunity he had to meet President Truman personally. Somebody had introduced Joe to the president as the photographer who took pictures in both Hiroshima and Nagasaki. The president shook his hand and asked him to walk with him somewhat away from other members of the group. At this point, Truman expressed something about the massive destruction of the bombs. He stated that he had not taken the initiative to drop the bombs. "It was something FDR wanted done, so I did it," Joe reported that the president told him.

Of course we know that even though he had earlier been a senator and then vice president, Truman knew nothing about the bomb until he became president after Roosevelt died. In public statements, Truman never expressed any regret or hesitancy about ordering the dropping of the bomb; and as far as I know, only this personal testimony of Joe O'Donnell exists to suggest any other emotion on Truman's part.

Little by little, understanding of the bombs' horrible effects grew among the U.S. public, especially after the New Yorker magazine devoted an entire issue to John Hersey's essay "Hiroshima." A government insider's "official" report was widely circulated to put a different spin on the event. It claimed falsely that without the bombs, the allies would have had to invade the Japanese main islands, resulting in loss of life on both sides totaling several millions. In fact, the Army Air Force had bombed practically all the cities in Japan. Hiroshima and Nagasaki were among the last three or four targets available. Military authorities such as MacArthur and Eisenhower knew that within reason, Japan could not survive more than a month at most, and people in the administration's

highest ranks knew that Japan had already put out feelers toward
surrender.

Among Joe O'Donnell's photographs were several he had taken along
the coast, showing telephone poles simulating cannons protruding from
bunkers. Photographs taken from space had been sufficiently realistic
to persuade some allies that Japan really was prepared for a last-ditch
resistance. The bombs were actually unnecessary evils, yet the U.S. public
was glad to believe the propaganda that this terrible evil was really a
wonderful good. That has become the general opinion ever since, even
though enough evidence has come to light to cause many people to doubt
it (see below in this book for more information on this point).

2.   Opposing Reagan's Contra War

2a.   With Witness for Peace in Nicaragua, 1987

The last two weeks of November 1987, I was one of about twenty
people from Kentucky who went to Nicaragua under the sponsorship of
Witness for Peace (WFP). Gail Phares was the remarkable woman chiefly
responsible for founding this organization. Gail had begun her career as
a Catholic nun serving in Guatemala, but she had to flee the country.
U.S.-supported terrorist regimes of several right-wing military dictators
had replaced the democratically elected government of Jacobo Arbenz
Guzmann. In President Dwight Eisenhower's all-out anticommunist
campaign, the CIA had planned and supported this coup, which
subjected Guatemala to decades of conflict that bore hardest on the
poor and the indigenous people that actually comprised the population
majority.

Yet another factor not widely known, the American-owned United
Fruit Company profited handsomely from this change of regime.
Besides the Dulles brothers, Secretary of State John Foster and CIA
Director Allen, both of whom had once been legal counsel to United
Fruit, Eisenhower's personal secretary was married to a high official of
the company, and several others with close ties to United Fruit occupied
various posts in the Eisenhower administration. The United Fruit
Company was the monopoly exploiter of banana plantations. They
dispossessed or used for cheap labor the majority indigenous Indian
population all over Guatemala. President Arbenz had made moves to

abolish the feudalistic system that impoverished the peasants. He began to enforce laws on the books regarding property valuation and tax obligations that United Fruit had heretofore ignored with impunity. He expropriated vast unused acreage of farmland from United Fruit, paying the very low price at which United Fruit had evaluated the land so as to avoid paying taxes. The CIA brought false charges that Arbenz was a puppet of communism to justify support for a military coup by right-wing extremists that began a reign of terror that persisted for over a decade. Gail Phares was among those who had been forced to return to the U.S. She subsequently left her order to marry, but she maintained an undying passion for justice for the people of Central America who were victims of exploitative governments, especially those aided by the U.S.

In the meantime, Nicaragua became the focus of popular resistance to the U.S.-backed dictatorship of Anastasio Somoza, the third-generation leader of a family that had ruled Nicaragua for over thirty years. The main resistance called themselves Sandinistas, honoring hero Augusto Sandino, who for three years had led guerrillas to resist the decade-long U.S. Marine occupying force. The marines organized and armed the National Guard, and the first Anastasio Somoza gained control of this force and had Sandino assassinated in 1934. From 1927 to 1979, the Somoza family dominated Nicaragua and enriched itself and its partisans at the expense of the general population. Once, somebody complained to President Franklin Roosevelt about the constant violations of human rights committed by Somoza, to which Roosevelt is said to have responded, "Well, yes, Somoza is a son of a bitch, but he's *our* son of a bitch."

The younger Anastasio Somoza commanded the assassination of Pedro Chamorro, editor of a newspaper that criticized the dictatorship, and Chamorro's widow Violetta became a member of the Sandinista leadership group. In 1979, with massive popular support, the Sandinistas defeated the National Guard, and Somoza fled the country. Daniel Ortega was elected president in an election certified without corruption by international observers. The U.S. sent no observers, and President Reagan refused to recognize the election. He embraced the remnants of the National Guard that fled to Honduras and plotted to return. Reagan offered them support as a counterrevolutionary force that he praised as heroes like the American founding fathers resisting British rule. He gave them both covert and overt aid, including the CIA destroying the main storage depot of Nicaragua's petroleum supply. The world court called this and other acts international crimes and imposed a multimillion-dollar fine on the U.S., which Reagan totally ignored.

Gail Phares now lived in Raleigh, North Carolina. She recruited and led a group to Nicaragua during this contra war. One day, near the front lines, they could see on a hilltop on the opposite side of a valley a troop of men with heavy arms. The Nicaraguans with Gail's group informed her that those were contras but that they were withholding fire because they knew that people from the U.S. were watching. The incident inspired Gail to bring more such delegations since their accompanying presence might be a protection for the Nicaraguans, and their witness back home to what they had experienced might lead toward peace. Since that time, Witness for Peace (WFP) has grown to nationwide scope and far outgrown Gail Phares's early efforts. WFP still sends delegations not only to Central America but also to other trouble spots such as Colombia. The policy of sending people from *el norte*—the North—to accompany indigenous people in dangerous situations has been adopted by other organizations, such as Catholic Pax Christi, Christian Peacemaker Teams, and the Presbyterian Peace Fellowship cooperating with both the Presbyterian Church (USA) Global Mission Unit and the Presbyterian Church of Colombia in accompaniment there.

Father Jim Flynn of Louisville provided orientation guidance for those of us who were to go on the November 1987 delegation, but Gail Phares herself was our on-site leader. In Managua, we visited both the Catholic and the Protestant agencies devoted to aid for the poor and the needy, who make up the bulk of the population. We learned that before the contra war, the Sandinistas had gained high praise from the United Nations for their programs to bring better medical and literacy services to the people at large, but the contras had pretty well disrupted and reversed the gains. At that time, Nicaragua received aid from the USSR. The cold war at that time was characterized by deadly conflicts in many places throughout the world in which the two superpowers each caused as much trouble as possible to the other by arming opposing sides in those surrogate wars.

On our trip into the country, we had to detour around a bridge that the contras had recently blown up. The immediate reaction of us Americans was "Our tax dollars at work!" We ended up in the town of Nueva Guinea, which had suffered a contra attack some while before. The water tower still lay where they toppled it, and the school had not been rebuilt since they destroyed it. There were still anti-Sandinista elements in the area, and a small post of government troops was outside the town. There was hard feeling between the two sides, and the troops were not above some violent acts. During our stay, a man was found shot dead outside the village. Though by the time we left, no final explanation had been given, we got the impression that he probably was a victim of the troops in retaliation for his well-known antigovernment activity.

Delegation members in pairs stayed in the homes of villagers. My partner was Livingston Taylor, retired political columnist of the Louisville *Courier-Journal* newspaper. The house had one electric drop cord with a single bulb, the floor was dirt, and we slept in hammocks in the main room. The wife seemed a bit sullen, and with the children, she stayed out of sight. Only later we learned that when Witness for Peace representatives had come to organize the stay in Nueva Guinea, the husband had attended the meeting and agreed to take two guests, but his wife didn't know anything about it till the moment we arrived.

We met several religious groups. In Central America, many Protestants (locally called evangelicals) belong to deeply fundamentalist anti-Catholic traditions. At least they deserve credit for helping some people recover from sexual promiscuity and alcoholism, concerning which the generally Catholic culture was apparently indifferent. The evangelicals in Nueva Guinea were fruit of efforts of a splinter sect I had never heard of. They had a song, I was told, that celebrated "the Gospel came from North Carolina."

The Somoza regime had exploited the sectarian rivalry between evangelicals and Catholics to solidify their control of the common people who had so much misfortune in common that should have united them. The Catholic hierarchy in Nicaragua followed the decree of Rome, which excommunicated several priests who had important posts in the Sandinista government. Other priests defied authority and lived among the poor. At some time in our visit, I heard somebody raise the question "Why should people criticize the government for accepting aid from the Soviets? It's made it possible for our people to get educational and medical benefits we never had before."

There were Catholic lay organizations nearly everywhere that practiced the liberation theology that spread all over Catholic Latin America in those days. We attended their meeting on the Sunday we were in the village. My Spanish was certainly not up to colloquial give and take, but I understood most of the scripture lesson and the message that Sunday. What sticks most firmly in my memory was hearing a woman's fervent prayer, which included a specific petition that God would bless President Reagan and help him change his policies.

2b. With Habitat for Humanity in Nicaragua 1991

Later, while I was a missionary in residence at Presbyterian College in Clinton, South Carolina, I went to Nicaragua for a second time. The contra war had ended, and next to Haiti, Nicaragua was the poorest country in the Western Hemisphere. The George H. W. Bush administration had given economic aid and encouragement to a faction including Violetta Chamorro that split from the mainline Sandinistas led by President Daniel Ortega. The Bush administration supported Violetta in national elections, and she was elected president. Ortega did not challenge the vote, and Chamorro did not disband the Sandinista army or remove local Sandinista officials in many places throughout the country.

My second trip to Nicaragua took place during Presbyterian College's spring break in 1991. The professor of Spanish led, and I accompanied a group of students to assist Habitat for Humanity in building some thirty small residences up in the mountains. I'm not clear about the origins of this project, but I understood that it was a cooperative farming group that now occupied property that had once belonged to a very wealthy man (presumably a partisan of Somoza originally). By mutual assistance, they were trying to improve their general livelihood, and they were energetically investing "muscle capital" to supplement housing aid from Habitat.

Our group occupied a house that was just being completed when we arrived. We were five males—three men students plus the Spanish teacher and me—and five women students. In the two rooms assigned to us were bunk beds to sleep four in one room and six in the other. The women were given the privilege of deciding which man would have a bunk in their room, and they chose me. During the day, we scattered out to our assigned workplaces. I was teamed with Teresa, a wiry woman who saw me carrying a sack of concrete up the hill, snatched it from me, and rapidly ran on ahead. We mixed cement to put into forms to make open-work cement blocks to be placed in the house walls to provide ventilation.

The massive destruction and debt from the contra war had made the early Sandinista medical and educational help for the people impossible.

Our neighbors in the community told us that parents had to pay school tuition and buy books, which many of them could not afford. The same was true with health care. I was deeply saddened to observe the dire condition in which so many Nicaraguan people lived, which might not have been so bad if my own government had let the Nicaraguans go their own way.

Some years before Margaret died, she and I both opposed the Israeli wars that displaced the Palestinians and that our country had aided. I knew that that problem had very deep and ancient roots and that there were serious religious factors involved. I thought that, in comparison, the Nicaraguan issue was much less complicated. If only we could leave little Nicaragua alone, things might be better. Silly me! I began to see that these were only separate facets of *one big* problem, namely, the imperial ambitions of the United States.

11

Wanda Rowe Myers

In between my two trips to Nicaragua, I met and married Wanda Rowe Myers. She was a member of the Strathmoor Presbyterian Church, which had been a supporter of Margaret and me as missionaries. The church was in walking distance from my house on Strathmoor Boulevard, and I had begun to attend it regularly.

1. Wanda and I Marry

I first met Wanda at the home of another church member, Mary Lee Kelly. Mary Lee was the widow of a medical doctor. Her overweight, diabetic son, George, and his equally overweight wife, Billie, lived with her. George had lost a leg because of his diabetes, and being confined to a wheelchair, he couldn't easily leave the house. None of the Kellys could drive a car, and Wanda Myers took them to grocery shopping and to doctor visits whenever necessary. Mary Lee had been accustomed to have someone do a weekly Bible study at her home because her son, George, no longer attended church. The person who had taught the class was in process of leaving Strathmoor, and Mary Lee asked me to take over the responsibility, which I agreed to do. (Only later, I learned that the other teacher was joining some strange local charismatic group.)

At my first meeting at the Kellys' home, I met a small group of people including Wanda. She was proudly showing a photo of her newborn great-grandson, an interracial child of Wanda's granddaughter Marsha Baldridge and her African American boyfriend. For our first session, we had in hand the pamphlets the former teacher had used, and we took up where he left off. The lesson was 1 Corinthians 14, Paul's dealing with the problems related to speaking in tongues in the Corinthian congregation. We had a good discussion of the issue, question and answer, with me more or less guiding somewhat away from the fervent approach of charismatics to tongue speaking as I had come to know of them. However, it became clear I would need to have some different material to follow in our subsequent weekly sessions, which I obtained from the Presbyterian publishing house.

The weekly sessions began in September 1989 and continued till just before Christmas. We intended to begin again after New Year 1990. George Kelly became seriously ill and grew worse till he died on February 14, 1990. We did not resume the Bible classes. Wanda and I had become friendly. She told me that she strongly objected to the former Bible teacher and didn't want to continue, but out of loyalty to Mary Lee, she came the first time. If she didn't show up after that, she probably wouldn't be missed. She was favorably impressed with the way I led the class, so she continued on until the class ended.

Wanda had a close friend, Marilyn Landers, another widow. They were co-moderators of the women's organization at Strathmoor Presbyterian and did many things together. In the spring, the Louisville Presbyterian Theological Seminary and the Louisville Bar Association cosponsored a series of discussions dealing with various issues in which legal and religious aspects overlapped, such as death penalty, euthanasia, gun violence, and others. I invited Wanda and Marilyn to go with me to the lectures. After the first two, Marilyn dropped out, but Wanda and I continued.

All this time, I was still occupied with Nicaragua and Witness for Peace. At the time I had gone to Nicaragua, one of the permanent staff had suggested that I consider becoming a member of the WFP team. I seriously thought that I might be able to build some connections among the evangelicals and the Catholics in the countryside to ameliorate their sectarian rivalries and cooperate to address social and economic problems that weighed equally on both. I thought that if I attended a "total immersion" class to learn Spanish, I might get fluent enough in a relatively short time to do it. By then, my brother-in-law Bill Hopper and his wife, Mollie, were on the Global Mission staff at the Presbyterian Center in Louisville, and I asked Bill to find out what sort of language study possibilities the Mission staff knew about and to let me know. He informed me that there was a good program in Antigua, Guatemala, where I would live with a local family and study the language formally several hours each morning, but the rest of the time I would be immersed in the local language and culture. However, he said there were no openings available for a new student till the following year.

I needed to buy a rug for one of the rooms in my house, so I asked Wanda if she would give me advice and counsel in the process. Wanda took me to a furniture store where she knew one of the clerks personally, and we picked out a nice rug. With an occasional movie and meal out, we continued our friendship over the next months. During this time, I accepted an invitation from Presbyterian College in Clinton, South Carolina, to serve the next academic year as missionary in residence to teach one class of freshmen Bible, plus a missions course in the spring. I declined the offer of payment for that academic year since I felt my Social Security and Presbyterian pension checks were more than sufficient for my needs.

Wanda was very knowledgeable about Louisville, being a member of the Louisville Historical Society and the Filson Club, a repository of significant historical documents and sponsor of lectures on historical subjects. With her, I had attended several functions. On the Fourth of July, she and I planned to attend an afternoon affair at a historic home in the highlands. A day or two before July 4, Mollie Hopper called to invite me to lunch at their place on the fourth. I accepted gratefully and asked if it would be OK for me to bring a friend. She assented promptly. (Bill told me later that when Mollie informed him of my request, he said he'd bet it was a woman friend.)

Lunch at the Hoppers' was delightful. The food was delicious, and the four of us felt instantly drawn together. Bill and Wanda had a great time reminiscing about the old days in Louisville, especially the 1937 flood. We left midafternoon to go to the next event, and from there, we ate supper at a small neighborhood restaurant where we had dined before. We went to Wanda's house for the end of a perfect day. As I prepared to leave, we stood up, and I took Wanda in my arms and kissed her. When we parted, she exclaimed, "I haven't had that feeling in a long time!"

The next time I was with Wanda at her house, I asked her to marry me. She promptly replied, "I'm not about to marry a man who's wearing two wedding rings!" She had taken note that in addition to the wedding ring Margaret had given me, I was also wearing the one I had given Margaret, which fit my finger perfectly. The following Sunday, I was scheduled to preach at the 11:00 a.m. service at Strathmoor Presbyterian, and Wanda invited me to Sunday dinner at her house afterward. I carefully removed both rings. After a very delicious dinner at Wanda's, as she sat on the sofa, I knelt down beside her and asked her to marry me. This time, she consented.

To fulfill my agreement at Presbyterian College, I was to show up on campus there before the end of August. I tried to persuade Wanda to get married at once and to go with me to Clinton, South Carolina. She demurred. She thought things had moved a bit too fast already, and she said she needed more time to prepare. She planned to move to my house since I had been there all alone and it had no signs of my first wife. She was already thinking of passing her house on to her daughter, Ellen. Wanda had all sorts of stuff she had collected over the decades. Hers was a house her first husband, Jesse Burge Myers, had bought with a GI loan following the war, and she had lived there ever since. So I went off on schedule to Clinton, where I had a nice two-bedroom apartment supplied by the college. There Wanda joined me at the beginning of the second semester in 1991 after we married.

We had lots of planning to do for our wedding. It would be at Strathmoor Presbyterian Church, conducted by David Montgomery, our pastor. He was so pleased—it was his first wedding. He had been a student at the seminary when Margaret and I were there in 1982-1984. David had come as a solo pastor at Strathmoor from an associate pastorate at a larger church in Nashville, Tennessee. The first Sunday he preached, I had written him a letter of comment. He had replied by asking me to arrange to meet with him one-on-one every week, which I was glad to do. That could in part take the place of his former experience, where the larger church staff had always met each Monday to review Sunday and plan ahead. David conducted two premarital counseling sessions for Wanda and me before I left for South Carolina. From there, I had to carry on a lot of our planning by phone and correspondence, but I did visit Louisville twice and Wanda came to Clinton once during the first semester.

Wanda had one daughter and two granddaughters who would stand up with her. I had three sons, but it was not easy to corral them. John, in Maine, had been alienated from the family since before his mother's death and had refused to visit her before she died. He declined both my request and also Wanda's. Bill, in New Hampshire, had agreed when I first asked him; and in consultation with him, we set the date as Thursday,

December 13, to fit a deadline he had on some bonus airline miles and also to avoid the pre-Christmas crowds of college students thronging the Boston airport. After that, he got back to me to say that he would not stand up with me because his convictions as a fundamentalist Baptist would not permit it. Telephone conversation could not persuade him, and I wrote an essay, "The Bible and What It Means to Me," trying to highlight the Bible's developing theme of God's inclusion of all people in divine grace, but it didn't convince Bill and his wife, Roberta. Still, he brought Roberta and their three sons, Ken, Ron, and Ben. They stayed in the home of George and Jean Edwards and attended the reception afterward at the church but were not present in the religious ceremony. My son Samuel was the only one of my three sons who stood up with me. He accompanied Wanda's daughter, Ellen, down the aisle. Wanda's son-in-law, Mike Potter, accompanied her granddaughter Marsha, and Wanda's nephew Greg Rowe accompanied her granddaughter Susan. It was a beautiful event well photographed by one of Wanda's neighbors

Wanda and I spent the first night at her house before setting off on our honeymoon, which was to end at Clinton, South Carolina. Mary Kute, my across-the-street neighbor on Strathmoor Boulevard, had been intensely interested in every detail. She had asked me about our trip. I told her we were going to spend a few nights in an Indiana state park, then head south to a nice bed-and-breakfast at Beaufort, South Carolina, before going up to Clinton. Mary's comment was, as I heard it, "Sounds like Wanda-lust to me," but I don't think that's what she really said.

2.   My Year at Presbyterian College

When I arrived alone on the campus at Presbyterian College, I immediately joined a daily morning gathering at the flagpole on the campus to pray for peace. President Saddam Hussein of Iraq had invaded neighboring Kuwait in August, and President George H. W. Bush was giving many indications of preparing to go to war.

2a.   Opposing George H. W. Bush's Iraq War

Saddam Hussein claimed that Kuwait was drilling oil from a supply that actually belonged to Iraq. It was the almost-inevitable fallout from

Winston Churchill's redrawing the map of the Middle East following the fall of the Ottoman Empire after World War I. What had once been Assyria, Churchill turned into Iraq, but he drew a line cutting off the southern point of Iraq to form a new state, Kuwait, in order to prevent one country from controlling too much of the oil resources in the region.

Ronald Reagan during his presidency had sent Donald Rumsfeld (who later became George W. Bush's secretary of defense) to cultivate friendly relations with Saddam Hussein to keep him from getting too close to the Soviets. During the deadly war between Iraq and Iran, the U.S. had secretly aided the Iraqis, among other things providing chemical weapons that they used in the war. Saddam had also turned those chemical weapons against his Kurdish minority. Now Saddam Hussein was apparently following a line more independent of U.S. wishes and needed to be checked.

I was suspicious of Bush's motives, especially in view of his successful invasion of Panama to capture dictator Manuel Noriega. Bush had been head of the CIA before becoming Reagan's vice president, and Noriega had been a paid CIA operative ever since the late 1980s. Thus, the CIA and the U.S. administration were not only aware but also not opposed to Noriega's rise to dictatorial power in Panama. Only when Noriega began to operate independently of U.S. direction and was also complicit in drug dealing did he become an enemy to be deposed. It looked to me as though a war against Saddam Hussein and Iraq might be a similar case of punishing a client who got out of line. At that time, I read that the military commander who would have to oversee any action against Noriega observed that government offices were in close proximity to a large slum area, and he planned to conduct operations so as to avoid destroying the slum area. As Bush's plans to attack progressed, the president replaced that commander with another, who did nothing to prevent destruction and the large loss of civilian life in the slum during the actual attack.

In Iraq, Saddam Hussein had summoned U.S. Ambassador April Glaspie to a meeting not long before the invasion of Kuwait. Some people suspected that Glaspie told Saddam that the U.S. would not oppose his invasion plan. Much later, the declassification of all the known documents and their interpretation by various experts seemed to show that Glaspie's diplomatically phrased statement to Saddam did not specifically oppose his invasion plan and that he had interpreted it to suit his purposes.

Kuwait bordered on Saudi Arabia, which was an important U.S. ally and whose oil supplies were considered even more essential to the U.S. economy than Iraq's. Tens of thousands of Iraqi troops were massed in Kuwait. Secretary of Defense Dick Cheney (later George W. Bush's vice president) had visited Saudi Arabia, whose king had requested military defense. Bush sent U.S. armed forces that were stationed in Saudi Arabia.

Vice President Dan Quayle had spoken publicly about the necessity of protecting the U.S. petroleum supplies, an obvious point that hardly needed mentioning. Bush laid most emphasis on Iraq's violation of international law by invading Kuwait and upon the presence of huge numbers of Iraqi troops, poised for a possible invasion of Saudi Arabia. War fever was inflamed in the U.S. by emphasizing the USSR's friendly relations with Iraq. Also, Kuwait hired a publicity firm in the U.S. that disseminated accusations that Iraqi troops had committed horrible atrocities in Kuwait, the worst of which—ripping out respirators for premature babies in a hospital—were later shown to be pure fabrications. The U.S. air attack on Iraqi forces in Kuwait began January 17, 1991, with terrible effect.

All this took place while I was finishing teaching first-semester classes at Presbyterian College, returning to Louisville to marry Wanda, and bringing her with me to Clinton. During the winter break, I went with the Spanish professor and eight students to Nicaragua for the Habitat for Humanity project. By the time I came back to the college, the Gulf War was over.

The U.S. offensive against Iraqi troops in Kuwait proceeded more rapidly than anyone had anticipated. Without any attempt at resistance, the Iraqis retreated up the main highway from Kuwait headed toward Baghdad. U.S. air attacks that proceeded unhindered destroyed so many tanks and armored troop carriers with their human personnel that the road came to be known as the Highway of Death. The air force inflicted further damage on infrastructure, causing the death of many civilians. Major U.S. media described the retreat and quoted American pilots comparing their attacks to "shooting fish in a barrel" or "a turkey shoot."

I was appalled to read about this. I wrote a letter identifying myself as "Missionary in Residence, Presbyterian College," condemning this slaughter as a war crime. I sent a copy to several newspapers, two of which printed it. The U.S. Army officer who taught the ROTC classes at Presbyterian College complained to the president, who called me in for a reproof, but I didn't back down.

Wanda and I attended the First Presbyterian Church in Clinton. The sanctuary was decorated with red, white, and blue symbols, and the pastor spoke in terms that supported the war. The first time I encountered this I was deeply angry, and as we returned home, I remained silent and a bit sullen. We were just now getting to know each other more intimately, and Wanda felt some anxiety at my silence. At least she asked me about it, and I was able to tell her the reason and reassure her that my negative mood was not at all directed against her.

Actually, our semester in Clinton was a very happy time. We did a lot of walking around the town and were constantly impressed by the cordial greetings we got from everybody we passed. We made friends with the college chaplain and his wife and with young Peter Hobbie who came as a new member of the Bible and philosophy faculty and had an apartment in the same building as ours. I had known his father, Welford Hobbie, slightly.

During the summer of 1991, a group of retired Japan missionaries who had gathered at Lake Nojiri during summers in Japan held a reunion at a small Baptist college near Greenville, South Carolina. The principal planner was Marion Moorhead, who with his wife Thelma was retired nearby at Easley and had a long association with that college. Most of those gathered for the reunion had known Margaret, so naturally, they were curious to meet Wanda. She passed with flying colors and continued to accompany me to other such reunions that took place every two years over the next decade.

3. Wanda and I at Home

When we returned to Louisville from Clinton, Wanda's daughter, Ellen, and son-in-law, Mike Potter, helped move some of her furniture to my house, and we settled down to a comfortable existence on Strathmoor Boulevard. Over time, Wanda used her car to transfer various other possessions from one place to the other. Her friend Marilyn Landers lived a few houses away, and we regularly attended Strathmoor Presbyterian Church. Wanda continued to drive Mary Lee and Billie Kelly for shopping and medical appointments. Every Sunday, we drove those two and another widow to and from church. I often thought of Wanda as a very effective deacon or deaconess because of her loving spirit and willing help for others. She told me that she had been asked to become a ruling elder in the church but had not consented. I thought it was too bad that Strathmoor was one of a few congregations that ceased to have both deacons and elders. She would have been an ideal deacon, setting a good example for others.

Growing up in Rockport in western Kentucky, Wanda had attended the Presbyterian Church there, and she often referred to Miss Betsy, who taught the children's Sunday school class. "God is love" was the theme of Miss Betsy's teaching, Wanda reported, and "God is love" was Wanda's standard response in any discussions at church. "God is love" was the principle by which Wanda conducted her whole life.

Several times, we drove down to western Kentucky where Wanda had grown up and where we met some of her friends from girlhood days. We also visited what had been the farm homestead of her grandfather Josiah Acton, who had been a Baptist preacher "at Hell's Neck," according to Wanda's mother, Bessie Katharine Acton Rowe. Grandpa's house was long gone, but we visited at a season when we could see blooming jonquils in what had been the front yard. Wanda's mother, Bessie was bedfast, nearly deaf and blind, in the King's Daughters nursing home in Louisville. Wanda went every day at noon to feed her mother lunch, not only providing tender loving care, but also serving as a presence to forestall any possibility of neglect or mistreatment.

Granny lived to be 103 years old and was already bedfast when I first met her. She had been the widow of Hetsley Rowe for over fifty years and lived in a house she had bought with government benefits received in compensation for three sons who served in the war. One was shot down over Leipzig and buried in Europe, one was shot up on Anzio Beach and invalided home, and the third had returned from battle with a serious case of what was called shell shock after World War I but now is called post-traumatic syndrome disorder (PTSD). He was seriously wounded not only bodily but also mentally and wandered around aimlessly in public for a while, but he was sent to a veterans' facility in Indiana, where he died. He was buried in the Zachary Taylor Cemetery in Louisville, and I went with Wanda to leave a wreath by his headstone every Memorial Day.

Granny was a remarkable person in many ways. She grew up in a place and time when girls were not given much opportunity for education, but she had built firmly on the little she had. Wanda said she used to take her mother to yard sales, and she always went first for the books. Next morning, she would call Wanda to report on a book she had already read. When women were given the vote, she responded enthusiastically; and when she owned her own home, she opened the front room for a voting place in her precinct. Wanda told me that once in the nursing home, somebody asked Granny what her work was earlier, and she responded firmly, "School teacher!" Wanda said that was not true, but it was indicative of Granny's secret ambitions and self-estimate.

Granny did some research in family genealogy, and she was instrumental in helping several women establish their credentials to join the DAR (Daughters of the American Revolution). Granny herself qualified for membership but never joined, for she thought the organization was basically racist. Granny helped a woman descended from a slave of one of her own ancestors to establish connections. Wanda corresponded with the woman for some years, and after we married, she and I visited her once and spent a night in her home in west central Indiana. She told us her grandfather had taken his family there from Kentucky, for he thought it would be less disadvantageous for nonwhites.

Wanda did not let the lack of advanced education prevent her career accomplishments. She graduated from high school in Rockport, where her father, Hetsley Rowe, held a clerical position for Louisville Gas and Electric Co. (LG&E) at a coal mine owned by the company. For the advantage of his children, he brought his family to Louisville. They lived in the neighborhood of James Lees Memorial Presbyterian Church, which Wanda attended and joined. Her father hoped to find his daughter a job at LG&E, but it was clear she needed clerical training in typing and shorthand, which she got at a local business school. After several minor office jobs, Wanda became personal secretary to the president of the First National Bank of Louisville and later of Mr. Walter Girdler, CEO of the Girdler Corporation and Tube Turns, recipients of a national award for excellence in defense effort during the war.

After Wanda's husband, Jesse Burge Myers, returned from military service, she resigned her secretarial job, and they started a family. Jesse "Red" Myers became the chief purchasing agent for the entire public school system of Louisville, Kentucky. When their girls Ellen and Betty were grown, Wanda taught young children at the weekday school at Strathmoor Presbyterian and also in the Sunday school there. She loved the children, and the children loved her.

When I met Wanda, she had been a widow for ten years and no longer taught at the church. She owned her own home and was provided for by her husband's pension. She had attended several Elderhostel events, and she had also joined a Louisville group that visited a number of Louisville's sister cities in Europe.

Wanda's younger daughter, Betty, had taught Spanish for a few years in a high school in Southern Indiana and had been killed by a drunk driver in a car wreck. There was a group of about half a dozen young women who had been dear friends of Betty, and when I met Wanda, these friends used to get together on occasion, and they invited Wanda to join them. The fondness of these young women for this woman old enough to be their mother was for me strong evidence of the kind of person Wanda was as well as the kind of person Betty had been. Even after we married, I still accompanied Wanda when she would see one or more of Betty's friends. Wanda was active in the local MADD chapter and the Compassionate Friends support group. I was also glad to join her in those meetings. We regularly attended the annual Race Relations Conference of Louisville and Jefferson County.

Wanda remained active at the church. I mentioned above that she and Marilyn Landers were joint moderators of women of the church. After coming back from South Carolina, Wanda had accepted the position of Strathmoor's representative on the Board of the Missionary Furlough Home on the seminary campus. She had the office of vice moderator, which put her in line for the next three-year term as moderator. The current moderator was the daughter of a former pastor of Central Presbyterian, but before the end of her first year as moderator, she got married, left Louisville, and moved her membership to a different denomination. Thus, with only minimum preparation beforehand, Wanda fulfilled the duties of moderator for five years. With her typical deaconess compassion and efficiency, she did a great job.

As moderator of the Furlough Home Board, Wanda had to go frequently to the seminary to pick up mail and check on other details related to the apartments. On one occasion, her foot rolled on some acorns on a slight incline. She fell and seriously injured her left ankle and lower leg. It required a hospital stay and the attachment of a metal plate secured to the bone with several screws. She had trouble getting into and out of our home, as it required thirteen steps up from street level, either front or back.

While Wanda was recovering, we kept our eye on real estate ads in the paper; and eventually, we found a condominium on the first floor at Salem Square that required only two steps into the main entry. I sold my house on Strathmoor Boulevard to a younger woman whom Wanda had come to know as a receptionist of the King's Daughters Home where her mother had stayed for so many years. She had a husband and a young son, and they had been looking for a place they could afford. Although I had the possibility of a bidding war between her and another interested couple, I let her have the place at a reasonable price.

Wanda and I enjoyed many travels and activities, including an annual trip to New England. Her brother Herbert Rowe, who had been wounded at Anzio Beach, lived in Maine with his wife, Anne Ayvaliotis, who was an artist. They lived in the rural village of Washington in an old farmstead house with a long history going back to the original owners, a family named Hilton. I liked to refer to their home as the Washington Hilton. Herb had built a studio for Anne separate from the house, and we attended displays of Anne's paintings that hung at local art galleries.

Wanda's younger sister Billy Davis lived in Vermont with her husband, Charlie. Billy and Charlie had married as teenagers, and Charlie had attended University of Louisville while working for the General Electric Appliance plant. Steadily, he worked his way up to head of the transportation division, charged with shipping out washers, driers, refrigerators, etc., all over the country. He also served as a greeter and host for company visitors to Louisville during the Kentucky Derby. Charlie had a very generous retirement package and had bought a farm in a small Vermont town and built his own house. His wife, Billy, kept horses. Their son Charlie Jr. (Buzz) lived with his family in a town not far away in his house that Charlie helped him build. In time, their daughter Kathy and her husband, Billy Clancy, also built a house on part of Charlie's land.

My eldest son, Bill, and his family lived in New Hampshire. My son John (whom Wanda had been instrumental in getting reconciled to the family) lived in Auburn, Maine, and a close friend of mine from college days lived in Brunswick. In addition to family visits, we also participated in several Elderhostel programs, including one centered on New England shipbuilding and another on lighthouses.

Though Wanda had made several trips to Europe, she had never wanted to go to any Oriental country until after she met me. We decided to visit Japan, but since we were crossing the Pacific, we might as well see China too, so we signed on with a tour to China first. The group was small enough to fit all together in a minibus wherever we went. From Beijing, we went out to the Great Wall. In southern China, we rode down the Li River, observing the magnificent Karst rock pillars, which are a famous attraction.

We spent several days in Shanghai on the fourteenth floor of a new hotel. This was the first time I had seen a plastic card used for a hotel room door key. From our room, we could look out over an area that had once been a slum, but the land had been cleared, and construction crews were in the process of building more multistory buildings. We were led to believe they were intended as housing for the people who had been displaced. There was still a lot of work done by humans assisted by some machinery. Cement was mixed in old-time cement mixers that men with wheelbarrows loaded with sand, gravel, and cement to which water was added. We could see other men working by hand to assemble the steel rods to put in deep holes in the ground to strengthen the foundation columns for the structure. Other men then used wheelbarrows to bring the cement mixture where two others would help roll it up a ramp and dump the cement into the hole. The whole process would have been greatly facilitated by trucks bringing in ready-mix concrete to each place needed, but that would have deprived hundreds of men of employment.

A recently married couple in our group consisted of Ann, a young woman who had finished her training and was expecting to join an obstetric-gynecological medical team when they returned, and her husband, Alex, who was going to work at Case Western University. Ann's mother was originally from a well-to-do family in Suchow, some miles outside Shanghai. The communist authorities had taken over their large residence and turned it into small apartments for members of the party faithful. The family fled to Taiwan, where her mother married a Taiwanese man, and they had subsequently emigrated to the U.S. where Ann grew up and got her medical training. Ann knew the address of her mother's former home, for one of Ann's aunts and her daughter still had a room in the building. Our tour guide took us there. We were able to gain entrance, and Ann had a brief reunion with her aunt and cousin.

Next, Wanda and I went to Japan, but our ten-day stay was interrupted by three typhoons. From Tokyo, we took a night train that was able to cross the Inland Sea on the recently completed bridge due to arrive at Takamatsu early the next morning. In my day, it would have taken parts of two days, including riding a ferry boat across the water. Because of the typhoon, we didn't reach Takamatsu till noon the next day. Some of the events planned for us had to be cancelled. From there, we went on to Shikoku Christian College. It was a school holiday. There were no students around, and some of the faculty and staff whom I had known were no longer there. We were hospitably welcomed into the home of my Korean faculty colleague Kim Junki and his Japanese wife, Watanabe Michiko. We spent one night as guests of the family who now owned the house Margaret had planned. The next-door neighbors, Professor and Mrs. Nishiwaki, were away on a trip because of a death in their family, so we didn't get to see them.

I preached on Sunday at the Kotohira Kyodan Church, where Margaret's ashes are kept in their cemetery plot. We went farther west on Shikoku Island to visit several other churches where I had friends. Despite the inconvenience of the three typhoons, it was a generally satisfactory visit.

4. Last Years with Wanda

While Wanda and I lived in our condominium at Salem Square, we customarily took a walk every day. There were half a dozen routes from which we could choose. I always took along a bag to pick up any plastic, glass, or aluminum waste I found along the way. The city recycling pickup did not include service within the campus of our condominium, so occasionally we would take our collected metal, glass, and paper items to a central recycling point.

On July 4, 2001, I had an episode of extremely rapid heartbeat. I lay down on the bed and seemed to calm down, but my pulse count was so high as to be alarming. I thought I'd better do something about it. Wanda went with me to an immediate care center. As soon as the admitting nurse took my vital signs, she called for an EKG test. When the doctor saw the results, he said I needed to go to the hospital at once. I told him I had my car, but he insisted on calling an ambulance, and Wanda followed in my car. It being a holiday, the hospital was shorthanded, but they gave me a pill meant to calm things down. Somebody brought a machine designed to give some information about my condition as the operator, with hands well lubricated, felt all around my chest while the machine did its thing, whatever that was. The medicine did not have the desired effect, so they took me to another room where they sedated me and shocked my heart back into proper rhythm. They said I had suffered atrial fibrillation. I spent one night in the hospital. As soon as possible, I went to Dr. Robert Shaw, our primary physician, who referred me to a cardiac specialist. He did various tests, such as monitoring me walking on a treadmill. They prescribed several medicines, two of which I still take daily, but I have not had any serious heart trouble since. I had a brief period of high blood pressure, for which I took some medication. However, an apparent disharmony with other medications caused noticeable discomfort. But since Dr. Shaw discontinued two of my heart medications, I seem to be OK, thankfully.

I became aware that sometimes in bed during the night, Wanda gave signs of apnea. I could hear her intake of breath growing steadily shorter till her throat would close momentarily and her breathing would stop and then begin again with a kind of snort to repeat the cycle. It is said that severe apnea tends to deprive the brain of oxygen and might lead to dementia. Dr. Shaw recommended she have a test to determine the severity of the case, for Medicare would cover the cost of a device to assist breathing. The test was to be given overnight. I took Wanda to the Norton Suburban Hospital one evening, where I would pick her up the next morning after the overnight test. Next day, she was waiting for me when I arrived, and she reported that all the wires and attachments necessary to monitor everything had made it impossible for her to sleep at all, so she had cancelled the test.

One Sunday afternoon, we each had an event we wanted to attend, so we took our cars for the purpose. I had already returned home when Wanda came back. She reported that she had had a slight accident. Her left front fender was bashed, and the steering had been damaged. I asked her where it happened, and we got in my car for her to show me. Downtown, she couldn't remember the place. However, the lady in the other car had given her name and phone number, so I called her to get the details. Fortunately, the damage was relatively minor, and a man paid Wanda a pretty good price for the car, which he intended to fix himself. She reluctantly gave up her driver's license, and we began to look for a retirement facility.

We checked out a number of places in Louisville, but when we visited Westminster Village across the Ohio River in Clarksville, Indiana, we immediately saw its superiority to any of the others. The campus was in a more beautiful setting, and the apartments were slightly larger than the others and less expensive. We were shown a two-bedroom apartment at the end of a long corridor. A weeping willow tree stood about twenty yards from the terrace exit, and beyond that was a small pond. The apartment was being renovated completely, as the former resident had recently died after living there for many years. While the redecorating went on, I was able to find a buyer for our condo at Salem Square, and we moved on July 2, 2003.

Wanda and I joined the thrice-weekly exercise group, and when the lady who led it had to give it up, I took her place. Nearly every day, Wanda and I took a walk of about a mile and a half. Lapping Park and Wooded View Golf Course adjoin our campus. A roadway separates the front and back nine holes of the golf course, leading to a lodge not far from Silver Creek. Surrounding woodlands have many paths, and the changing of the seasons brings constant delight. Sometimes we walked on the golf course at twilight, and once in a while, we could see half a dozen deer grazing.

As time went on, Wanda's dementia got noticeably worse. I was slow to adjust to the realization that repeating directions on how to use the phone answering machine for an elderly person with dementia is the opposite of repeating directions to a child. I still feel a sense of shame for my slowness to catch on. Wanda recalled her mother's last decade of life in the nursing home and had often said she did not want to undergo that style of dying. She often said, "I'm losing my mind" or "I've lived too long."

At one of our annual physical examinations from Dr. Shaw, an X-ray showed a spot at the top of Wanda's right lung. Our natural assumption was that it must be cancer. Dr. Shaw prescribed a PET scan and referred us to a lung specialist. He looked at the various plates and prescribed an endoscope test. Besides that one spot, the lungs seemed otherwise healthy, but they had not obtained a tissue to perform a biopsy. The surgeon said, "I believe that I can easily remove it all by surgery." Wanda looked him in the eye and, without a moment's hesitation, said, "No indeed!" Wanda was nearly ninety, actually older than me. She still had sense enough to know that even if the doctor's prognosis was correct, freedom from cancer was not a good exchange for radical surgery and survival with progressive dementia.

In actual fact, Wanda survived for nearly two years without significant pain or discomfort. Our walks became slower and shorter. We had to go twice to have the fluid removed from her lungs. It got worse so we couldn't travel, for she was completely disoriented in a place outside home. I couldn't leave her alone at home, but on a few occasions, a friend came to stay with her when I had to be away. It seemed desirable to consider hospice care. We had the sixteenth anniversary of our marriage on December 13, 2006, and two days later, a very kind, efficient lady came to interview us for hospice. Because Wanda had refused to have a formal biopsy, we had no certainty about her actual ailment, though we had assumed all along it must be cancer. This proved a technical problem, but the lady stayed with us and used her cell phone for many calls until she finally got official approval and formally enrolled Wanda in hospice care.

Wanda's family moved her double bed and antique dresser out of our bedroom, and the hospice installed an adjustable hospital-type bed for Wanda. I slept on a mat beside the bed. In this way, Wanda could stay in her most familiar surroundings, and I could remain at hand. For a few days, I took her in a wheelchair for the evening meal in the main dining room, but that soon stopped, and she was fully confined to bed. She still gave no signs of pain but had some restlessness of her legs, which a mild sedative relieved. A little after midnight on December 28, I gave her the drops of sedative; and when I woke up the next morning, she was dead. I called hospice immediately, and a nurse came. Since Wanda had bequeathed her body to the University of Louisville Medical School, I called the number to give notice. The nurse and I waited quite a while till two men came to receive the body. They had been delayed by an accident on the bridge over the Ohio River.

I knew that Wanda's sister Billy Davis and her husband, Charlie, were on a trip to Europe, so I set the date for a memorial service at James Lees Memorial Presbyterian for January 12 to coincide with the Martin Luther King holiday weekend on January 2007. By that time, the Davises were back, and other friends and family were able to attend. The loving support of the congregation and helpful suggestions from Irene Rawlings about posting some appropriate photographs and having a book for people to sign meant a great deal to me at this particular time. I really felt as though I saw the face of Jesus in their faces. In this time of grieving for the loss of Wanda, I also relived my sense of loss of Margaret so many years before. Both these women were truly gifts to me from God, and I can never fully express how they enriched my life.

PART SIX

My Life as Activist and Writer

12

Pearl Harbor, Hiroshima, and Nuclear Weapons

In addition to the traveling and other pleasures that Wanda and I enjoyed during these years, I continued to be active in various campaigns for peace, nonviolence, and justice. As time passed, more and more information was coming to light concerning the bombing of Hiroshima and Nagasaki, the unusually severe effects on humans, and doubts about the decision to drop the bomb in the first place.

1. The Failed Effort at the Fiftieth Anniversary

The Smithsonian Institution planned a retrospective exhibition in 1995 covering the first fifty years of the atomic age. From the museum in Hiroshima, they had borrowed a number of artifacts to present stark evidence of the bomb's effects. Among them were the mangled remains of a child's tricycle. Another was a section of concrete wall that showed effects of the bomb's radiation that hit the surface directly, but it also showed the silhouette of a human who had been sitting in front of the wall and whose body had absorbed the direct radiation, leaving that part of the wall's surface unaffected. I had seen these and many other vivid examples when I had visited Hiroshima some years before, so I knew how effective the exhibition could be.

Some veterans' organizations got wind of the plans and mounted a vigorous campaign against it. They insisted that the bomb had been a good thing by ending further conflict. They wanted to downplay the suffering of the Japanese victims and to emphasize Japan's atrocities in the Far East and perfidy in the Pearl Harbor attack. They wanted to make a special exhibit of the restored *Enola Gay*, the B-29 bomber that had actually carried the bomb to Hiroshima. Their campaign got popular support and was carried up to Congress, and in the end, the Smithsonian called the whole thing off.

Following this fiasco, I kept reading all I could find about the decision to drop the bomb. My Methodist missionary friend David Swain had done extensive research into the history of Japan's rapid mastery of Western science after Commodore Perry had shocked the Japanese out of their two centuries of isolation. David, as an expert in that field, had made the English translation of the published report of the physical and social effects of the nuclear bombs on Hiroshima and Nagasaki. He became my source for the great deal of information I used when I wrote up my account of the Pearl Harbor attack and the nuclear bombs.

When Harry Truman became president after FDR's death, he learned about the bomb for the first time, and he knew little of the discussions that had been going on. The White House staff was divided. Some urged response to feelers put out by the Japanese to end the war, but others wanted to carry on to unconditional surrender. General Walter Groves, manager of the Manhattan Project working to produce the bomb, wanted to keep going till the bomb was finally perfected so it could be used. Henry Stimson, secretary of war, had appointed Groves to that job and supported him in his zeal to use the bomb whenever it became available. Stimson had criticized the firebombing of German cities, but he had specifically advocated such a policy for Japan. Army Air Force General Curtis Lemay oversaw the firebombing not only of Tokyo but also of most of the other cities of Japan, using thousands of bombers and tens of thousands of incendiary bombs. There were actually only a few cities that were not already burned out. General MacArthur, seconded by General Eisenhower, thought Japan could not hang on much more than a month or so without using the bomb. After the bomb was dropped, they refrained from criticizing it, and their earlier remarks became known only much later.

Researcher Gar Alperovitz brought to light another important factor that led to the decision to drop the bomb, which he presented in the book *Atomic Diplomacy, Hiroshima and Potsdam: The Use of the Atomic*

Bomb and the American Confrontation with Soviet Power.[16] Germany had surrendered on May 7, 1945, and President Truman, Great Britain's Winston Churchill, and the Soviet's Joseph Stalin met at Potsdam to discuss postwar policy toward Germany and the Eastern European countries. Alperovitz used abundant documentation to show what transpired there. Stimson did not want to start such negotiations till after "the bomb was laid on Japan." The bomb was not yet tested, and Truman delayed the Potsdam meeting as long as possible but finally went to the meeting in July. While there, Truman was informed of the successful test of the bomb called Trinity on July 16. He told Churchill, who remarked that with the bomb, the allies could be "all-powerful and capable of dictating to Stalin" now. Truman followed up by ordering the bomb to be dropped on Hiroshima. Experts may differ on how to evaluate the weight of various issues, but there can be no question that Japanese cities were victimized at least in part to demonstrate an implied threat to the Soviet Union. Stalin knew all about the bomb from spies, and he only hardened his own policies toward Germany and other European countries during the cold war that dragged out for many years.

During the eighteen months after the 1945 bombing, the U.S. public learned more about the actual effects of the bombs, and feelings of revulsion began to grow. General MacArthur in Japan absolutely forbade the publication of any photographs depicting the human consequences. Nevertheless, details of the stupendous damage to humans leaked out, and respected American citizens expressed criticism. John Hersey's essay "Hiroshima" that occupied a complete issue of the *New Yorker* magazine had a lot to do with a general change of public opinion. At last, members of the inner circle prepared a public report that bore Stimson's name as author that claimed falsely that everything possible had been done to avoid using the bomb, that it struck only militarily significant targets, and that using it had saved millions of lives on both sides.

Thus, as the fiftieth anniversary of the bomb approached, I wrote up a mimeographed 8.5 by 5.5 inch pamphlet to explain why the bombs were not needed to end the war. Concerning Pearl Harbor, there was available *Pearl Harbor Final Judgment* by Major Henry Clausen, whom Secretary of War Stimson had commissioned and authorized to compile

---

[16] Gar Alperovitz, *Atomic Diplomacy, Hiroshima and Potsdam.* New York: Penguin Books, 1985.

what became the official report of the attack that brought the war to the U.S. Clausen presented damning claims of dereliction of duty and interservice rivalry in Hawaii between Navy Admiral Kimmel and Army General Short, but he also mentioned serious deficiencies all the way up to President Roosevelt. Clausen's report gave the impression that a combination of many mistakes, major and minor, that should have been avoided had made possible Japan's surprise attack.

2. Questions about Pearl Harbor and Hiroshima

The fiftieth anniversaries of both Pearl Harbor and Hiroshima came and went with no noticeable progress of understanding on either side. Before the sixtieth anniversary, I read an important new book, *Day of Deceit: The Truth about FDR and Pearl Harbor.*[17] Author Robert B. Stinnett had expected to be one of the navy men involved in the final invasion of Japan. After the war, he had been a reporter of the *San Francisco Times*, and he believed the story that the Japanese fleet had proceeded across the Pacific with total silence of their wireless before the attack. He read something that indicated that there was evidence of wireless communication by the Japanese that was actually picked up, thus providing evidence that something was in the offing.

Spurred by this knowledge, Stinnett, through the Freedom of Information Act, obtained access to and examined over two hundred thousand declassified documents. He also personally interviewed many people all around the Pacific basin as the basis for his book. Stinnett's presentation convinced me that President Roosevelt had followed a careful plan to entice Japan to attack Pearl Harbor. This attack shocked the American public out of their broad reluctance to get actively involved in the war, which was already ravaging Europe. It enabled Roosevelt to keep a promise he had made during the election campaign for his third term as president. "I will not send your boys to fight a foreign war." On carefully reading this book, I was fully persuaded of its accuracy, and I set

---

[17] Robert B. Stinnett, *Day of Deceit The Truth about FDR and Pearl Harbor.* New York: Simon and Schuster, 2000.

out to revise my earlier pamphlet with a book that gave more detail about both events: *Pearl Harbor, Hiroshima, & Beyond: Subversion of Values.*[18]

I was late getting started on this work, and I kept finding other information I wanted to add, so I did not complete the book soon enough to find a publisher, and I ended by paying to have it published. I developed a thesis that had been growing stronger in my mind over the years concerning what I saw as Americans' false self-image. We Americans are good and honorable people, but we are sometimes misunderstood and attacked by nations with bad motives. We respond only in self-defense as the last resort, but we mobilize such overwhelming power that we completely defeat the evil enemy. Then we follow a program that helps them recover. In this way, we turn what appears to be evil, Pearl Harbor, into what is really a great good, Hiroshima. If one nuclear bomb produced so much good, then thousands of bombs must be so much better.

That was the prime example of "subversion of values," but there was much more. Following the Allies' victory over Germany, the U.S. had immediately proceeded to exploit Nazi secret files on the Russians to strengthen our struggle against the red foe. We had brought Werner von Braun and other German expert rocket scientists who had made possible Germany's V-2 rocket attacks on London to design the missiles to carry our nuclear warheads aimed at Russia. In Japan, General MacArthur, instead of arresting and trying Emperor Hirohito for his complicity in the war, had proclaimed the emperor's innocence and allowed him to keep his throne as a figurehead fronting MacArthur's assumed authority as supreme Allied commander. In other words, Japan's surrender was not unconditional.

MacArthur imposed on the Japanese the Peace Constitution renouncing war and armaments. Thoroughly exhausted by the war, the Japanese people in general gratefully accepted the Peace Constitution and seriously sought to learn democracy and maintain a policy of nonalignment with either the West or the East. When the Korean War began, MacArthur immediately turned around and organized the Japanese Self-Defense Forces, land, sea, and air, which have since become one of the most powerful armed forces in the world.

---

[18] Arch B. Taylor, Jr. *Pearl Harbor, Hiroshima, & Beyond: Subversion of Values.* Vancouver: Trafford, 2005.

In the U.S., we assumed that the postwar economic assistance to Japan had been similar to the Marshall Plan for Europe generously provided by us. In fact, the funds used were actually plundered by the Japanese from all over Southeast Asia during their imperial advance. When the U.S. discovered these assets, instead of trying to return them to their rightful owners, they took possession of them and doled them out in such a way as to help Japanese elements that would advance U.S. anti-Soviet purposes. Early funds to start the Japanese National Police force (the beginning of the Japanese army, navy, and air force) came from that fund. Likewise, the Liberal Democratic Party (which is neither liberal nor democratic) received special economic help from the U.S. to such an extent that they controlled the Japanese government for nearly three decades. Some of the early leaders of the Lib-Dem Party had been convicted war criminals. Their regimes approved a mutual security pact with the U.S., which effectively made Japan a subordinate partner with the U.S. in the cold war years and thereafter. Popular demonstrations against the mutual security pact were of such a scale and intensity that President Eisenhower had to cancel his planned visit to Japan, yet the pact was kept firmly in force.

Since Trafford was not a regular commercial publisher with a sales staff, it was more or less left up to me to publicize and sell the book, but that was not the kind of thing I had ever done, nor was I good at it. Besides, the book did not hit the market until after the strategic moment of the sixtieth anniversary. It's certainly not a best seller by any means, but as the years have passed, more and more facts are coming to the surface that corroborate what I have written, and some thoughtful people are seeing things as they really were.

3.   General U.S. Indifference to Nuclear Weapons

"Out of sight, out of mind" seems to be the prevailing U.S. attitude when it comes to nuclear weapons. Hiroshima Observance in Louisville has all but faded completely away. The only thing that gets the American public excited is the evidence that North Korea possesses nuclear weapons and the charge that Iran is trying to produce atomic weapons. Iran insists that it is only doing what it is permitted to do by terms of the Nuclear Non-proliferation Treaty, namely, developing nuclear power for civilian purposes, such as generating electricity, which they need because Western sanctions make it impossible for Iran to exploit their own resources of petroleum.

Observing that the U.S. did not follow its obligations in the Nuclear Non-proliferation Treaty to begin dismantling our stockpile of weapons, both India and Pakistan refused to sign that pact and proceeded to build their own bombs. Their ongoing quarrel over the control of Kashmir has several times brought them to the brink of nuclear war. Pakistan's instability linked to the war in neighboring Afghanistan tends to deflect attention from Kashmir, but the fact that these two mutually hostile nations both possess nuclear weapons is a real cause for concern.

The Presbyterian Church (USA) annually publishes the *Presbyterian Mission Yearbook for Prayer and Study*, a compendium of information about our church's ministry in every presbytery and synod throughout the United States and in all the countries around the world where we have partnerships in mission. We follow the liturgical calendar that is recognized by many denominations, and we take note of special days such as World Day of Prayer, World Communion Sunday, Human Rights Day, Earth Day, etc. For some years, Hiroshima Day was recognized every August 6 in our yearbook. But with no fanfare or debate, it was dropped, to the great disappointment of many of us who wanted it reinstated.

When the General Assembly met in Cincinnati some years ago, I was among the members of the Presbyterian Peace Fellowship who went to advocate for restoring Hiroshima Day by making our argument before the committee that was in charge of discussing many peace issues and making recommendations to the plenary session of the Assembly. Each speaker had only three minutes to speak during the committee's consideration of our issue, and we could not be present during the committee's discussion and decision.

The committee rejected our proposal. We heard afterward that the prominent Presbyterian who chaired the committee had swayed the decision by claiming that he himself had been one of many whose life was spared because the bomb relieved them from having to invade Japan. Only some time later, I heard that he was said to have understood that he had been mistaken, that the bomb was not necessary to end the war, and he regretted opposing the reinstatement of Hiroshima Day. Recently, I have spoken with one of the staff at the headquarters about the possibility of restoring Hiroshima Day to the Mission yearbook, and it remains to be seen what the result will be—the general spirit of indifference and undercurrent of militarism in the American public convinces me that we need to step up a campaign of education on many issues, not only concerning nuclear weapons, but also about gun violence in our own land that takes about thirty thousand lives a year.

4.   OREPA—the Oak Ridge Environmental Peace Alliance

The Oak Ridge Environmental Peace Alliance in Tennessee continues the struggle to abolish nuclear weapons with weekly vigils at the Y-12 facility and an annual observance of Hiroshima and Nagasaki. Ralph Hutchison and his companions do everything they can, including appearing at hearings supposed to allay people's fear of nuclear weapon production, while the government continues to advocate updating the bomb-making capability in violation of the Nonproliferation Treaty. So far OREPA has not succeeded in halting the Department of Energy (DOE) and the National Nuclear Security Administration (NNSA) plans to build more nuclear warheads in an expanded new Uranium Processing Facility (UPF) that can cost billions of dollars. All the scare tactics to increase national security are actually resulting in undermining our national well-being.

Several times, I personally participated in OREPA's Hiroshima Day Observance. I used to take several Louisville people along by car, but I have stopped driving that distance. The program is a two-day affair, including sleeping on the floor throughout the Church of the Good Shepherd, a local United Church of Christ congregation that makes its premises available. There are educational classes and training in peaceful protest and nonviolent actions. Those who plan to commit civil disobedience by crossing the line into the facility itself receive special instructions along with the partner they have chosen to be their companion, support, and liaison when they are arrested and taken to jail. The whole group gathers in a park downtown and marches to the Y-12 plant over a mile away. Every year, a Japanese Buddhist group finishes a longer pilgrimage to take part in the demonstration. People hang folded paper cranes along the barrier fence, read the names of bomb victims to the tolling of a bell, and cheer those who do the civil disobedience.

Once, I met an old fellow named Gordon Maham and heard his story. He was a worker at the Y-12 plant from the beginning, but at that time, nobody knew what exactly they were doing. When the Hiroshima bomb was dropped and the workers at the Y-12 plant learned that they had produced the weapons-grade plutonium explosive material that caused all the death and destruction, Gordon was shocked and outraged. He immediately quit his job in protest, but he lost his exemption from the draft. The Selective Service nabbed him because he had not registered, and he spent three years in federal prison. Once out of prison, Gordon devoted the rest of his life to activism for peace and nuclear disarmament.

OREPA regularly publishes a booklet called *Reflections for Nonviolent Community* with appropriate sayings plus notices of dates of historical peace and war events or birth dates of well-known peace activists on each day of the year. The issue for August-September 2013 reports that Gordon Maham died on July 9 at the age of ninety-six, and it tells a few details of his activism. Gordon called himself a peaceful planet person. He used to grow flowers in his garden at home, and he would bring one in a pot to Oak Ridge. After crossing the line, he would replant it inside before the guards could prevent him. For this kind of peaceful, nonviolent action, Gordon was arrested and jailed at least nine times.

You can check their Web site, OREPA (Oak Ridge Environmental Peace Alliance), for lots of information. The present nuclear facility dates back to the earliest times, and some of the buildings are in bad condition and pose threats to the environment. It is still needed for the U.S. to fulfill our obligations to reduce nuclear weapons according to the START Treaty. We still have over a thousand armed missiles ready for launch, but we have removed warheads from hundreds of missiles. We should be dismantling those warheads, but we are keeping them and planning to make them even more powerful. The George W. Bush administration discussed building new bunker-busting bombs it might use against Iran. It is clear to everybody that the facility is in need of renovation to fulfill our obligations, and in 2005, an estimate of $600 million to about $1.5 billion for that purpose was proposed. As plans proceeded, the Department of Energy and National Nuclear Security Administration (DOE/NNSA) proposed an all-new Uranium Processing Facility (UPF) with cost estimated at up to $6.5 billion, capable of building eighty new warheads per year besides preserving older warheads and making them more powerful.

Ralph Hutchison and the staff at OREPA keep careful watch over all these proposals and try to educate the public to the fact that such a new UPF will be the most expensive bomb-making facility in all history and its purpose will be contrary to the obligations we have taken on by signing the Nuclear Non-Proliferation Treaty and the START Treaty to reduce nuclear weapons. Unquestionably, the deteriorating facility is a threat to the environment and is incapable of efficiently carrying out our legal obligations. But we can fulfill our obligations by renovating the present facility at a fraction of the cost of the proposed new facility. It is difficult for OREPA and others to get clear estimates and proposals, but they have already learned that after spending some millions of dollars on various plans, it is clear that the proposed buildings themselves are not large enough to provide the actual workspace needed for all the operations projected to take place there.

In view of the recent recession and the acknowledged need to reduce federal spending, deciding *not* to build the new Nuclear Processing Facility at Oak Ridge sounds like a no-brainer.

13

Other Activities

When I retired from Japan, I remarked that I was tired of acting like a shotgun. I wanted to act more like a rifle. Still, as my years of retirement (retread) went on, I availed myself of the opportunity of taking part in a number of other campaigns for peace and justice. It might be called still acting like a shotgun.

1. The Fairness Campaign

Beginning before I retired from Japan, people in Louisville and Jefferson County were quietly working toward local ordinances to overcome discrimination against lesbian, gay, bisexual, and transgender persons (LGBT). After returning home, I was among a number of ministers in Louisville who formed the group Religious Leaders for Fairness. We met at regular intervals to plan strategy, participate in actions, and spread education and publicity on behalf of fairness. We wanted to demonstrate that serious-minded religious people could take a positive approach to the question of homosexual orientation, though in popular view, Christians tended to condemn homosexual people not only as sinners before God and unfit for membership or office in the church but also as objects of social discrimination.

My interest began many years previously when Margaret and I read a book on the subject containing a chart showing that every individual's nature lies somewhere on a continuum between exclusively heterosexual and exclusively homosexual orientation (about 16 percent each).[19] On another occasion, she and I had spent some time in the home of Dr. Paul S. Crane, who, having served as a Presbyterian medical missionary in Korea, retired early and joined a team of doctors in Nashville, Tennessee. In Paul's library, I found several journals and books describing cases in which a variation in an individual's genetic makeup might cause any of a variety of abnormal physical and/or psychological conditions. Thus, I was prepared to believe those who insisted that their homosexuality was not a choice—it was simply something about themselves they had to acknowledge. Newspaper advice columnist Ann Landers asked homosexual readers who were willing to respond whether or not they chose that lifestyle. She reported that among 75,875 respondents, a majority of thirty to one reported it wasn't a choice, and they're glad to be gay.

Concerning the daughter of a friend of ours, we heard that in her early teens, she heard the term *homosexual* and looked it up in the dictionary. "That's me," she told herself, "and I can't tell anybody about it." Fortunately for her, later on, she *was* able to tell her parents. They not only accepted and loved her but also participated in a telephone hotline to talk to young people or to their parents who might be facing this question.

I never had such a close relationship with persons or families for whom the question of sexual orientation was a problem, but I learned enough about it, and I came to know people who had "come out of the closet" and told their stories. I could readily participate as a member of Religious Leaders for Fairness with understanding. We got the Louisville City Council and the Jefferson County Council to pass the anti-discrimination ordinance. When the local city and county government amalgamated to form Metro Louisville, opponents failed in trying to make us go through the whole campaign again. Metro Louisville is an example of increasing fairness that is still lacking in many areas throughout Kentucky and the rest of the nation.

---

[19] Ralph W. Weltge, ed., *The Same Sex: An Appraisal of Homosexuality.* Boston/ Philadelphia: Pilgrim Press, 1969, pp 6-9.

2.   Effort to Abolish the Death Penalty

When Wendell Ford ran for governor and Ben Chandler ran for attorney general of Kentucky, they made a promise to speed up the resumption of applying the death penalty. For some years, there had been a moratorium on capital punishment after the Supreme Court had raised some serious questions about the way it was administered, but new methods were devised to make the penalty "acceptable," and Kentucky had passed another law that permitted the resumption of the practice. There was a number of prisoners on death row who had been there for years already, but there was always an extension whenever the question of setting a date for execution was brought up. After Ford and Chandler won the election, they set out to fulfill their promise of a faster execution process. A group in Louisville rallied to oppose their move.

I joined together with my friend and colleague George Edwards in this effort, along with Carl Wedekind of the local American Civil Liberties Union (ACLU). We drove monthly to Frankfort, Kentucky, to meet with members of the public defender's office to get updates on the status of several death-row inmates whose cases Attorney General Chandler was pursuing. We also did a bit of lobbying with members of the legislature. Governor Ford refused to see us, but Chandler did receive us one time. We gave him statistical evidence that all of the death-row inmates were poor people and poorly educated, and their legal defense was inadequate. Chandler acknowledged that the budget and personnel of the public defenders were inadequate, but he would make no promise to make improvements.

At the top of the list for exhausting appeals and having an execution date set was Harold McQueen. We learned a lot about Harold and his case. Harold was said to have become an alcoholic while still a child at home (if he could be said to have had a home). He had early dropped out of school, and he was judged to be borderline mentally retarded. He had actually joined the military service in the hopes that a disciplined life would get him straightened out. The most noticeable result was that while in the army, he became a drug addict in addition to being an alcoholic. Harold was trying to get money for his drug addiction by robbing a convenience store one night when he killed the young woman clerk. McQueen's lawyer was totally incompetent and offered no evidence of extenuating circumstances due to the misfortunes of Harold's childhood. He was now the first target of the speed-up campaign.

By the time Harold's case became prominent, he had undergone a thorough experience of regeneration in response to the compassion and friendship of Paul Stevens, a volunteer visitor at the Eddyville Prison. Paul himself had had a transformative experience. One evening at home, Paul had received a call that his daughter, who was babysitting at a home in the neighborhood, had been attacked. He hurried to the house, and as he entered, a young man who had been dating his daughter rushed by him and fled. Paul went in and found his daughter brutally killed. It was soon established that the killer had been the person who left the house as Paul was coming in.

The young man was arrested, tried, and convicted of murder. However, due to various irregularities of the legal procedure, he was released after serving only a brief time in prison. In Paul's eyes, he had escaped practically unpunished for his awful crime against his daughter. His rage, hatred, and craving for revenge grew stronger every day. Paul quit work and stopped attending church where he formerly had gone regularly to receive mass, and he spent more and more time simply brooding over this terrible thing. At length, friends persuaded him to go with them on a spiritual retreat; and during that time, he was able to understand that he was literally destroying himself. The only way he could survive was to surrender himself to God and commit that young man also into God's grace.

Healing began to take place, but Paul went farther. Having already given up his job, he went to the Eddyville Prison nearby and volunteered as a lay chaplain. It was in that capacity that he became acquainted with Harold McQueen. Through Paul's mediating the love of Jesus to him, Harold's life had been transformed. Harold became a believer and member of a Catholic parish. Deprived of drugs and alcohol in prison and guided by Paul, Harold went on to make up for lost years of schooling. He volunteered to help keep the premises clean. When teachers brought groups of schoolchildren to visit the jail, Harold would meet and speak about the evils of addiction and would offer himself as a prime example of the wrong way to go. It was obvious to any observer that Harold McQueen was a changed man, certainly not an unrepentant killer.

None of this had any effect on the determination of the governor and the attorney general who rejected our appeals for clemency. They determined to go through with the execution. We heard that the governor had even replaced the chief warden of the Eddyville prison because it was thought he might not be totally committed to death penalty. In due time, all appeals were exhausted. So after all those years without an execution and in spite of the efforts of people like us, Harold McQueen was led from his cell, holding in his hands the crucifix that had formerly belonged to Paul Stevens's daughter, and was strapped into the electric chair and shocked to death.

During our efforts on behalf of Harold McQueen and others farther down the list of the death-row inmates, we had called on members of the Kentucky General Assembly to urge them to replace capital punishment with life in prison without the possibility of parole. Carl Wedekind continued to devote himself to the cause, publishing two books, one on the general subject of death penalty and Kentucky's history of violence, and the other recounting some of his personal experiences as an advocate for abolishing the death penalty. Others besides Harold McQueen have been executed, and capital punishment has not been abolished in Kentucky. The electric chair has been retired as possibly too cruel, and some executions have been delayed by reason of scarcity of the poisons needed for lethal injections.

Carl Wedekind died a few years ago without seeing the success of the campaign, even though in recent years, surveys of public opinion in Kentucky consistently indicate that a majority of the citizens of the Commonwealth favor the alternative of life without parole. In conclusion, I can do nothing more than ask the familiar question: why do we kill people who kill people, to show that it's wrong to kill people?

3.   Bible Study Groups

All this time, I was occupied in the study and interpretation of the Bible. From the time that David Montgomery had asked me to meet weekly with him, our meetings had grown to include several other ministers. I participated in several groups that met weekly to study the lectionary. The lectionary consists of a set of four biblical passages each week, two each from the Old and New Testament passages, continuing over a period of three years, thus ostensibly covering most of the Bible. An ecumenical committee picks the texts for each week, and the Catholic Church participates, making only some minor changes in the list of texts, which it requires priests to use in preparing their homilies or sermons. The Presbyterian Church does not require that pastors use the lectionary texts for sermons as some denominations do, but many Presbyterian pastors now follow them to some extent. The practice has the virtue of encouraging a preacher to avoid the temptation of getting in a sort of rut and to pay more comprehensive attention to the total contents of the Bible. I've noticed that the committee that chooses the biblical selections may avoid a text that might raise a difficult question. I complain that sometimes the chosen text avoids problems by "cutting off" the head or the feet (or both) of a section in order to make things easier. In my view, that encourages people to have a simplified and basically mistaken attitude to what the Bible really says.

Online by computer, I also contributed to discussions of the lectionary texts and sermon preparation with a much broader interdenominational group. I was retired, and my pension was secure, and I knew some active pastors might have to take care when mentioning certain subjects that might be controversial to some of their ruling elders. Whenever appropriate, I tried to call attention to a note of social or political significance or ameliorate tendencies in the Bible to adopt an ancient patriarchal cultural stance that is prejudicial against women. In fact, I have written at least two essays that attempt to point out how the development of biblical faith shows a clear pattern of overcoming patriarchal prejudices that ancient people of all religions shared. Tracing that tendency in the Bible demonstrates clearly that starting from God's creation of humankind, male and female together in the image of God, to the history of Israel and the example and teaching of Jesus and Paul, the Bible really does support the oneness of humanity and the basic equality of women and men.

I could share my experiences as an activist and of having lived in foreign lands and cultures. I tried to do this in the light of the biblical principle of the oneness of God whose plan of salvation embraces all humanity. This idea had its root in my teaching Bible in Japan, and it had grown stronger as my son Samuel and I spent time in China and Pakistan on our trip home in 1986.

It proved to be a difficult task to deal with the whole of scripture using universal salvation as the basic principle of interpretation. The Bible is not really a monotheistic document. It contains evidence of a growth of faith from polytheism toward monotheism. I wrote a pamphlet I called *My Spiritual Pilgrimage toward Universalism* to trace my own development in that direction. From the beginning, I knew that mine was a minority view in the Presbyterian Church and among members of most other Christian denominations who were convinced that Christianity is the only religious guide to human salvation from sin and gaining eternal life in heaven. Several people I respected cautioned me that the word *universalism* might immediately rouse negative reactions in the minds of most Christians, so in a more recent edition, I changed the pamphlet's title to *Finding God's All-Embracing Love in Scripture* and using the original title as a subtitle.

Over time, I changed my approach and developed my theme at greater length. I finished the manuscript for a book-length work entitled *God for All: The Biblical Foundation of Universal Grace*.[20] I continued to work on this book, *A Goodly Heritage*, which is more autobiographical and personal in nature.

4.   The School of the Americas Watch

Another cause that attracted my attention was the SOA Watch. That is a group of volunteers whose purpose is to keep watch on, to publicize, and to seek the closure of the School of the Americas. Originally, it was established in Panama with political and financial support from the U.S. Department of Defense. The SOA is a training facility where army and police personnel from countries all over Central and South America come for training in counterrevolutionary planning and action by experts from the U.S. The training manual was shown to be replete with instructions on mass crowd control and so-called counterterrorism techniques including assassination and torture. So many graduates of this school returned to their home country and fomented military coups to install dictatorial governments with U.S. support that it came to be called the School of Coups (*La Escuela des Golpes*). In Panama, it became so malodorous that the army relocated it to Fort Benning, Georgia.

Nonviolent demonstrations against the school take place annually outside the gates, and meeting with representatives and senators in Congress has gradually gained support for a bill to close it entirely, but so far not by a majority vote. The Department of Defense claims that the worst features of the curriculum have been eliminated and that it really does teach democratic procedures. They even changed the name to

---

[20] Resource publications, Wipf and Stock, Eugene, Oregon, 2013

WHINSEC—Western Hemisphere Institute for Security Cooperation—but people familiar with the facts claim there is no evidence of substantive change.

Some years ago, a Roman Catholic priest missionary to South America, Roy Bourgeois, observed such prevalence of antidemocratic violation of human rights by many graduates of this school that he determined to do something about it. A particularly notorious crime was the assassination of Archbishop Oscar Romero of El Salvador. On his elevation to archbishop, Romero had been expected to be a passive supporter of the status quo, but experience and observation changed him once in office. The murder of several of the rural priests under his authority who had tried to assist the peasants radicalized him. He severely criticized the ARENA political party and the armed forces, among whose leaders were graduates of the SOA. In a speech on national radio, Archbishop Romero appealed directly to members of the armed forces. He urged them to disobey any officer who ordered them to kill peasants or drive them off their land. A day or so after that speech, the archbishop was celebrating mass at a public event; and at the moment he elevated the cup symbolizing the blood of Christ, he was shot to death by none other than a graduate of the School of the Americas.

Father Bourgeois, armed with a tape recording of the archbishop's speech, made his way into Fort Benning and managed to get next to the dormitory where personnel from Spanish-speaking military forces were sleeping. He put the boom box up in a tree and turned the tape on at full volume. The voice of Archbishop Romero repeated his command of disobedience. The timing of this event was precisely the date of Archbishop Romero's assassination, November 19. From that beginning and with increasing international support, Roy Bourgeois has organized an annual demonstration every November 19 outside Fort Benning. People who gather from all over the hemisphere join in the march, each one carrying a small white-painted wooden cross bearing the name of a certified victim of violence perpetrated by SOA graduates.

In the course of the demonstration, every year, several people would trespass beyond the set limit into the precincts of the facility and be arrested for civil disobedience. Following trials, they would be fined and jailed for up to six months. At the hearing, the judge always prohibited them from making any statement to explain why they were protesting. One November, I went to Fort Benning to participate in the demonstration. I was among several hundred who crossed the line into the fort. We were all herded on buses and taken several miles out in the country, where each of us received an official warning never again to attend an action at the School of the Americas. Then we were let loose and had to hike back into town. I myself had been prepared to be arrested and was gratefully surprised when we were not. We learned later that the total number of line crossers had been so many that the local jail and court system was incapable of handling us, so they let us go with a reprimand. My first and only experience committing civil disobedience did not land me in jail! I alternated between feeling grateful and disappointed.

Since that time, the authorities have erected higher fences and made it much more difficult for demonstrators to cross the line. I participated in another demonstration or two, going by charter bus with a group from Louisville and joining up on site with members of the Presbyterian Peace Fellowship. But with increasing age, I have stopped that annual trek, just as I have stopped going to Oak Ridge for the Hiroshima event.

As for Roy Bourgeois, he began to be active in the movement within the Roman Catholic Church to advocate ordaining women priests. Not only did he write and speak out on behalf of the women, but he also attended an ordination service for a woman. Though he received notices of warning from the hierarchy, he refused to back down. Most recently, the Catholic authorities have stripped Roy Bourgeois of his ordination and expelled him from his religious order. He persists in his leadership of the SOA Watch and his efforts on behalf of women.

14

Presbyterian Peace Fellowship
Delegation to Israel and Palestine

Dating all the way back to Margaret's and my days in Japan, we both had felt concern for the conflict between Israelis and Palestinians. Oddly enough, before we ever started out for China, while we were in New York City buying equipment of various kinds, we happened to be at Times Square where the famous running lights around the top edge of the Times Building continually flashed the latest news. We actually saw the flashing message stating that President Truman had given recognition to the unilateral declaration of the establishment of the State of Israel. I still had memories of dispensationalism and its expectation of the return of the Jews to their ancient homeland, so naturally, this news attracted my attention. In justification of his prompt announcement, Truman is said to have remarked that he had no Palestinian or Muslim voters to consider, but he did have to satisfy a large bloc of Jewish voters.

As time went on, this political consideration resulted in more and more support from the U.S. for the State of Israel. Margaret and I hadn't been able to ignore the question, even while we lived in Taiwan and Japan. With her characteristic instinctive sense of fairness, Margaret had very soon recognized that as an alien and inimical force dropped down in the middle of a predominantly Muslim region with a fairly large Christian minority, Israel was like a sort of cancer. About that time, I read a remark by a Roman Catholic priest whose name I can't remember, who said, "We are being told that Israel is the only friend the U.S. has in the Middle East, but before Israel, we didn't have any enemies there."

Back home in retirement, I became more and more convinced that the State of Israel has claimed a totally unjustifiable special privilege to pursue ethnic and economic policies toward Palestinians in contravention of international law and human rights. In the U.S., the Jewish lobby, abundantly assisted by powerful Jewish forces in public media plus present-day Christian sects that follow a revised Scofield Reference Bible system of interpretation, has built a formidable pro-Israel political atmosphere of obfuscation in the U.S. that is almost impossible to dispel.

From the early days, the Presbyterian Church (USA) has taken a strong stand on behalf of peaceful coexistence of two people in two states according to the UN decision. That was also the firmly proclaimed opinion of famous Jewish biblical scholar Martin Buber, whose books exerted a powerful influence on my understanding of the Bible. Presbyterians have long since rejected dispensationalism, with the belief that Jesus would return to earth to snatch up all true believers and set up a thousand-year kingdom in Israel with a new temple in Jerusalem. After the General Assembly meeting of 2000, the Presbyterian Peace Fellowship began planning a delegation to Israel/Palestine to be hosted by the Christian Peacemaker Teams. CPT is a voluntary group mostly comprised of members of traditional peace churches such as Mennonites, Quakers, and Church of the Brethren, but they welcome and assist participation by other concerned individuals and groups.

With Wanda's approval, I applied as a member of the Presbyterian Peace Fellowship delegation scheduled to take place in November 2001. From the time of that decision, I began attending the weekly Friday noon vigil in downtown Louisville, and Wanda usually accompanied me. This vigil was the local enactment of similar vigils held in many places in solidarity with a group of Women in Black, Israelis who stand silently outside the Knesset in Israel to demonstrate against the occupation of the Palestinian West Bank and Gaza by Israel Defense Forces and to appeal for the Palestinians' human rights. The Louisville Committee for a Two-State Solution had sponsored this vigil already for several years, but in anticipation of my going to Israel later, I began to take part.

At a Christmas holiday party at the home of an old friend of Wanda's, I met a retired member of the faculty of the University of Louisville. He had been a professor of Spanish and Italian. I had met his daughter, who was fluent in Spanish and who participated in Latin American peace and justice actions. I knew who her father was, and he evidently knew who I was. He engaged me in conversation and told of a recent trip he made to Israel. He was Jewish, but nonobservant and not actively engaged in the Israel-Palestine issue, though naturally interested in the matter. Unable to speak or read Hebrew, he felt himself not fully competent to observe and comment knowledgably on the issue, but he had seen the Women in Black outside the Knesset. He learned that one of the women demonstrators had come to Israel from Italy, and he began to talk to her in Italian. She told him that a strong motive for her to "go up" to Israel had been the deep anti-Jewish attitudes and policies she encountered growing up in Fascist Italy. Once in Israel, she soon realized that the policies of the Israeli Jews toward Arabs were very similar to those that she, as a Jew, had suffered from the Italian fascists. He said she told him, "Here in Israel, the Jews are the fascists."

Plans for a group of about twenty Presbyterians to go to Palestine had been pretty well completed when the attack on the World Trade Center took place on September 11. This momentous event naturally raised a serious question whether we should cancel our delegation or not. After careful consideration, we decided we might as well go ahead with our plan, and we were in Israel and Palestine from October 23 to November 3, 2001. The greatest danger I experienced was riding around some of the hilly streets of Jerusalem in taxicabs!

Rather than try to summarize my experiences in Israel and Palestine, I include here a copy of the report I wrote immediately after returning. To any who read this report, I state up front that all you read here describes conditions *years ago*. If things seem bad according to this report, realize that over the years since then, things have gotten *progressively worse* for the Palestinians.

A Report of the Presbyterian Peace Fellowship Delegation to Israel and Palestine, October 23 to November 3, 2001

Hosted by the Christian Peacemaker Teams and ably led by LeAnne Clausen of CPT, we had an impressive learning experience. I wish to thank all who expressed interest, concern, and support for me and to share my observations and conclusions. This is my personal report. I do not speak for our team as a whole.

1. The Context

Arriving just a little more than a month after the September 11 terrorist attacks against the USA, we saw close up what life can be like for Palestinians living under Israel's military occupation of the West Bank and Gaza. The U.S. only makes things worse by supplying weapons and economic aid to Israel while ignoring Israel's violations of the Palestinians' basic human rights, international law, and worse, UN Security Council resolutions. Both Israelis and Palestinians who spoke to us insisted that the U.S. holds the key. September 11 has caused the Bush administration to take some initiative in negotiations for peace in the Middle East. This issue demands attention in the broader context of what peace and justice affinity groups consider a misguided war on terrorism by the U.S.

Israel's occupation of the West Bank has continued since the war of 1967 when Israel gained control of all of the area west of the Jordan River originally designated for the Palestinians by the UN decision of 1948. This occupation has grown ever more oppressive, especially during the second intifada or uprising by the Palestinians protesting Ariel Sharon's entry into the sacred area of El Aqsa, Dome of the Rock, accompanied by hundreds of Israeli soldiers in September 2000. For years, Israel has refused to conduct substantive negotiations for peace while subjecting Palestinians to economic stranglehold, armed attack, and violation of human rights and personal dignity. In hopeless desperation, some Palestinians have responded with armed violence, including suicide bombings killing Israeli civilians. Israel has massively retaliated using heavy air and ground weapons made in the USA. Some eight hundred Palestinians have died in the most recent conflict, most of them civilians including women and children. Only about two hundred Israelis have died.

2. Deceptive Propaganda in the U.S.

In a one-sided manner, the U.S. government has supported Israel against the Palestinians. On October 25, 2000, the U.S. Congress passed resolution 365-30 placing the blame on the Palestinians for the second intifada, exonerating Israel and expressing "solidarity with the state of and people of Israel at this time of crisis." It urged President Clinton to use U.S. veto power in the UN Security Council to prevent "unbalanced resolutions" that might criticize Israel.

The major media in this country have abetted this trend by their acceptance of Israel's terminology. For example, Palestinian attacks against Israelis are "terrorism," while Israel's often massively unequal retaliation or preemptive killing of Palestinians is "self-defense." Israel has militarily taken over the West Bank and Gaza, "occupied territory" in international law. Israel claims the area was not part of any recognized national entity, and therefore, they call it "disputed territory." Regardless of terminology, the U.S. and the international community must not ignore the human tragedy.

Palestinian actions against Israel receive far more attention in the U.S. media than the more numerous and more damaging actions of Israel against Palestinians. When Palestinians killed Mr. Ze'evi, an Israeli cabinet minister, the incident that sparked the immediate conflict, it was branded "assassination." Israel has killed many more persons of rank in the Palestinian political system but calls these events "targeted killings" for the purpose of national security.

Conveniently ignoring the basic illegality of Israel's occupation of the West Bank and Gaza, the media have publicized what Israel claims as its generous offer to settle the issue by trading land for peace. The land the Israelis offer has been held by them against international law and in the strictest sense is not theirs to offer. When the Palestinians refuse to accept a final plan that does not recognize the rights due them in international law, they are called unreasonable. Columnists George Will and Cal Thomas repeat the lie that the PLO wants to drive Israelis into the sea, although before the Oslo meeting, the PLO changed its charter to recognize Israel's right to exist. The media ignore the fact that Israel has never officially recognized the Palestinians' right to their own land, and Prime Minister Sharon has expressed his purpose to drive all Palestinians away.

3. My View of Terrorizing Palestinians

Unquestionably, this is a very complicated issue, and neither side is without blame. In the Western world, there has been a proper revulsion against the Holocaust and all it symbolizes as the climax of centuries-long policies by European nations and people to segregate, to discriminate against, and finally to try to annihilate Jews. Still, such considerations should not blind us to the fact that as a modern nation state, Israel has put into effect policies against the Palestinians that replicate some of the most egregious policies under which earlier generations of Jews suffered at the hands of the Gentiles. People of fair mind and goodwill should not allow this to go on.

Without in any way attempting to deal fully with this matter, I wish only to testify to what I saw and heard during my visit with the Presbyterian Peace Fellowship/Christian Peacemaker Teams delegation, understood and interpreted in the light of considerable background reading before and after. I hope to help people here get a more balanced understanding of the problem to acknowledge the responsibility our nation and people bear for allowing the Israeli/Palestinian question to reach such a critically dangerous point and how we might work to effect some change in our national policy.

During my stay in Palestine/Israel, I took a number of photographs, some of which I have organized in a slide show to demonstrate what I see as Israel's state-sponsored policy of terrorism against the Palestinians. This terrorism may be divided into three categories.

3a. Terrorism by armed invasion

We arrived in Israel a few days after Israel had invaded and occupied several major Palestinian cities, including (for the first time) Bethlehem. The army called this invasion Operation Knife through Butter, an apt description of the disparity between the heavily armed invaders and the civilian victims. This major attack was said to be a retaliation for the Palestinians' assassination of Israeli Tourism Minister Ze'evi. Ze'evi had criticized the Israeli government for being too soft on the Palestinians and had announced his resignation from the cabinet. Some Palestinians believed that the Israeli government, fed up with Ze'evi as a troublemaker, had allowed Hamas to pick him off precisely to rid themselves of a nuisance while gaining a pretext to attack.

When our delegation entered Bethlehem, we had to go through narrow side streets because of machine gun fire in the center of town. From the hostel where we stayed, we could see an Israeli army post on top of a hill overlooking Bethlehem. Early on, the Israel Defense Force assassinated three Palestinians whom they suspected of complicity in the Ze'evi assassination or connections with groups considered by Israel to be terrorist. Besides these "targeted killings," Israeli snipers randomly killed a number of civilians, including seventeen-year-old Johnny Thaljiah as he left from worship in the Church of the Nativity. Our delegation visited the home of his family. We have learned of others—a nineteen-year-old young man killed as he stood behind the curtain of the window of his home, a woman from Jerusalem who came to check up on her elderly parents, a deaf man who did not hear the soldiers' orders, and a young mother, wounded by a sniper, who died in the rubble of the shop where she took refuge when a tank wrecked the place. In the space of ten days, the Israelis killed twenty-two people in Bethlehem. A woman in labor with complications was refused passage at the military checkpoint and prevented from getting proper care, resulting in the loss of life for her and her baby.

Israeli tanks rampaged down Manger Street, the main thoroughfare of Bethlehem and location of tourist shops. They wrecked cars, shops, and restaurants at ground level on both sides of the street and strafed residential quarters above with machine guns. They set fire to upscale shops at the Paradise Hotel, and the flames spread through the entire six-story building. We visited the home of the owner of one of the shops, and we saw windows broken by gunfire, which forced his family to take shelter in rear rooms. Tanks shelled the Bethlehem University and maternity hospital.

These acts can be described as nothing other than terrorism wantonly perpetrated against the civilian population: murder, destruction of homes and businesses, damage to essential institutions such as schools and hospitals. I mention Bethlehem simply because I went there and witnessed the immediate results of this army terrorism. But similar acts take place periodically all through the West Bank, and Palestinians in the Gaza Strip suffer from almost-constant military terrorism.

Although this was the first time that Bethlehem was militarily attacked and occupied, it had suffered great economic loss because Israel had prevented international tourists to visit the sacred city to celebrate the birth of Christ at the turn of the millennium in 2000. We saw the unfinished shells of several hotels that had been part of the plan to accommodate the tourists.

3b. Terrorism by Jewish settler encroachment

Among the Israeli practices most highly resented by the Palestinians is the establishment of settlements for Jews built within Palestinian territory on property most often taken illegally from the original owners. Prime Minister Ariel Sharon has been the most avid promoter of settlements. Perhaps the majority of settlers take up residence there because the government subsidizes the facilities, and modern, comfortable housing is available to them at a very reasonable cost.

A minority of settlers, however, are motivated by extremist, fundamentalist religious ideology, which they express in outbursts of violence against Palestinians living near their settlements and constant harassment of neighbors with the aim of driving them away. The very first settlement was established in Hebron, site of the Ibrahimi Mosque, built at the Cave of Machpelah, the traditional burial place of Abraham and Sarah, Isaac and Rebecca, and Jacob and Leah. In Hebron, King David also first solidified his kingship over all Israel and Judah.

In 1968, following the occupation of the 1967 war, a group of Jews claiming to be tourists registered in the only hotel in Hebron. But instead of leaving in due time, they simply took possession of it by arms. The Israeli government gave them possession of a military installation outside Hebron where they set up Kiryat Arba, now a very large settlement with modern facilities. A large contingent of the IDF provides protection for these settlers. Most live there for economic reasons, but a militant minority harasses their nearest Palestinian neighbors and constantly pushes the limits to take more land by surreptitiously placing trailer homes and water tanks on adjacent hills.

In Old Hebron, in the neighborhood of the Tomb of the Patriarchs, Israelis have built the settlement called Avraham Avinu—Abraham, our father. It looms above the wreckage of what used to be the central fruit market, which settlers destroyed in early 2001. Some shops were rebuilt, but they were soon demolished.

With some of our delegation, I visited a Palestinian home adjacent to the settlement. Only one family remains in what was originally home to as many as five households in an extended family. They have vowed to stay until they regain their freedom or until they are killed. Thickly planted flowers and shrubs on their third-floor patio shield them from the view of a military post not twenty yards away. From the other side of the patio, one can see the remains of a Palestinian home partially destroyed when the settlement was built. The owners are not permitted to repair and reoccupy their home. From the kitchen window, one can see the play area for the settlement children and large tanks holding abundant water supply. Palestinian houses have metal water tanks about the size of fifty-gallon drum cans on the roofs to hold the meager amounts of water allotted to them. Settlers sometimes amuse themselves by shooting holes in the drums.

In another home nearby, we found two women, wives of a man who has gone to Jerusalem to work and send money back for them and four little children. When his secondhand shop was destroyed, the man piled all his remaining stock in one of the rooms of this large residence once the home of several families. The women dare not leave the place for fear settlers will harass them on the street or even take over the property. Their water drums were shot up recently. Neighbors and CPT members do their shopping for them and keep them supplied with water.

In the same area, two other small fundamentalist settlements now stand in immediate proximity to houses, shops, mosques, and municipal offices. In 1994, a militant settler from the U.S., Dr. Baruch Goldstein, massacred twenty-nine Muslims at prayer in the Ibrahimi Mosque. Rioting Arabs killed a number of settlers, but IDF soldiers killed many more Arabs. Afterward, Israel closed Al Shuhada Street, the main thoroughfare through the old city, to all Palestinian vehicles. Shops all along this broad street have been destroyed or permanently shuttered, many with graffiti proclaiming "death to Arabs." Some narrow streets in the old city have wire netting above them to catch trash and garbage thrown down from the settlements above.

Israel has never stopped expanding existing settlements and building new ones. IDF soldiers outnumbering the settlers themselves in Palestinian cities protect the residents from attacks by the Palestinians and do nothing to restrain settlers from attacking the Palestinians. In my view, this policy constitutes another clear example of terrorism perpetrated against a largely civilian population.

3c.   Terrorism by fragmentation into Bantustans.

Delegation members in small groups visited and stayed in Palestinian homes one night during our time in Hebron. I spent the night in the home of Abdel Ra'of, and next day, I visited the home of Yusef al Atrash. They both live in the village of Al Sendas, but a paved Israeli highway has cut their village into two. They can come and go only by foot. Access to the highway by vehicles is blocked by mounds of stone and earth thrown up across the village street.

Israel is in the process of building a network of these roads within the West Bank. They permit easy travel among Israeli settlements and allow the IDF to deploy men and arms rapidly at will. These highways may cut through fields, vineyards, orchards, even residential areas, wherever the occupiers determine. On either side of the highways, a certain strip of land is designated as a buffer for Israeli security, from which Palestinians are to be gradually removed.

Both houses I visited have received notices of demolition, though there is no date specified. In fact, Yusef's present house, only partially built, is his third home. Israeli bulldozers wrecked his first house. Neighbors and friends in the U.S. alerted by CPT helped him build a second house. Less than a month after he moved in, that one was demolished. Beside his third house is the tent in which he and his large family live while rebuilding.

Yusef lives partway up the hill Jabal al Sendas. Within the last month or so, on the opposite side of the hill behind Yusef's house, the IDF bulldozed a track up to the top and has established an army post allowing surveillance of a number of villages in the surrounding area. Often, in similar cases, settlers may follow the army, bringing in mobile homes and water tanks to assert possession, leading eventually to the building of permanent housing on confiscated land.

Alongside the main highway north and south along the Jordan River, Israel has built a fence and a second highway, cutting off Palestinian access to the river and its life-sustaining water. These highways, military posts, and ever-spreading settlements have been deliberately designed to encircle major cities such as Hebron and Bethlehem and to divide up the larger territory into fragmented and disconnected enclaves. In effect, Palestinians would be confined to areas similar to the Bantustans in which South Africa's apartheid government limited the black Africans.

Israel made a "generous offer" to turn over to Palestine all West Bank and Gaza, except the settlements and the land for the connecting roads. The total area that Israel would keep under these conditions amounts to less than 10 percent. On paper, Palestine would control all the rest. As Jeff Halper, an Israeli university professor who takes direct action to prevent demolition of Palestinian homes, told us, this would be similar to a jail, where the prisoners actually occupy and use up to 90 percent of the space, but the jailers occupy the remainder, which gives them total control of the entire facility. Alexandra Lusak of our delegation affirmed the appropriateness of the comparison from her experience of prison ministry.

Even now, Israel exerts such total control of the West Bank that it has effectively shut down the Palestinian economy and closed off the Palestinians' access to jobs in Israel. In Jerusalem, I saw a group of Oriental-looking men, whom I addressed in Japanese. They gave no sign of response, and I learned that they are some of the many Chinese and other third world people brought in by Israel to do the physically hard, dirty, low-paid kind of work which Palestinians used to do but have now been denied. This sense of imprisonment, which envelops all Palestinians, is the third and most pervasive and most subtle of all the forms of terrorism to which Israel subjects them.

4.   The Need for UN observers

The rest of the world has no understanding of the reality of the prison-like conditions under which Palestinians live. Unlike prisoners, they have been condemned to this existence not for any crimes they have done, but to satisfy the desire of the dominant power of the State of Israel supported by the U.S. The Israeli power structure seems to believe they can guarantee national security by the kind of terrorist pressures they constantly impose on the Palestinians. When frustration, hopelessness, and sense of abandonment by the international community drive Palestinians to resist with violent and terrorist acts of their own against Israel, it is they, not the Israelis, whom the U.S. political authorities and the major commercial media condemn.

Carol Drew, a member of our delegation who works closely with abused women in upstate New York, observed the close similarities, magnified many times, in the relationship between the Israelis and the Palestinians. Like a husband or boyfriend wielding all the physical and economic power, Israel subjects the Palestinians to constant insult, psychological assaults on dignity and self-respect, and physical abuse from battering to murder. These attacks usually come, so the perpetrators say, because of something the other person did wrong or failed to do properly. If an abused woman finally responds with physical injury or even death for her abuser, she may come in for horrified condemnation from society at large. Blame the victim!

In Bethlehem, we met with Mr. Zoughbi Zoughbi, director of the Wi'am Conflict Resolution Center. "Israel doesn't know what to do with us," he said. "They won't marry us (form a single state with common citizenship), and they won't divorce us (allow us to have our own viable independent state)." The second alternative is the one Palestinians desire, and since September 11, the George W. Bush administration has begun to say that Israel should withdraw from the West Bank and begin negotiations leading to a Palestinian state. Unfortunately, the administration has not accompanied such talk with realistic action to bring about those objectives. The U.S. continues to give Israel unconditional support not only in words but also in billions of dollars and military equipment in aid while continuing to place the most stringent conditions on Arafat and the Palestinians to restart the process.

I fear that the U.S. administration and congress are at present incapable of taking the steps necessary to force Israel to change. Without that, Israel will drag out the "negotiations" as it always has done while continuing to create "facts on the ground" by expanded settlements and keeping its stranglehold on the Palestinian economy and maintaining its military occupation. In my view, the first step would be to have United Nations observers on the ground throughout the West Bank to document and report on abuse by both parties. If enough voices are raised by U.S. citizens in favor of such a move, the U.S. might go along with it instead of bowing to Israel's objections and vetoing such a move. I believe that a truly objective report by UN observers will convince the world community of Israel's crimes against international law and against humanity in their treatment of the Palestinians. This might result in a rising tide of understanding and sympathy for the Palestinian cause, such that our allies would put the pressure on the U.S. administration and congress to do the right thing. It is for us, as U.S. citizens, to make a start immediately to pressure our government to vote for and to support fully a UN initiative to observe and report on the Israel/Palestine crisis as soon as possible.

When I reached this point in my report, we had news of the series of suicide bombings by Palestinians, which killed twenty-six Israelis and injured dozens in early December 2001. A week previously, Israel had assassinated Mahout Abu-Hound, leader of Hamas, and all Israelis expected Hamas to respond sooner or later. Prime Minister Sharon has capitalized on this latest reaction to his policy of incitement and is launching all-out military attacks and complete travel closure on West Bank and Gaza, Palestine. The U.S. now encourages Israel to respond as we have done with our terrorist war against the Afghan people. The cycle of violence rushes upward. Hatred for the U.S. and our client Israel cannot but rise along with it.

15

Concerning Israel, Present and Future

After I returned from Israel/Palestine, Wanda and I resumed standing vigil every Friday noon in solidarity with the Israeli Women in Black. I had made a slide show from photographs and prepared a program that I presented to a few audiences, several in private homes and in several churches. I wrote a brief report that appeared in the Louisville *Courier-Journal* that drew forth a negative response from one of the local rabbis. For some years, the James Lees Memorial Presbyterian Church that I attend had cosponsored an event with the synagogue of which that person was the rabbi and with the local Muslim Cultural Center: an annual Thanksgiving celebration of the Children of Abraham. Our pastor had taken the lead in organizing this event, and I had happily taken part regularly. We rotated among the three congregations year by year, and we had a common meal shared by all and a worship service that included liturgical features of all three faiths. To my disappointment, the rabbi had written directly to the newspaper, criticizing me by name and calling me unfair.

In those days, our Friday vigil was pretty well attended. We regularly had over a dozen, including mostly Christians, but some secularists and several Muslims and one Jew, with whom I had first become acquainted when I met with solidarity groups protesting Reagan's contra war on Nicaragua. This Jewish friend was a union organizer at the local Philip Morris cigarette plant, and for a while, he was a national officer of the New Jewish Agenda involved actively in many peace and justice issues, including human rights for Palestinians. He suffered bitter opposition from fellow Jews. On several occasions, when other Jews learned that he had been invited to be a panelist at a public meeting to discuss a question, they very pointedly refused to participate themselves and boycotted the meeting. My friend told me his grandfather had been an Orthodox rabbi. He himself was nonobservant and admittedly uninstructed in the Bible. He asked me to instruct him in some of the teachings of the Hebrew prophets who addressed political and economic justice issues. I was flattered that he would ask me, and I readily obliged. Together with him and with a Palestinian faculty member of the University of Louisville, I jointly wrote an op-ed piece on Israel/Palestine that the *Courier-Journal* published.

It is painfully obvious that many Jews are so closely committed to the State of Israel that they seem to have a knee-jerk reaction of branding as anti-Semitic anyone who criticizes Israel. Although I fully recognize the deep relationships among Israel as a nation state, Jews as a people, and Judaism as a religious faith, it seems clear to me that they are not identical. I can appreciate the values of Judaism and admire much about many Jews while still judging the State of Israel as grossly violating international laws and the Palestinians' human rights, claiming an exceptionalism that the world community does not recognize for any other nation. Sometimes it seems to me as though the U.S. thinks of itself as specially entitled. I agree wholeheartedly with a well-known Presbyterian public figure, the late William Sloan Coffin, who said, "It's time for the U.S. to join the world and stop trying to lead the world."

For my own part, I have been a lifelong student and teacher of the Bible, believing that the Old Testament—adapted from what was originally written in Hebrew and is the Bible of the Jews—is authoritative scripture for me as is the New Testament translated from Greek. I appreciate the interrelations between the two parts of the Bible and the close relations between Judaism and Christianity as I have come to understand the two faiths. I have long since rejected the exclusivist view called supersessionism—that Christians now supersede or replace Jews because Jews rejected Jesus as Messiah. That is a key emphasis of the Scofield Bible and dispensationalism, which Presbyterians have long since judged to be inappropriate as a means of interpreting scripture.

I wrote a brief essay entitled "Israel, Jews, and Judaism" to state my case and had it duplicated locally for distribution. I can also send it on line directly to those who request it. A point made in the Hebrew Bible confirmed by the New Testament that impresses me deeply is that God has never abandoned Israel/Jews as the *people* (Hebrew *'am*) of God, yet their desire to be like other *nations* (Hebrew *goyim*) led to the formation of the Kingdom of Israel, which reached its zenith under King David. As a kingdom like other nations, the Israelites became involved in international power politics and the whole round of war and peace that characterized the ancient Near East nations. Split into northern Israel and southern Judah, the two Jewish nations fought each other as well as other nations. Both eventually fell before the assaults of Assyria and Babylonia, the rival superpowers of the time.

I believe God wants the people of God to be witnesses in the world to God's sovereign plan of grace, mercy, and peace for *all* people. Under the minor priestly family of Hasmoneans (nicknamed Maccabees), the Jews again became like other nations and established a dynasty that combined priestly, military, and kingly authority, enjoying client status under Roman hegemony.[21] After surviving for about a century, the Kingdom of Judea self-destructed in corruption and internal strife to be overthrown and placed under direct rule by Rome.

As I read the New Testament, especially the writings of the apostle Paul and of those influenced by him, God's plan for humanity includes the Gentiles among the people of God without requiring them to become Jews. The Jewish people of God are likened to an olive tree with root, trunk, and branches into which Gentiles are grafted as wild olive branches (Romans 11:11-35). Another text speaks of "the commonwealth and covenants of Israel" from which Gentiles were originally aliens until brought near through Christ (Ephesians 2:11-22). The New Testament anticipates the early consummation of God's kingdom when "all Israel will be saved" (Romans 11:26), and both Jews and Gentiles will together be "one new humanity in place of the two" (Ephesians 2:15). That's an expectation that is as yet still unrealized.

It's impossible for me to imagine how that "one new humanity" could express itself long ago. Of course it didn't reach that consummation,

---

[21] This latter-day Judean Kingdom or Hasmonean dynasty may be approximately dated as follows: About 161 BCE, Judas Maccabeus received Rome's recognition for the kingdom of "the nation of the Jews." Thereafter, still as clients of Rome, the Hasmoneans continued to rule but became increasingly quarrelsome and corrupt. Brothers Hyrcanus II and Aristobulus II fought each other with such violence that Roman General Pompey overthrew them in 63 BCE and imposed direct rule by Rome.

and in the succeeding centuries, the increasingly populous and powerful Christians perpetrated horrible persecutions and pogroms against the Jews, reaching a climax in the Nazi Holocaust. That was a concerted effort to exterminate the Jews, along with other racial groups and individuals whom the Nazis considered to be racially, physically, or mentally "abnormal" or "deviant." Therefore, they unilaterally rejected them as not pure Aryans and tried to destroy them all.

1.   Israel's dependence on military domination

One can only sympathize with Jews who looked to the Zionist movement in hopes for relief and freedom. Some have returned to Palestine and reestablished their own state. In anticipating that accomplishment, Chaim Weizmann, who became the first president of modern Israel, wrote, "Our relations to the other races and nations would become more *normal* . . . We shall revert to *normal* . . . like unto all the nations."[22] At present, among Zionist Jews, most are secular, but others are fervent believers. Some fundamentalist Christians (in the Darby/Scofield tradition) also deserve to be called Zionists—literally interpreting various biblical texts, they are willing to give unconditional support to the State of Israel and anticipate rebuilding the temple, and they expect Jesus to return to establish the kingdom after there is a temple for him to return to.

I see all this as a modern expression of the ancient Israelite tribes' desire to have their own king to lead them out and fight their battles (1 Samuel 8:4-22). It is also a modern counterpart to the Maccabean/Hasmonean Kingdom of Judea. Some of the most powerful and influential of the founders of the modern Jewish state were members of terrorist gangs, and they have always based their quest of security on complete military and economic domination of the Arab population of Palestine.

General Moshe Dayan was a leader of Israeli troops in their wars of independence that destroyed hundreds of Arab villages and permanently made refugees and exiles of their inhabitants. He was a major figure

---

[22] Jacqueline Rose, *The Question of Zion*. Princeton University Press, 2005, p.76, emphasis original.

in the government while Israel continued its policy of geographical expansion and repression of the Palestinians. At a memorial service for an Israeli officer ambushed and assassinated by Palestinians from Gaza, Dayan delivered a brief speech that has become famous as a statement of Israel's basic policy toward Arabs. Dayan said:

> How can we blame them for hating us? For eight years they have been sitting in refugee camps, while in front of their very eyes, we turn their land and the land of their forefathers into our homeland. Not of the Arabs of Gaza must we demand an answer but of ourselves. How could we have been so blind as to forget our destiny, the destiny of our generation, cruel as it may be? (. . .)
>
> It is the destiny of our generation, the core of our existence, to remain alert and armed, strong and unyielding, for if the sword were to fall from our fist—we will be cut down.[23]

Modern Israel is supposedly a secular democracy, a majority of its citizens being secular Jews, yet conservative religious Jews demand and receive special privileges. Until recently, their privileges have included exemption for full-time rabbinic scholars from otherwise universal military service (including both men and women). They clamor most loudly for the advantages they gain from policies that dominate and humiliate Palestinians. In actual fact, Israel's discriminatory practices against the Arabs who live as citizens in Israel are comparable to some of the worst cases of Jim Crow laws against Negroes in the U.S. South. Treatment of Arabs who live in the occupied territories is much, much worse.

Ancient Rome supported the Jewish Hasmonean kingdom until it destroyed itself by violence and corruption. Similarly, ever since President Truman gave instant recognition to Israel's declaration of independence, the U.S. remains the most powerful supporter of Israel. Besides the numerous times the U.S. vetoed UN Security Council resolutions

---

[23] This quotation from Dayan is contained in an article by Miko Peled, "What Israel's Best Friend Should Know" in the publication of Americans for Middle East Understanding (AMEU), *The Link*, Vol. 46 No 4, September-October, 2013, p. 5.

condemning Israel's violations of international law and the human rights of the Palestinians, we also supply Israel with at least three billion dollars of aid every year, much of it in the form of military assistance. While displaying an unmistakable bias in favor of Israel, the U.S. continues to promote "negotiations" between Israelis and Palestinians, though there has never been any advantage accruing to the Palestinians. There are Jews who honestly recognize the basic error of Israeli policy toward the Palestinians.

2. Jewish critics of Israel

Henry Siegman, the director of the US/Middle East Project and head of the American Jewish Congress from 1978 to 1994, wrote an essay entitled "The Great Middle East Peace Process Scam." Siegman developed the thesis that Israel has *never* envisioned a Palestinian state that Israel does not completely dominate and has *never* participated in good faith in the so-called peace process. Israel always uses the times of peace process negotiations to strengthen its own facts on the ground. Israel always blames the Palestinians for stopping the negotiations when they refuse to accept an impossible proposition from Israel. For the most part, people in the U.S. accept Israel's account and blame the Palestinians.[24]

In 2013, the Israeli filmmaker Dror Moreh produced a documentary entitled *The Gatekeepers.*[25] It consists of interviews with five men, each of whom has served as the head of Shin Beit, Israel's top-level secret intelligence agency, their counterpart to the American CIA. The Shin Beit is charged with the responsibility of maintaining surveillance of Palestinians to prevent terrorist acts if possible and to track down and destroy those who succeed in carrying out such acts or are suspected of plotting them. These interviews are interspersed with footage depicting various incidents of Shin Beit agents carrying out their duties destroying Arab terrorists or rounding up suspects.

---

[24] Henry Siegman, "The Great Middle East Peace Process Scam" London Review of Books, August 16, 2007.

[25] I was able to view this film, renting it from Amazon.com.

The five men interviewed agree that Israel's policy of suppression of Palestinians only encourages a vicious circle of mutually destructive incidents of attack and counterattack that has no foreseeable end. As I watched this film, I received the following inescapable impressions:

1) During their training and experience over time in the Shin Beit, these men received training in the use of the Arabic language to the point of ability to understand it in its various subtle nuances. They circulated among Arabs and came to know and respect the humanity of their "enemies," whom Israelis customarily refer to as terrorists. One section of the film is entitled "One Man's Terrorist Is Another Man's Freedom Fighter."

2) Those who spent their careers in Shin Beit came to understand that there is no place for morality in the work Israel expects them to do. Several of them expressed outrage at some acts of the army such as cruelly killing bound Arabs whom they had already captured. That is symptomatic of the underlying policy of Israel toward the Palestinians. The Shin Beit has at its disposal sophisticated technology that enables them to identify, keep track of, and assassinate specific targets. They expressed concern to avoid killing innocent civilians or family members nearby, but they say that is impossible, regrettably.

3) They criticized politicians as being untrustworthy, especially for showing no interest in meeting or knowing Arabs. Politicians have no general strategy but follow only tactics designed to destroy as many "terrorists" as possible.

4) The militant conservative residents of the settlements aim to drive out all Arabs and take over all the territory. Some of them see the Israeli government as an enemy for opposing them. It was such an Israeli who assassinated Prime Minister Yitzhak Shamir for signing the Oslo agreement with the Palestine Liberation Organization (PLO). Shin Beit has had to take measures to prevent Israeli settlers (whom they called their own "flesh and blood") from committing atrocities of such a scale that they might result in embroiling the entire region in war.

5) These former Shin Beit heads stated clearly they would be willing to talk with any other party, even those considered the most violent and inimical.

6) They gave the unmistakable impression that they believed Israel's policy toward the Palestinians was mistaken and that it could not succeed. "You cannot make peace by military means," one of them stated flatly. Israel cannot achieve final victory and is destroying the character of its own people by taking young Israelis out of high school, inducting them into the army, giving them a gun, and placing them in authority over Palestinians of all ages and both genders.

3. A road not taken

Listening to these men I was reminded of something I read in one of the English language newspaper when I was in Jerusalem in 2001. (I deeply regret that I didn't preserve a copy of that paper.) It was an interview with a visitor who had at one time been a high official of the South African government. He drew a clear parallel between that white apartheid regime and the current Israel/Palestine situation. The white minority in South Africa had total control of military, economic, and political power over the black majority. The two sides had been locked in a desperate struggle for decades. The conditions of the blacks grew worse all the time, yet their resistance showed no signs of weakening or ending. There was, moreover, no expectation of the whites gaining a final victory. Eventually, the white power structure acknowledged that the only way to end the cycle of violence was for the party in power to stop. They stopped. The visitor stated that the Israel/Palestine violence would end only when the stronger side, Israel, takes the initiative to stop. Regrettably, Israel has given no sign of stopping. The ghost of Moshe Dayan still walks.

I recall that there is another wholesome result of the end of that South African violence. When the former white power structure was negotiating with newly elected President Nelson Mandela for a smooth transition to a multiracial government, both sides agreed to stop the production of nuclear weapons and to get rid of the weapons they had on hand. White South Africa had built several atomic bombs with technical and other assistance from Israel. With its new beginning as a multiracial state with a unity government, South Africa became the only nation in the world to give up voluntarily their complete nuclear weapons enterprise. I find it a bit curious, yet easy to understand: devout Jews use various locutions to avoid pronouncing YHWH, the name of their national God. The secular State of Israel will not officially and publicly name or acknowledge the existence of their nuclear arsenal, the supreme power on which they depend for what they call security.

Here I would like to refer to a book that came to my attention only after I had finished this work.[26] Author Blumenthal includes a sweeping historical background from the earliest days before the actual establishment of the new state. His book's starting point is Israel's barbaric war against Gaza in 2008-09, which brought to power the nation's most right wing government. Israel has become a country where right-wing leaders, such as Avigdor Lieberman and Benjamin Netanyahu, sacrifice democracy to their power politics; where the media and opposition stand aside and watch the assault on civil liberties, where state-funded Orthodox rabbis publish books that teach how and when to kill Gentiles; where Jewish youth refuse to sit in a classroom with an Arab; and where mob violence targets Palestinians scapegoated by leading government officials as "demographic threats."

Blumenthal interviews the demagogues and speaks with political leaders behind the organized assault on civil liberties. He illuminates the present by uncovering the ghosts of the past, the histories of Palestinian neighborhoods now gone and forgotten; how that history has set the stage for the current crisis of Israeli society; and how the Holocaust has been turned into the justification for occupation. More and more Israelis join the "exodus" for America, while Germany is the next most popular destination. Those who choose to remain or have no choice seem more and more coarsened in character and impervious to humanitarian impulses.

In ancient times the Maccabee/Hasmonean dynasty monopolized religious, military, and political authority over the Kingdom of Judea with recognition and assistance as one of Rome's clients for almost a century between 161 and 63 BCE. Over time the Hasmonean siblings became so greedy, so corrupt, and so ferociously competitive that Rome overthrew the warring parties and established authority under the Edomite Herod, called King of the Jews. The modern state of Israel has perhaps a decade or so to reach its century mark, but can it really last so long without

---

[26] Max Blumenthal, *Goliath: Life and Loathing in Greater Israel.* New York: Nation Books 2013. I have not been able to study this book in depth, but I have read parts of it, and I have used exerpts from the review at Amazon.com.

American aid? Given the extent to which the U.S. has entangled itself in complicity with what goes on there, we must expect to suffer a share of whatever fate awaits it.

4.   Some signs of hope

The primitive Christians' expectation of Christ's early return has gone unfulfilled for neatly two thousand years, but throughout history since the time of Emperor Constantine of Rome, Christians too have attempted to exercise religious domination by means of governmental force, including military coercion, instead of fulfilling the call to all people to witness God's sovereign grace for all. Gradually, some Christians seem to be accepting this role of witness separate from governmental power, but by no means all Christians conform to the principle. In the twenty-first century, the United States is home to the greatest variety of religious faiths of any other nation on earth, and I believe that with care and mutual respect, we may succeed in showing a living example of true religious freedom and cooperation to promote world peace.

I have read a number of books by Jews and by Christians who show a decided interest in and sympathy toward the other faith. They consistently seek to discover and join in embracing the positive aspects of the other tradition while honestly acknowledging the shortcomings of one's own. I consider myself a member of that growing group. For the foreseeable future, there will undoubtedly be members of both faith groups who insist on the superiority and exclusiveness of their respective position, but participants in a third way are growing in number. I am hopeful that in time, the small number of concerned Muslims will increase and that the three major monotheistic faiths can point the way for an even more comprehensive realization of the one new humanity, with warm and open welcome for any and all to participate simply as sister or brother human beings.

Edwards Brothers Malloy
Oxnard, CA USA
May 13, 2014